D

th

Discworld and the Disciplines

Critical Approaches to the Terry Pratchett Works

Edited by ANNE HIEBERT ALTON *and*
WILLIAM C. SPRUIELL

CRITICAL EXPLORATIONS IN SCIENCE FICTION AND FANTASY, 45
Series Editors Donald E. Palumbo *and* C.W. Sullivan III

McFarland & Company, Inc., Publishers
Jefferson, North Carolina

LIBRARY OF CONGRESS CATALOGUING-IN-PUBLICATION DATA

Discworld and the disciplines : critical approaches to the Terry Pratchett works / edited by Anne Hiebert Alton and William C. Spruiell.
     p.   cm. — (Critical Explorations in Science Fiction and Fantasy ; 45)
    [Donald E. Palumbo and C.W. Sullivan III, series editors]
    Includes bibliographical references and index.

    ISBN 978-0-7864-7464-6 (softcover : acid free paper) ∞
    ISBN 978-1-4766-1601-8 (ebook)

    1. Pratchett, Terry—Criticism and interpretation.
2. Discworld (Imaginary place)   I. Alton, Anne Hiebert, 1963– editor of compilation.   II. Spruiell, William C., editor of compilation.

PR6066.R34Z58 2014
823'.914—dc23   2014010343

BRITISH LIBRARY CATALOGUING DATA ARE AVAILABLE

McFarland & Company, Inc., Publishers
  Box 611, Jefferson, North Carolina 28640
  www.mcfarlandpub.com

Table of Contents

Acknowledgments

We would like to thank Sir Terry Pratchett, for obvious reasons, and his agent Colin Smythe for his assistance and his patience in fielding incessant e-mail queries. In addition, we would like to thank series editor Donald Palumbo for his comments and suggestions.

We would also like to thank the following artists, publishers, and representatives for their permission to reprint the illustrations in the essay "Coloring in Octarine":

- Colin Smythe, on behalf of the Josh Kirby Estate, for *Hogfather* and *Reaper Man*.
- Paul Kidby, for *Granny Weatherwax Standing, Granny Weatherwax with Bees, Rincewind in XXXX, Cohen the Barbarian,* and the cover image from *Nanny Ogg's Cookbook*.
- Stephen Briggs, *Turtle Recall: The Discworld Companion ... So Far* by Terry Pratchett and Stephen Briggs, and The Orion Publishing Group London for *A View in the Shades* and *Armoured Raven*.
- David Wyatt and HarperCollins Publishers for *No Rat Shall Kill Another Rat* from *The Amazing Maurice and His Educated Rodents*.
- Stephen Player for a selection from *The Streets of Ankh-Morpork* and *Feegles*.
- The Discworld Emporium for *Twilight Canyons* from *The Compleat Ankh-Morpork*.

The librarians at the Clarke Historical Library and the Park Library, Central Michigan University, and especially those at the Documents on Demand office, were very helpful in obtaining numerous hard-to-find copies of articles and books we needed for our chapters and for the Annotated Critical Bibliography—and we strongly appreciate all of their efforts.

Finally, we hereby impose personal thanks upon the following, be the recipients willing or not:

- Trey Jones for his feedback on the probability section; all remaining issues are, of course, one hundred percent Bill's fault.
- The students in Anne's English 460: Interdisciplinarity and Terry Pratchett class (Fall 2012) for their enthusiasm and commentary during the research process.
- Administrative secretaries Jamie Fockler and Denise Abbey for their technical expertise and assistance throughout this project.
- Anne's family, Colin and Matthew, who not only put up with a lot of single-topic conversations (and/or monologues) during the duration of our work on this book but also, in Matthew's case, joyfully embraced the chance to explain game rules to slightly befuddled adults.

Introduction

ANNE HIEBERT ALTON *and*
WILLIAM C. SPRUIELL

Terry is now read in thirty-eight languages, with sales now in the
region of 70 million books worldwide: put side by side, they'd stretch
from London to Rome—over a thousand miles.—Colin Smythe,
"Terry and Discworld"

Terry Pratchett is one of the most prolific and successful fantasy novelists
of the last several decades: knighted in 2008 for his contributions to literature,
he has been referred to in reviews as "the Dickens of the twentieth century"
(Hunt 91), though, since a number of his influential works have appeared after
the turn of the millennium, that moniker may need to be adjusted. He has
won numerous awards for his writing, including the prestigious Carnegie
Medal for *The Amazing Maurice and His Educated Rodents* (2001), the Margaret A. Edwards award (2011), LOCUS awards for best fantasy novel (2008)
and best young adult novel (2004, 2005, 2007), and the British Book Award
in the Fantasy and Science Fiction category (1994), among others. His Discworld series, which has forty volumes to date (not counting the various companions, maps, and other satellite works),[1] has captivated readers of all ages,
backgrounds, and nationalities. In 2002, one percent of all books sold in
Britain were written by him, and it has been joked that "no British railway
train is allowed to depart unless at least one passenger is reading a Pratchett
novel" (Hunt 91). Few other contemporary popular authors find their work
referred to by people working in as wide a range of fields as robotics, business
management, elementary education, philosophy, and medicine, to name but
a few.[2]

1

The sheer number of adaptations and complementary works that his work has motivated is also significant. In addition to audio books (abridged and unabridged) and plays, several novels have been adapted in different modes: animated or live-action films, graphic novels, or illustrated screenplays. Three books have also been lavishly illustrated—~~Faust~~ *Eric* (illustrated by Josh Kirby), *The Last Hero* (illustrated by Paul Kidby), and *The Illustrated Wee Free Men* (illustrated by Stephen Player). Pratchett has also collaborated with other writers and artists to create satellite works[3] that provide more detailed information about the Discworld and its inhabitants, such as *Nanny Ogg's Cookbook*, which contains, among other things, recipes for a number of delicacies including Nanny's (in)famous Carrot and Oyster pie. Other collaborations include several maps of the Discworld, *The Unseen University Cut-Out Book* (in collaboration with Alan Batley and Bernard Pearson), and two picture books set within the Discworld. Pratchett's created context has also been enthusiastically adopted by gamers, who have shaped text- and action-based games around it. Most traditional are trivia quiz books like David Langford's *The Unseen University Challenge* and *The Wyrdest Link*, complemented by the on-line Discworld University Challenge,[4] which provides a daily quiz of ten questions and posts a new tournament each month. Interested players can make use of companions like Pratchett & Stephen Briggs' *Turtle Recall: The Discworld Companion ... So Far* and Andrew Butler's *An Unofficial Companion to the Novels of Terry Pratchett*. In addition, conventional board games like *Thud!*, *The Discworld Board Game*, and *Guards! Guards!* sit alongside role-playing games, computer games, and other online games.[5] While some of the earliest retailing may have begun with the now-defunct Clarecraft Discworld figurines,[6] a large variety of Discworld merchandise is now available including stamp covers, greeting cards, jewelry, sweatshirts, miniatures, aprons, mouse pads, stickers, tote bags, mugs, and magnets, among other ephemera. Collectors can also purchase calendars, desk diaries, and a variety of prints as well as original artwork. Several volumes devoted to the art of Discworld have also been published.

For dedicated fans, there are a number of conventions devoted entirely to Discworld, and these are attended by fans from all over the globe. The premier event is the Discworld Convention, started in England in 1995 and now a biannual four-day event that includes talks and panels, theater, a charity auction, musical performances, and a myriad of other events. Moreover, as Colin Smythe notes,

> Eric and Arthur Wall have produced a number of alcoholic beverages to entertain fans—"Nanny Ogg's Scumble," "Ridcully's Revenge," supplied with a bag of hops, and a drinking horn designed and produced by "the Cunning Artificer,"

and "Black Hogswatch" (which came with a Cunning Artificer mug portraying the Hogfather and a bag containing nuts and chocolate coins). And while I am on the subject of alcohol, the Australian company marketing the Discworld II computer game produced bottles of white wine which they called the "Fountain of Youth," 1996 vintage [Smythe "1996–1998"].

Other conventions include those held in Australia (Nullus Anxietas), Ireland (Irish Discworld Convention), Germany (Scheibenwelt Convention), and North America (NADWCon). In addition, Wadfest is a fan-organized, family-friendly camping weekend with the intention of providing attendees with the opportunity to dress up as their favorite characters and participate in a masquerade, purchase limited edition merchandise, listen to stories and a variety of other performances, and meet people with similar fantasy- and specifically Discworld-related interests.

This proliferation of Discworldiana not only encourages us to redefine our notions of what exactly constitutes a "text"—which, in keeping with the traditions of a variety of literary theoretical frameworks,[7] for our purposes will include not only works of literature but also films and other adaptations, games, and memorabilia associated with the Discworld—but also suggests that Pratchett's work holds an immense as well as diverse cultural significance. Given that millions of people are willing to trek, either in person or virtually via the internet, to the ends of the earth (quite literally, in some cases) to attend a conference or play a game or find a T-shirt or watch a play, or to do any of a number of other Discworld-related activities, clearly something in Pratchett's creation of Discworld has appealed enough to them to galvanize them into pursing action of some sort, beyond their initial reading of the novel(s). While one hesitates to label any single author as "universal," Pratchett's particular and individual flavor of writing appears to cut a narrow swath across a very broad band of readers: though his books by no means appeal to everyone in a single cultural group, they do have a broad appeal across cultural barriers and divisions, and speak to—at least in our world—humans of a similar mindset.[8]

In other words, this is exactly the sort of thing that people who like that sort of thing like—a statement also true of happiness, and oxygen.

Pratchett and Interdisciplinarity

In her 2002 article, "Is There Hope for the Humanities in the 21st Century?," Susan Bassnett notes that she would like to see "Terry Pratchett on every degree program in English Studies" (109) as an example of a writer whose work encompasses the most important elements of interdisciplinarity. A decade later, Pratchett's work—and here we refer specifically to his Discworld books—has become even broader (if possible) in terms of the fields it invokes: in addition to such staples as literary (and non-literary) genre-play, socio-political satire, and commentary on such apparently diverse areas as economics, mythology, geography, and folklore, his *oeuvre* now also includes treatments of sports, racism, picture books, and science—to name but a few very broad categories that Pratchett has absconded with and made his own through the witty and at times acerbic use of humor embedded throughout his fantastic narratives.

Pratchett's Discworld books are inherently multidisciplinary. He merrily deploys innumerable genres and literary conventions (often within the same book), only to overturn them and transform them into self-critiques as well as often highly targeted social satire. One of the best examples appears in *Night Watch*, perhaps Pratchett's most complex novel, which utilizes elements of criminal justice, history, philosophy, economics, geography, politics, and even a nod to physics in terms of the time travel conceit to present a scathing critique of society's penchant for reinterpreting history from the perspective of the winners.

Inasmuch as an awareness of disciplinary conventions, including those involving language use, is a prerequisite for interdisciplinarity, encouraging readers to practice metalinguistic and metageneric discourses prepares them to encounter disciplinary discourses at an analytic level. Pratchett often does this by making readers aware of the ways in which language catalyzes meaning. While wordplay is not typically perceived as part of the formal critical toolkit for making reader perceptions of the text even more complex, its effects—encouraging consciousness of multiple readings, manipulating the poetic dimensions of text, shifting language from background to foreground—arguably develop the same faculties as are required for critical analysis. Indeed, the major differences between humor and criticism may lie less in what the participant is doing than for whom s/he is doing it. When readers encounter a line such as "'A night watchman in crappy armor is about your métier,' said Colon, who looked around proudly to see if anyone had noticed the slanty thing over the e" (*Arms* 238), they probably do not directly perceive it as a scholarly comment on the intersection of orthography, pronunciation, and the marking of social class—but their resultant shift in worldview can be exactly the sort professors devote a good bit of energy to encouraging.

His tendency to invoke multiple disciplines surfaces frequently throughout his novels, both in terms of their foci—ranging from rock music to religion to economics to sports to geography to mythology to politics, to name but a few—and in the way Pratchett uses humorous paratextual devices such as footnotes to achieve a number of ends. They often contain comments on language:

not only grammatical commentary, but also comments on specific words— like *Wyrd Sisters'* "Quaffing is like drinking, but you spill more" (15)—as well as translations of dwarfish. They include background information about different kinds of groups, like wizards and witches and dwarfs and Igors, and individuals like Archchancellor Ridcully and Bergholt Stuttley (Bloody Stupid) Johnson; on urban as well as Unseen University politics; on food, like Dibbler's sausages and Troll beer and what kind of vegetable the Big Wahooni is (*Truth* 55); on geography, like the miasmic river Ankh in the city of Ankh-Morpork or the lethal waterfalls of the Edge; and on Discworld folklore, like the Yeti of the Ramtops (*Thief*) or Anoia, "a minor goddess of Things That Stick in Drawers" (*Postal* 334). The footnotes also often contain jokes and humorous asides—one-liners or more complex witticisms like the notion of Rogers the bull thinking that there must be two of him because his eyes face in opposite directions (*Clay*)—as well as pithy insights about life and human nature, like the observation that "deafness doesn't prevent composers hearing the music. It prevents them hearing the distractions" (*Music* 146).[9]

At times these apparently tangential bits work their way into other texts that Pratchett writes. A brief mention of the Death of Rats in *Reaper Man* foreshadows the development of this small personage into a minor character in a number of later novels, including *Soul Music, Hogfather, Thief of Time,* and *The Amazing Maurice and His Educated Rodents,* among others. A lengthy footnote about the Hogfather in *Soul Music* eventually morphs into a whole novel that focuses on this folkloric manifestation, and Pratchett's practical attitude towards folklore—"I think of folklore in much the same way a carpenter thinks about trees" (Pratchett and Simpson x)—eventually led him to collaborate with English folklorist Jacqueline Simpson on *The Folklore of Discworld*. Other tangential information of a quasi-scientific nature found outlets in Pratchett's four *Science of Discworld* books, which Pratchett co-wrote with science writers Ian Stewart and Jack Cohen. Pratchett appears to view disciplinary discourses in much the same way Feegles view sheep: coming at them from ground level does not appear to be as much an impediment as an opportunity for surprise. By his appropriation and reconstruction of discourse types, he provides readers with models for gaining a measure of conscious and playful control over what can otherwise be an impenetrable hegemonic maze.

Overview of the Book

Over the last decade, increasing awareness of the need for and benefits of interdisciplinary communication has resulted in an increasing number of publications exploring the intersections between literature and philosophy, ecology, political science, mathematics, psychology, music, science, religion, and art. Many of these have considered popular literature as well as canonical works, with such titles as *Harry Potter and International Relations* (2006), *The Unimaginable Mathematics of Borges' Library of Babel* (2008), *The Physics of Star Trek* (2007), *Sensation and Sublimation in Charles Dickens* (2011), and "Flavor Pairing in Medieval European Cuisine: A Study in Cooking with Dirty Data" (2013), the last of which considers the long-overlooked area of intersection between corpus linguistics, biochemistry, and history of cuisine. Our collection presents a multidisciplinary selection of essays that provides a variety of scholarly approaches to Terry Pratchett's *Discworld* series, which, over the last two decades, has begun to garner serious critical attention. Numerous individual essays and shorter critical pieces on Pratchett have appeared, along with an increasing number of scholarly articles and book chapters discussing topics including allegory, witches, heroes and the heroic tradition, myth and folklore, and genres such as *Bildungsroman* and parody. Pratchett's work also has begun to appear on K-12 school reading lists and in university classrooms, and several master's theses have been written on Pratchett, applying such approaches as feminism and stylistic analysis to explore topics including humor, allusion, and intertextuality. Despite this increasing critical interest, the marked dearth of book-length scholarly/critical works leaves an enormous gap in terms of providing scholarly analysis and commentary. This collection aims to help fill that gap. In response to the growing trend in scholarship and academe for interdisciplinary studies, it offers readings that approach Pratchett's *Discworld* series from such diverse perspectives as language and linguistics, literary criticism, visual and performance art, and popular culture studies. Though all of the essays in the collection are written in English by scholars who participate in humanities and social science research, and also serve as one form or another of literary criticism, they nevertheless represent and reflect some of the diverse perspectives that Pratchett's Discworld invites.

The first essay, Roderick McGillis's "*The Wee Free Men*: Politics and the Art of Noise," provides an investigation of the Tiffany Aching books, exploring the ways in which Pratchett's treatment of noise and silence comment on constructions of childhood in both its ethical and political senses, and on relations between individuality and community. McGillis uses Italian Futurist painter and composer Luigi Russolo's theory of the "Art of Noises" and the idea that noise "is, in short, art—revolutionary art" as a springboard into his exploration of Pratchett's treatment of noise and his notion that books for younger readers tend to have a narrative perspective that "is more attuned to sound" than those for older readers.

Anne Hiebert Alton's "Coloring in Octarine: Visual Semiotics and Discworld" considers the various images that complement the Discworld books and traces the trajectories of meanings that arise from a visual analysis of Discworld. While artists Paul Kidby and the late Josh Kirby have produced the lion's share of Discworld art, others including Stephen Player, David Wyatt, Melvyn Grant, Stephen Briggs, and Bernard Pearson and the Discworld Emporium have also contributed to the vast array of images, including but not limited to cover art, the decorative art of frontispieces, chapter headings and ornaments, and tailpieces, illustrated books, and hypotrochoidal texts such as picture books and maps. When considered together, all of these images not only amplify Pratchett's already vividly described world but combine with it in a kind of creative synergy that creates a larger imaginative whole.

Gray Kochhar-Lindgren's "Tell It Slant: Of Gods, Philosophy and Politics in Terry Pratchett's Discworld" focuses on relations among fantasy, religion, and philosophy in the Discworld novels. It examines the ways in which Pratchett remixes religious traditions and how the act of writing in the genre of fantasy repositions traditional philosophical discourses of truth that depend, to a large extent, on some version of correspondence matching language with "real" objects in the world. Kochhar-Lindgren presents the act of making fantasy worlds as creating a narrative site—one full of puns, wordplay, and linguistic invention—that gives Pratchett an opportunity to critique and then to reclaim religious and philosophical traditions for an emancipatory purpose.

Caroline Webb's "The Watchman and the Hippopotamus: Art, Play and Otherness in *Thud!*" considers Pratchett's study of the nature of racial conflict and how the use of art (story, painting, game) empowers people to examine not only notions of the Other but also the tensions within the individual, as well as between groups, "that obscure the commonality of the human." She argues that *Thud!* illustrates how readers can learn significant lessons about the power of empathy or the importance of diversity, among other things, from a variety of art forms—paintings, games, children's picture books—and thus "engage with our own potential for civilization" in addition to forming a more tolerant and culturally sensitive identity.

William C. Spruiell's "Counting Dangerous Beans: Pratchett, Style and the Utility of Premodified Bits" demonstrates the application of basic techniques from linguistic stylistic analysis and corpus linguistics to Pratchett's prose, illustrating several ways in which quantitative observations can be brought to bear on discussions of readers' perceptions of stylistic features—for example, the extent to which readers' native language-variety might influence their sense of how marked a particular expression is in Pratchett's novels.

The final essay, Gideon Haberkorn's "Debugging the Mind: The Rhetoric of Humor and the Poetics of Fantasy," considers the place of Pratchett's novels in relation to their generic concerns with both humor and fantasy and argues that the Discworld series displays a fusion of aspects typical to both. Grounding his argument in the theories of both poetics (of fantasy) and rhetoric (of humor), Haberkorn contends that Pratchett's novels explore the ways we spin meaningful patterns, or stories, out of our sensory perceptions while concurrently encouraging us to think about how we create these patterns "to explore the role of the words in our heads, and how they control us."

Our collection concludes with a Primary Bibliography of Terry Pratchett's Works Published in English plus an Annotated Critical Bibliography comprising entries for known published criticism on Pratchett's Discworld novels, including monographs, critical articles, book chapters, and biographies; in addition, it includes a list of interviews, dissertations, and theses. Not surprisingly, these pieces have employed a variety of approaches, with feminist, genre-based, and stylistic analyses predominant, and have addressed a multitude of topics, including allegory, witches, heroes and the heroic tradition, myth and folklore, as well as Pratchett's use of humor, allusion, and intertextuality.

Pratchett marries entertaining prose with a kind of edgy humorous insight into the human condition that, in an arena other than fantasy, would be regarded as high art—indeed, in many ways he could be regarded as the Chaucer of our time. However, Pratchett's prose is of the sort that very large numbers of people, unfortunately, *voluntarily* read, thus making it not very well suited as an intellectual in-group marker and hence not as attractive for literary critics as it might be otherwise; one can only hope that at some point he learns to talk about bricolage instead of merely doing it masterfully. Borrowing from one of his own comments on fantasy as being "the proper diet for the growing soul" and adapting it more generally to his own work, we might say that "all human life is there: a moral code, a sense of order and, sometimes, great big green things with teeth" (Pratchett 205).

NOTES

1. See bibliography for a full list.

2. See, for example, works by Michael Allen; Liam Farrell; Paul Fitzpatrick; Alison Rostron; and Karl Sprachken.

3. Although this term will be examined more closely in Alton's essay in this volume.

4. As of August 2012 its web address is http://www.funtrivia.com/private/main.cfm?tid=22299.

5. One of the earliest role-playing games was *GURPS Discworld* (1998), reissued in 2002 as *Discworld Roleplaying Game*. GURPS is the acronym for Generic Universal RolePlaying System.

6. Clarecraft "produced handmade Discworld figurines" that became very pop-

ular with not only collectors but also Pratchett himself (L-Space Librarians). The company, founded by Bernard and Isobel Pearson in 1980, "acquired Discworld rights in 1990" but shortly thereafter they sold the company to Bob and Trish Baker and it eventually stopped trading in 2005 (McCrea).

7. For example, structuralism, poststructuralism, and semiotics present different interpretations of what exactly constitutes a "text." As Bernard Radloff suggests, "In narrower usages 'text' is restricted to linguistic unities, in wider usages any group of phenomena, and even being itself, may be understood as 'text'" (639).

8. One example of his broad appeal appears in Francis Lyall's law book entitled *International Communications: The International Telecommunication Union and the Universal Postal Union*, which includes five references (four in footnotes and one in his Preface) to Discworld novels—*Going Postal, Thief of Time, Men at Arms,* and *The Fifth Elephant*—because "Terry's insights were so relevant" (Lyall "Letter").

9. While many of these comments are strewn throughout the Discworld books, another striking one appears when Ridcully wants to pry open a door that has been nailed shut and labeled with the words "Do not, under any circumstances, open this door" because he wants "To see why they wanted it shut, of course"; his comment is accompanied by the footnote, "This exchange contains almost all you need to know about human civilization. At least, those bits of it that are now under the sea, fenced off or still smoking" (*Hogfather* 13).

WORKS CITED

Note: This list excludes Discworld novels, which appear in the Primary Bibliography.

Allen, Michael. *Misconceptions in Primary Science*. Berkshire, England: Open University Press, 2010. 178. *MyLibrary*. 23 July 2012.

Bassnett, Susan. "Is There Hope for the Humanities in the 21st Century?" *Arts & Humanities in Higher Education* 1:1 (2002): 101–110.

Farrell, Liam. "Don't Look Now." Soundings. *British Medical Journal* 312: 7025 (27 Jan. 1996): 255. JSTOR. 7 Aug. 2013.

Fitzpatrick, Paul Michael. "From First Contact to Close Encounters: A Developmentally Deep Perceptual System for a Humanoid Robot." Diss. MIT, 2003. *CiteSeer*. 7 Aug. 2013.

Hunt, Peter. "Terry Pratchett." *Alternative Worlds in Fantasy Fiction*. Ed. Peter Hunt and Millicent Lenz. London: Continuum, 2001.

Langford, David. *The Unseen University Challenge: Terry Pratchett's Discworld Quizbook*. London: Gollancz, 1996.

L-Space Librarians. "Clarecraft Figures." Merchandise. *The L-Space Web*. N.d. 7 Aug. 2012.

Lyall, Francis. *International Communications: The International Telecommunication Union and the Universal Postal Union*. Burlington, VT: Ashgate, 2011.

_____. "Letter to the Editor." *Discworld Monthly* 182 (June 2012): n. pag. 23 July 2012.

McCrea, Erik. "Links to Micro-National and Fantasy Coins." *GeoCities.ws.archive*. 7 Aug. 2013.

Moran, Joe. *Interdisciplinarity*. 2002. 2d ed. New York: Routledge, 2010.

Pratchett, Terry. "Let There Be Dragons." *Science Fiction Chronicle* 15:1 (1993): 5, 28–29.

Radloff, Bernard. "Text." *Encyclopedia of Contemporary Literary Theory: Approaches, Scholars, Terms*. Ed. Irena R. Makaryk. Toronto: University of Toronto Press, 1993. 639–41.

Rostron, Alison. "Building from the Middle: How Middle Managers Construct Their Identities Both as Leaders and Followers." M.A. thesis. University of Chester, 2009. University of Chester. 7 Aug. 2013.

Smythe, Colin. "1996–1998: From Convention to Convention: Two Years on the Discworld." *Terry Pratchett*. Colin Smythe Limited. N.d. 23 July 2012.

_____. "Terry and Discworld—2008–2010." *Terry Pratchett*. Colin Smythe Limited. N.d. 23 July 2012.

Spracklen, Karl. *The Meaning and Purpose of Leisure: Habermas and Leisure at the End of Modernity*. London: Palgrave Macmillan, 2009.

"Story of Wadfest." *Wadfest*. N.d. Web. 23 July 2012.

A Note on the Text

In the essays we will be adopting American spelling, except in those cases where British is required for quotations or editions published only in Britain. Russian names will be transliterated using the U.S. Board on Geographic Names system, except where otherwise required in article titles. As Pratchett is a popular and contemporary writer, there is not yet a "standard" edition for his works, and so authors have used different editions according to availability.

Abbreviations

Parenthetical references throughout the essays and notes will use the following abbreviations:

Abroad	*Witches Abroad* (1991)
Academicals	*Unseen Academicals* (2009)
Almanak	*The Discworld Almanak* (2004)
Arms	*Men at Arms* (1993)
Art	*The Art of Discworld* (2004)
Blink	*A Blink of the Screen: Collected Short Fiction* (2012)
Clay	*Feet of Clay* (1996)
Colour	*The Colour of Magic* (1983)
Companion	*The Discworld Companion* (1994)
Compleat	*The Compleat Ankh-Morpork City Guide* (2012)
Continent	*The Last Continent* (1998)
Cookbook	*Nanny Ogg's Cookbook* (1999)
Cow	*Where's My Cow? A Discworld Picture Book* (2005)
DeathMapp	*Death's Domain: A Discworld Mapp* (1999)

DiscworldMapp	*The Discworld Mapp: Being the Onlie True & Mostlie Accurate Mappe of the Fantastyk Magical Dyscworld* (1995)
Elephant	*The Fifth Elephant* (1999)
Eric	~~*Faust*~~ *Eric* (1990)
Folklore	*The Folklore of Discworld* (2008)
Footnotes	*Once More, with Footnotes* (2004)
Free	*The Wee Free Men* (2003)
Gods	*Small Gods* (1992)
Guards	*Guards! Guards!* (1989)
Hat	*A Hat Full of Sky* (2004)
Hero	*The Last Hero* (2001)
Hogfather	*Hogfather* (1996)
Jingo	*Jingo* (1997)
Jugulum	*Carpe Jugulum* (1998)
LancreMapp	*A Tourist Guide to Lancre: A Discworld Mapp* (1998)
Light	*The Light Fantastic* (1986)
Lords&Ladies	*Lords and Ladies* (1992)
Maskerade	*Maskerade* (1995)
Maurice	*The Amazing Maurice and His Educated Rodents* (2001)
Midnight	*I Shall Wear Midnight* (2010)
Money	*Making Money* (2007)
Mort	*Mort* (1987)
Music	*Soul Music* (1994)
NightWatch	*Night Watch* (2002)
Pictures	*Moving Pictures* (1990)
Poo	*The World of Poo* (2012)
Portfolio	*The Pratchett Portfolio* (1996)
Postal	*Going Postal* (2004)
Poster	*The Josh Kirby Poster Book* (1989)
Pyramids	*Pyramids (The Book of Going Forth)* (1989)
Reaper	*Reaper Man* (1991)
Recall	*Turtle Recall: The Discworld Companion ... So Far* (2012)
Regiment	*Monstrous Regiment* (2003)
Rites	*Equal Rites* (1987)
ScienceI	*The Science of Discworld* (1999)
ScienceII	*The Science of Discworld II: The Globe* (2005)
ScienceIII	*The Science of Discworld III: Darwin's Watch* (2005)
ScienceIV	*The Science of Discworld IV: Judgement Day* (2013)
Snuff	*Snuff* (2011)

Sourcery	*Sourcery* (1988)
StreetsMapp	*The Streets of Ankh-Morpork Being a concise and possibly even accurate Mapp of the Great City of the Discworld* (1993)
Thief	*Thief of Time* (2001)
Thud	*Thud!* (2005)
Times	*Interesting Times* (1994)
Truth	*The Truth* (2000)
Wintersmith	*Wintersmith* (2006)
Wyrd	*Wyrd Sisters* (1988)

The Wee Free Men
Politics and the Art of Noise
Roderick McGillis

"Why was it, Tiffany Aching wondered, that people liked noise so much? Why was noise so important?"—*I Shall Wear Midnight* [1]

My epigraph asks the question I hope to answer. At the beginning of *I Shall Wear Midnight*, Tiffany Aching is attending a fair where the air sounds like a "great cauldron of noise" (1). The various noises "made by people trying to make noise louder than other people making noise" were the sounds of people "*having fun*" (1–2; my italics). Noise, then, is a testament to fun. We might see and hear the truth of this in schoolyards at recess or in dimly lit nightspots or on crowded beaches or at sports events. But like everything else, noise is not one-dimensional. Pratchett notes that fairs are "deceptively cheerful" (3). He does not go on to examine the deception, but he does let us know that along with the noise of the fair, the fair also has its silences, the silences of pickpockets and thieves. Elsewhere in his work, Pratchett complicates the noise/silence binary when he notes that silence itself may be loud. Some silences speak louder than any sound can manage. The quiet voice can seem like a scream: "Eskarina did not shout; she spoke very quietly and in a way that seemed to make more noise than a scream would have done" (*Midnight* 337). Without intending to diminish the complexity of this rich invocation of noise in Pratchett's work, I will concentrate on his Tiffany Aching books in order to associate noise with childhood, but childhood in an ethical sense and even a political sense.

The noise of these books' children, the Nac Mac Feegle or the Wee Free Men, is the exuberance of childhood coupled with the acceptance of respon-

15

sibility. The delirium of these small pictsies is the expression of fun and high spirits, but also of their dedication to freedom and independence. The noise that we hear from the Nac Mac Feegle is the noise of the future in the sense that it prompts us to accept humanity in all its confusion and discord to go forward with a sense of life's loudness, the loudness of togetherness and community. Pratchett's work is nothing if not dedicated to equality and community, and to be dedicated to equality and community is to be forward-looking—in a word, futurist. I do not argue that Terry Pratchett is a Futurist. No one is a Futurist today, although many live in the future. And sometimes the future is the past or at least a version of the past (I think of Steampunk). In any case, I do argue that the Futurist painter Luigi Russolo's letter to Francesco Balilla Pratella in 1913 offers a useful entrance to Pratchett's Discworld, especially to his creation of the Nac Mac Feegle. Listening to the atonal music of the composer Balilla Pratella, Russolo came up with what he termed the "Art of Noises," a combination of "the most complex succession of dissonant chords" (5). Noise, he argued, is the sound of industrial civilization, civilization removed from the silence of nature (4). Noise is a characteristic of modern life. Russolo put the case succinctly: "Today noise reigns supreme over human sensibility" (4). Noise, white or otherwise, is a constant feature of contemporary life and it is easy to conclude that noise functions as a *negative* feature of contemporary life. Noise infiltrates our peace of mind, distracting us from focusing on important aspects of daily life. Noise makes it difficult for us to relax and find a space outside the stresses of modernity, especially urban modernity. Conversely, noise might soothe and quiet our nerves; it may prove reassuring. Noise reminds us of certain spaces, and it may stretch time. Russolo thinks that noise has its beneficial uses, and that "our ears far from being satisfied [with the sounds we hear], keep asking for bigger acoustic sensations" (6). Noise is not simply irritating static, the sound of brouhaha, or the unquiet condition of contemporary and future life. For Russolo noise is provocative, creative, and stimulating. To envisage a time and place without noise is to envisage a post-apocalyptic future emptied of life's bustle and life's fullness. For a Futurist like Russolo, noise is youthful and challenging to the status quo. Noise keeps us forever young. Noise is, in short, art—revolutionary art.

Noise is a feature of urban living, and perhaps it is no accident that Pratchett has described his novel, *I Shall Wear Midnight*, as an "urban fantasy" (Mullan). This is the book in which Pratchett asks the question quoted above in the epigraph to this essay: "Why was noise so important?" (1). The book delivers more than one answer to this question, but in a nutshell we can say that the answer is (as always in Pratchett's world view) because noise makes us human, keeps us human, and brings us together. It is in its own way leveling, just as the fair that opens the book is leveling. Like the fair, noise is a feature of the carnivalesque; it reflects the body in all its excesses. Noise describes the sound of protest as well as the sound of victory. Noise expresses joy as well as pain. Noise assures us that the future will hear about what matters. Noise carries the sound of humanity in all its roughness and charm.

On the subject of noise, Russolo is thinking specifically about orchestral music. He concocts six categories of noises for the orchestra he would like to hear. I will not list all the sounds in these six categories, but a brief survey gives us (1) roaring and bellowing, (2) whistles and snorts, (3) whispers, rustlings, mutterings, and grumbles, (4) cracks, shuffles, and buzzings, (5) wood or rocks knocked together, and (6) voices moaning or shouting or screaming (10). This list reminds me of the various sounds we might associate with the Nac Mac Feegle in Pratchett's Tiffany Aching Books (and in their first appearance in another Discworld book, *Carpe Jugulum*). The Nac Mac Feegle are nothing if not loud. They are loud much of the time, but they can rustle and they can be silent when hiding from the Big Jobs (you and me). But even their silence has a certain loudness: Tiffany tells Miss Tick, in *A Hatful of Sky,* that she knows the Feegles are watching her when she can't hear anything: "It's always a bit quieter if they're watching me" (27). The Nac Mac Feegle are pictsies (not pixies), small people with red hair, blue tattoos, kilts and swords. They are clannish and rural. Some of them live in a burial mound, reminding us just how life-affirming they are; they do not quake in the presence of death (or Death, for that matter. See *Wintersmith* 295). They have a seemingly endless supply of gold coins that they do not value highly. They inhabit a world removed from Russolo's urban cities with their constant cacophony of sound. But they are noisy and they like nothing more than finding a busy pub or tavern in which to carouse. What might the Nac Mac Feegle and their noise have to do with Pratchett's sense of value?

The Nac Mac Feegle first appeared in the "adult" fantasy, *Carpe Jugulum*. I place "adult" in quotation marks because Pratchett's work can and does appeal to readers of pretty much all ages from the young adult years to old codgers like me. Having said this, I make note that Pratchett's work, at least in the marketing of that work, falls into adult and children's books. Interestingly, the Nac Mac Feegle first appear in an adult book, but thereafter appear as a group only in the series of four children's books featuring the young witch, Tiffany Aching. In an interview with Ann Giles, Pratchett remarks that "it's probably true to say there is not a massive difference between my children's books and my adult books.... The books go out there and I've always been aware that fantasy is uni-age and the kids who read, read anything" (Giles). The line between adult and children's fiction may be unclear, but publishers and writers do acknowledge such a line. In various interviews Pratchett points out that he is able to address larger issues in children's books and that the language of a children's book must be somewhat clearer (simpler) than the language of an adult book. The simpler language of a children's book accounts for the readability of the Nac Mac Feegle's speech in the Tiffany Aching books. In *Carpe Jugulum*, their speech is impenetrable. So far, so good. Fantasy appeals across the age spectrum; books for children do differ from books for adults.

In *The Hidden Adult*, Perry Nodelman lists forty-five qualities that distinguish children's books (76–81). Might we add to this list that books for younger readers are noisier than books for adults? Noise appeals more to youth than to age, as anyone above, say, forty-five, who has tried to have a conversation in a well-populated bar or even in many restaurants will recognize. At least noise impinges on one's consciousness less the younger one is. The young take noise for granted. I think we might argue that narrative perspective in books for the young is more attuned to sound than in books for adults. Often we have a narrative voice that mimics orality. Perhaps the most spectacular example is Tolkien's *The Hobbit*, a fantasy whose narrator provides sound effects and speaks directly to readers. Noise has been a feature of children's books for a long time. *Alice's Adventures in Wonderland* is a loud book. At one point, Alice engages in a shouting match with the Queen of Hearts, and we have splashing water, a barking dog, and much cavorting and mirth. The Disney version of this book is also suitably loud, most emphatically so in the zany Mad Tea Party scene. In *A Hat Full of Sky*, Granny Weatherwax prods Tiffany until she is shouting, screaming, and full of fury. Granny maneuvers Tiffany until she is so angry that she becomes noisy and this noise is a feature of an anger that keeps Tiffany free of fear and able to confront the hiver, this book's villain (252–255). Noise serves the function of catching readers' attention. It also reflects the energy of youth. Noise has something of the exuberance (and possibly the anger) of childhood. It is also a challenge to routine and to the complacency of a settled and composed life. It shakes things up. It keeps us awake and perhaps even alert. Noise cuts through complexity. A strain of English comedy stretching from the *Goon Show* on BBC radio from 1951 to 1960, to *Monty Python's Flying Circus* (1969–1974), to *Black Adder* (1983–1989), to Pratchett's Discworld books (1983–ongoing) joys in noise, the noise that will make ye free. Laughter itself is a form of noise, and laughter is, or can be, an expression of the carnivalesque. Laughter is a stay against confusion; it brings people together. The noise of laughter is a feature of childhood at its best.

In other words, noise has its place in the world of children's books if we accept that these books not only socialize young readers, but also set out to alert young readers to the possibilities of transgression. Transgression need not be anti-social or ruthlessly disruptive of community. It can be educative, healthy, and necessary for the free individual. We might remember that the Nac Mac Feegle are the Wee *Free* Men. Noise is often transgressive, but at the same time it can form community as we see in many children's games in which shouting and cacophony are the rule. Just as Russolo was eager to hear sounds that expand sensibility, sounds that will turn "every factory ... into an intoxicating orchestra of noises" (12), sounds that take us into the future, so the noises perpetrated by the Nac Mac Feegle expand our sensibilities and allow us to appreciate the almost anarchic fun these characters represent. In *Wintersmith*, the Feegles are relieved to hear that Rob Anybody has a plan: "They always felt happier when Rob had a Plan, especially since most plans of his boiled down to screaming and rushing at something" (170). Their oft-repeated cry of "crivens," delivered in an oval-shaped, twenty-point font near the end of *I Shall Wear Midnight*, is as good an example as any. Crivens is the Nac Mac Feegles' most familiar cry; it serves as war cry, expression of joy, expletive, and general signal of presence and identity. It is rude, but also a hearty expression of high spirits. It may be a shortened form of "Christ Defend Us," or "Christ in his Heavens," or simply a way of saying expletively, "Christ!" (see Velten) with an emphatic exclamation mark. In effect, "crivens" is lightly disguised profanity in the manner of W. C. Fields's "Godfrey Daniel." It is a word uttered loudly. It is the signature of the Nac Mac Feegle. In a children's book, "crivens" is a reminder of language that ought not be spoken in polite company. It is transgressive.

The Nac Mac Feegle are transgressive; they lie and steal and drink to excess. The Nac Mac Feegle may be loud, they may be inebriate, and they may be aggressive to the point of violence, but they are also loyal, persistent, and joyous. These small pictsies with their blue tattoos teach us that to be human is to err, but they also teach us to engage in life whole-heartedly. Their boisterous antics are reminiscent of the antics of children. They are even known to dress up, as when they make themselves into a Big Job and enter a tavern in Ankh-Morpork in *I Shall Wear Midnight*. Like children, the Feegles run about, gambol, take what they want, and generally live a life of boisterous fun. As far as they are concerned, they live in heaven where anything is permitted. Living the way they do means they steal and carouse. Their life style might indicate that they are criminal and selfish, but if they are, then they are the way the fabled Robin Hood is criminal and selfish. As their leader Rob Anybody (and his name is a nearly accurate descriptor) points out, "we never steal from them as has nae money, we has hearts of gold, although maybe—OK, mostly—somebody else's gold, and we did invent the deep-fried stoat" (*Midnight* 172).

Tiffany explains to Petulia, in *A Hat Full of Sky*, that the Nac Mac Feegle are fairies, but "not the sweet kind." She goes on to say that they are "good ... well, more or less ... but they're not entirely nice" (281). The Feegles are attractive precisely because they are good but not nice. Their goodness manifests itself in their willingness to help those in need, and their not niceness manifests itself in their fierce individuality and independence.

Perhaps the good-not-niceness of the Feegles is most evident in their penchant for lying. The Feegles rarely tell the truth. They seem to have a pathological aversion to the truth. Their lies, however, are not malicious; the Feegles think lies are necessary for their survival. And they lie so often that lying becomes, strangely, a method of telling the truth. In their lying, they are akin to Discworld's most complex and admirable character, Granny Weatherwax. In *A Hat Full of Sky*, Tiffany reflects on Granny: "She lied all the—she *didn't tell the truth* all the time" (257; original italics). Granny's lies serve a purpose, and more often than not that purpose is the betterment of humanity. As Granny notes in the same book: "the start and finish, is helpin' people when life is on the edge. Even people you don't like" (251). She cautions Tiffany when she advises her to "tell people a story they can understand" (258). Telling stories is another way of saying "tell lies." What matters in the end, as Granny again asserts, is helping people. Tiffany asks Granny why she and Miss Tick sent Tiffany to learn witchcraft from the ditsy Miss Level, and Granny replies that they did so because Miss Level cares for and about people:

> She cares about 'em. Even the stupid, mean, dribbling ones, the mothers with the runny babies and no sense, the feckless and the silly and the fools who treat her like some kind of a servant. Now *that's* what I call magic—seein' all that, dealin' with all that, and still goin' on. It's sittin' up all night with some poor old man who's leavin' the world, takin' away such pain as you can, comfortin' their terror, seein' 'em safely on their way ... and then cleanin' 'em up, layin' 'em out [250; original italics].

The sentence goes on for another nine lines, presenting the ethics of humanity. Granny's speech pattern itself is important. She is a common person, educated in the ways of humanity but with little in the way of "higher education." Characters like Granny, Tiffany, and even the Feegles have their flaws—they are human, even when they are pictsies—but when you get right down to it, what defines them is their humanity, their willingness to help others without prejudice.

Another connection between Granny, Tiffany, and the Feegles is their status as outsiders. Granny and Tiffany are witches and witches are by definition "other" than the rest of the members of a community. Witches stick out by virtue of their pointy hats (and for the most part their black clothes), but also by what other members of the community perceive to be their magical ability. As Pratchett and Granny Weatherwax make clear throughout the Discworld series, magic is as much perception as it is fact. Or magic is a fact by virtue of people accepting it as fact rather than it being a matter of spells, charms, or potions. "Headology" is a word Granny uses for magic. In any case, witches are othered. As for the Feegles, they are "other" because they are fairies, because they are small, and because they come from away. They are foreign among the likes of Big Jobs. That othered characters like Granny or the Feegles sacrifice themselves for the good of those who other them is testament to their goodness. The ethics of the other in Discworld are tolerance and assistance without prejudice. Pratchett's world may have its hierarchies, but ultimately what matters is the human instinct for cooperation and care. Ministering to others is the lot of the witch in Discworld, and the Feegles who live on the Chalk take as their lot the protection of the big wee hag, Tiffany Aching. When Pratchett says that he can tackle more difficult themes in his children's books than in his other books, he refers, in part at least, to this theme of communal responsibility and collective assistance. The Feegles are willing to put themselves in danger to help the wee big hag because they admire and respect her for what she is, a Big Job who helps others and who puts herself out for others.

These small pictsies fit the ingredients of a children's book precisely because they are children, or at least they are like children. Not only do they run about and make loud noises, but they also are on the verge of literacy. Much is made in the books of their respect for literacy; the new kelda (their matriarch) has decided that literacy is something her people should master. They know that Tiffany is a reader, and they look up to those who have the ability to read. With Rob Anybody, we have a character who is, somewhat reluctantly, learning to read. In *A Hat Full of Sky*, the Feegles go inside Tiffany's mind in order to discover how to save her from the dreaded hiver that threatens to infiltrate her thinking. They have the ability to travel between worlds, even when the world is inside a person's head. In Tiffany's mind, they come across her grandmother's old shearing hut, but Tiffany is nowhere about. As they scout the place, words begin to appear on the door. Awf'ly Wee Billy begins to read, but he is abruptly cut off by Rob who snaps, "I ken weel what they say! ... I ha' the knowin' of the readin'" (218). What follows is a painfully funny attempt by Rob to read the words that keep appearing. For each letter Rob "reads" as if he were looking at a pictograph: "that's the snake, an' that's kinda like a gate letter, an' the comb on its side. Two o' that, an' the fat man standin' still, an' the snake again..." (218). In case you missed it, the word Rob has just read is "SHEEPS." He goes through another four words in the same fashion, and then proudly announces, "There! Is that readin' I just did, or wus it no?" (218).

The exclamation mark after Rob's "There" deserves notice. The Feegles more often than not speak in exclamation marks; that is, they speak loudly, in an exclamatory manner. Noise is their element. When Rob announces that the meaning of the words he so descriptively reads is that the Feegles "are gonna go *stealin'*!" they reply with a resounding cheer (219; original italics). The Feegles, like children, live life in exclamation marks. The exclamation mark, as we see in *I Shall Wear Midnight*, constitutes one aspect of Pratchett's art of noise. As part of his noise exposition in this book, Pratchett differentiates between the noise churned out by the Cunning Man, this book's villain, and the noise raised to thwart fear or the noise raised to indicate the Feegles' zest for life. Tiffany and Laetitia go shopping and while they are looking at various articles of apparel, the Cunning Man attempts to invade Tiffany's mind with a view to taking it over. The Cunning Man represents hate and paranoia and when he gets into your head, the world turns dark before your eyes. Tiffany hears the voice of the Cunning Man croaking in her head: "*I will take you and your confederacy of evil!!!!!*" She thinks that "she could actually see the exclamation marks. They shouted for him, even when he spoke softly" (324; original italics). Here is loud writing, the volume indicated by the combination of italics, exclamation marks, and of course the word "shouted." The noise of the Cunning Man is unpleasant and counter to the enjoyment of life. This is the sound of the death principle as opposed to the noise of the Feegles that is the sound of eros, of life lived to the fullest. The Feegles have experienced easeful death, or so they think. They have passed through the magic casements and live with unabated energy. The Cunning Man, on the other hand, is jaded. He is the cruelty and intolerance and superstition of the world. He is the unpleasant adult to the Feegles' buoyant children. A witch hunter, the Cunning Man represents the dour and decidedly dark deliverer of gloom. He renders the world devoid of charm.

The Feegles are not, literally, children; they are, however, childlike. The childlike, in the words of George MacDonald, "is the divine." For MacDonald, the child is the type of essential humanity, willing to serve others and to look up to and obey authority. The childlike knows no age. The Nac Mac Feegle are adamant that they are not pixies, not cute small humanoids with pointy hats. Rather they are a warrior-like race, "the most feared of the fairy races" (*Folklore* 103). In *The Folklore of Discworld*, Pratchett and Simpson refer to them as "out-and-out rebels against any authority whatsoever" (104), and in *The Wee Free Men*, the lawyer toad says they are rebels against anyone and everything (77). This is not exactly the case, as they do follow what their kelda directs them to do, but they follow direction in an independent, and usually wild and wooly way. They live by their own rules, which is to say they live without the benefit of rules.

If heaven lies about us in our infancy, then the Nac Mac Feegle have died and gone to heaven, or at least this is what they believe. *A Hat Full of Sky* opens with an excerpt from *Fairies and How to Avoid Them* by Miss Perspicacia Tick; this excerpt includes a section on the history and religion of the Nac Mac Feegle. Here we learn that these little pictsies used to live in Fairyland, but they were exiled for some reason. In exile, they found themselves in "our world [i.e., the Discworld, a world intriguingly like the world of readers], with its sunshine and mountains and blue skies and things to fight" (10). How could such a wonderful place, they reason, not be "a heaven or Valhalla?" Therefore, they must be dead. If, in the heat of battle in this world, they die, then they fret that they will go to a boring place where nothing much happens and they will have no one to fight.

When they appear in *Carpe Jugulum*, the Nac Mac Feegle speak a language well nigh impenetrable. Here is a brief example of their speech: "Yings, yow graley yin! Suz ae rikt dheu" (209). Whatever this may mean, it most likely sounds better when uttered loudly. The "Yings" and the exclamation mark seem to signal the need for loudness. We should not assume that noise exists only in the three-dimensional world of matter, that noise is something only for the ears. Eyes too can hear. Noise, as we have seen, may be an aspect of silence. The loud silence that our eyes can see lies at the origin of Pratchett's Nac Mac Feegle. They are, we remember, pictsies, members of the fairy crew, and Pratchett finds his fairies in nineteenth-century art and literature. In *The Wee Free Men*, Tiffany goes to the land of the fairies to rescue the Baron's son Roland from the Fairy Queen. The chapter in which she does this has the title, "Master Stroke." When Tiffany approaches the place of the fairies, she hears "a loud *crack*!" Then she pushes her way through the tall grass and observes the following scene: "On a flat rock, a man was cracking nuts half as big as he was, with a two-handed hammer. He was being watched by a crowd of people" (220; original italics). In the Author's Note at the end of *The Wee Free Men* and also in Pratchett and Simpson's *The Folklore of Discworld*, Pratchett gives the origin of these fairies and this scene: the famous painting by the Victorian artist Richard Dadd called *The Fairy Feller's Master-Stroke* (1855–64). The painting depicts the cracking of a nut, and it is the cracking of this nut, or at least the blow that tries to crack the nut, that Tiffany hears. As she passes by the fairy feller, she remarks: "Best of luck with the nut-cracking" (221).

The passing joke here is that the nut-cracking is akin to cracking a joke.

The "crack" is both the sound of the master-stroke and a witty remark—a joke. It is also a colloquialism for something that makes you burst out laughing, something that cracks you up. Crack is a loud sound as well as a small space; in other words, a crack is something that we can both see and hear. The crack of dawn, for example, is the sliver of light on the horizon as the sun begins to rise and the sharp sound of the alarm clock as it jangles in the morning. Crack contains the noise that we can see reverberating through Discworld, the noise that gives life. The allusion to the Dadd painting is nice because it combines noise and silence, ears and eyes and allows them to share sense impressions. The painting is, in effect, something of a synesthetic moment. Synesthesia is evident later in the book when Tiffany smells snow; she thinks that "snow had a smell like the taste of tin" (249). Synesthesia reminds us of the Romantic aesthetic at the heart of these books. And by looking back at a Victorian moment, as he does when he invokes the Richard Dadd painting, Pratchett catches the craziness at the heart of Discworld. This craziness is what Lewis Carroll refers to in *Alice's Adventures in Wonderland* as madness: "We're all mad here. I'm mad. You're mad" (58). The madness Carroll alludes to and that pervades the Discworld is not the madness of Richard Dadd incarcerated in a psychiatric hospital, but rather that fine madness that allows one to create. The poet, the madman, the lover, and the Feegle have much in common.

One thing these four people have in common is their hope for the future. The mind that loves, creates, and carouses joys in the things of the world. The world is not too much with the poet, the madman, the lover, or the Feegle. But the future is a delicate sound. Tzvetan Todorov has recently outlined the Futurist manifesto of the early twentieth century, connecting its aesthetics to its political desire for revolution. He assures us that we are politically savvy in these days of the early twenty-first century: "We now spurn peddlers of political dreams—utopians who promise us that happiness is just around the corner—because we have learned that promises such as these served in the past to hide the sinister designs of Lenin, Mussolini and Hitler" (89). Todorov cautions us that "Romantic images, in their artistic perfection" participate in the drive to a totalitarian organization of community. The Futurists were complicit with dictatorship.

I began by connecting Pratchett with Luigi Russolo and the Futurists. Like the Futurists and members of other movements in the arts in the early to mid-twentieth century, Pratchett works in the Romantic tradition. However, we need not see this tradition in the elitist or politically sinister way that Todorov outlines. The privileging of art that we see in Romantic ideology, a privileging that can have as its political manifestation the championing of heroic figures, is not simply a projection of the artist as great person speaking from his or her particular Olympus. The vision of the artist in Romantic thinking is more often than not egalitarian. Everyone is an artist. In Pratchett's world this view of the arts manifests itself in the power of story. We see just how powerful story is in the myth of Wintersmith and his love for the Lady Summer. As Granny Weatherwax says in *A Hatful of Sky*: "A story gets things done" (258). Witches are, after all, just storytellers. The Wee Free Men inhabit the world of story. What Pratchett calls "the narrative imperative" (*Folklore* 22) organizes the world, and all of us are participants in story. Like the past, the future consists of stories and more stories. Generations may pass, but story remains forever young. Story is perhaps just a shout-out to the human race. Terry Pratchett's books for young readers offer stories of a world fraught with a complexity compromised by the simple act of shouting.

WORKS CITED

Alice in Wonderland. Dir. Clyde Geronimi, Wilfred Jackson, Hamilton Luske. Disney, 1951.

Black Adder. BBC1. 1983–89.

Carroll, Lewis. *Alice's Adventures in Wonderland.* 1865. Ed. Roger Lancelyn Green. Illus. John Tenniel. New York: Oxford University Press, 1982.

Giles, Ann. "Terry Pratchett—'I know the books have their heart in the right place.'" Interview with Terry Pratchett. *Bookwitch.* 24 Apr. 2012. Web. 29 Mar. 2012.

The Goon Show. BBC Home Service. 1951–60.

MacDonald, George. "The Child in the Midst." *Unspoken Sermons.* First Series. London: Alexander Strahan, 1867. *Project Gutenberg.* 8 Aug. 2013.

Monty Python's Flying Circus. BBC. 1969–74.

Mullan, John. "Terry Pratchett talks to the Guardian Book Club." Interview with Terry Pratchett. Guardian Book Club. 18 Dec. 2009. *Guardian.* Web. 20 Mar. 2012.

Nodelman, Perry. *The Hidden Adult: Defining Children's Literature.* Baltimore: Johns Hopkins University Press, 2008.

Pratchett, Terry. *Carpe Jugulum.* 1998. London: Corgi, 1999.

_____. *A Hat Full of Sky.* 2004. London: Corgi, 2005.

_____. *I Shall Wear Midnight.* 2010. London: Corgi, 2011.

_____. *The Wee Free Men.* London: Doubleday, 2003.

_____. *Wintersmith.* New York: HarperTempest, 2006.

Pratchett, Terry, and Jacqueline Simpson. *The Folklore of Discworld.* 2008. London: Corgi, 2009.

Russolo, Luigi. "The Art of Noise." 1913. Trans. Robert Filliou. N.p.: Ubuclassics, 2004. 1 Apr. 2012.

Todorov, Tzvetan. *The Limits of Art: Two Essays.* London: Seagull, 2010.

Tolkien, J. R. R. *The Hobbit.* 1937. 2d ed. 1951. London: Allen and Unwin, 1979.

Velten, Alexandra. "English Dialects in Modern British Fiction: 'Ach Crivens': The Language of the Wee Free Men." 2008. *L-Space.* 6 Apr. 2012.

Coloring in Octarine
Visual Semiotics and Discworld
ANNE HIEBERT ALTON

"No poet, no artist, of any art, has his complete meaning alone."—
T. S. Eliot, "Tradition and the Individual Talent" [55]

T. S. Eliot's comment seems a perfect place to begin an exploration of the relevance of illustration in relation to the hermeneutics of Terry Pratchett's Discworld series. The enormous range of visual material created for and about the Discworld and its inhabitants serves to amplify Pratchett's vibrant prose by providing additional depth, flavor, and shading, giving it supplementary meanings that fluctuate and shift depending on the artist being read or remembered at any moment of reading. These multiple images, when taken together, can color our imaginations and steer them so that we imagine Discworld and its people and places along certain lines. We have wiggle room, of course, and for most readers Pratchett's prose likely plays the most significant part in influencing their imaginations: after forty-plus novels, the lines have fallen into certain patterns, and the fantasy Pratchett created some thirty years ago has taken on a certain *gravitas* or resonance—a critical mass of suspended disbelief, perhaps—which means that experienced readers of Pratchett may not veer too far away from the imagery that they have created in their minds' eyes. That said, while readers have shaped these images largely based on the words that they have read on the page, they have also—in some cases inadvertently, in others deliberately—had these images informed by the amazing variety of illustrations that exists to accompany the books; book covers, media adaptations, companion works, and other images have (perhaps unconsciously) helped to solidify the ways that Discworld and its inhabitants appear in our imaginations in terms of their general shape and/or specific details.[1] The artists who create these images participate in what I think of as coloring in octarine, or Discworld-meaning-creation. Discworld readers know that octarine is Pratchett's color of magic, but for my purposes it is also the resulting meaning that we, as Discworld readers, construct when we read the books in conjunction with their images.

To explore these artists of octarine in a way that is possible within this essay, I have necessarily defined some parameters and exclusions, since it was impossible to consider all of the visual interpretations of Discworld (had we but world enough and time...). Thus, even though they are part of a larger discussion of visual semiotics and phenomenology, this essay does not discuss adaptations of Pratchett's works, Discworld-inspired and related games, and Discworld ephemera such as jigsaw puzzles, wine labels, Clarecraft figurines, jewelry, tea towels, and many other objects created over the years as collectible items for Pratchett fans.[2] In the case of both adaptations and games, my grounds for exclusion rest on the lack of a direct line of connection between the original text and the illustrations: in most of these cases the illustrations are based on something that is not directly a Pratchett text, even though the text on which it is based may be. For instance, the illustrated animated screenplays for *Wyrd Sisters* and *Soul Music* correspond with the animations of these works, which in turn are adaptations of Pratchett's titular novels; thus, their artwork is at least one step removed from Pratchett's original text. Similarly, the artwork that appears in the graphic novels of *The Color of Magic* and *The Light Fantastic* and the "big comic books" of *Mort* and *Guards! Guards!* is based on adaptations rather than the original novels.[3] The illustrated screenplays for the live-action films of *Hogfather* and *The Colour of Magic* are likewise one step removed from the originals: their screenplay text, illustrated with film stills, was written by Vadim Jean (albeit "mucked about with" by Pratchett) before being performed by actors, after which the films were edited by a group of producers and cinematographers, and as a result have a series of interpreters separating them from the originals. In none of these cases am I suggesting that these adaptations are not works worthy of further study; instead, they fall so clearly into the larger fields of film and media studies that they warrant a far more detailed discussion than can be achieved here. The same argument holds for the case of artwork for the games, which encompasses not only covers and graphics for a variety of computer, role-playing, and board games[4] but also game-cards and instruction booklets. Finally, in relation to the delightful abundance (or plethora, depending on one's perspective) of Discworld ephemera, for the most part it has been left out due to the sheer volume of merchandise that exists, available through internet shops and dealers, among other places.

This essay thus focuses mainly on the art of two-dimensional illustration as it has been created in response to particular Discworld texts and to Pratchett's concept of the Discworld as a whole. This artwork includes the cover art of Paul Kidby and the late Josh Kirby, which moves from the realm of decoration and representation into that of homage and parody. It also includes the decorative art of frontispieces, chapter headings, and tailpieces that appears in several Discworld books, including *The Josh Kirby Discworld Portfolio, The Art of Discworld, The Pratchett Portfolio, Night Watch, Monstrous Regiment,* the four Tiffany Aching books, *The Amazing Maurice and His Educated Rodents, The Folklore of Discworld,* and the *Discworld Companions* and *Diaries.* In addition, this essay considers the illustrated books written by Pratchett: Josh Kirby's ~~Faust~~ *Eric,* Paul Kidby's *The Last Hero,* and Stephen Player's *The Illustrated Wee Free Men,* where the illustrations not only decorate Pratchett's text but also interpret, supplement, and at times extend it. It concludes with a discussion of the artwork that appears in what I refer to as the hypotrochoidal texts, works generated from within the Discworld novels— *Where's My Cow?, The World of Poo, Nanny Ogg's Cookbook, The Discworld Almanak,* and the maps—that have concurrent implications outside Pratchett's multiverse. Despite the many variations and potencies of images that appear throughout the Discworld books, they come together in a substantial body "to illuminate text, to throw light on words" (Shulevitz 120), which is one of the main purposes of illustration. In doing so, all of the images necessarily interpret the written text into other, more visual, formats, and consequently they contain an implicit element of translation of medium as they move from the written word to the visual image.[5] Moreover, many of these images go a step—or several—further and supplement the text of Discworld to extend it, often with Pratchett's blessing. Taken together, all of the illustrations establish some of the shades and hues of the color of octarine. This essay considers the key visual contributions to Discworld and explores their visual semiotics in order to trace the trajectories of meanings that arise from a visual analysis of Discworld.

*****

Ursula Le Guin once commented, "I write in the 'despised' genres: children's literature, science fiction, women's literature, fantasy" (Le Guin). Certainly fantasy has taken longer than some other genres to claim its respectability in the areas of literary study well established within the so-called literary canon. Fantasy illustration similarly embodies Le Guin's notion and magnifies it.[6] Illustration is an art form that also exists on the margins, the poor cousin at the table; it occupies a similarly side-lined place in relation to fine art as fantasy does to mainstream literature. As Steven Heller notes, "All painters know that the word 'illustration' is the kiss of death" because of the old notion of pure art necessarily being separate from commercial art, as commercial art—read: illustration—is considered as "the beginning of selling out" (3). Some of the reasons for this may be traced to audience as well as genre expectations. Our western culture, at least, traditionally has regarded pictures in most literature as being elements that, while occasionally decorative, are either unnecessary or appropriate only for immature readers—echoes of Le Guin's "despised" genres—and thus something that readers need to grow up and out of.[7] Take, for example, literature for children. We often assume that contemporary books published expressly for children must include illustrations, and it is virtually impossible to find a book today marketed for younger readers that does not contain pictures of some sort, be they cute decorations that ornament books of instruction like alphabet books or early word books, or the double-page spreads that dominate picture books. Even chapter books and juvenile novels tend to regularly include full-page images. However, the art of reading pictures is not something that is either taught or emphasized as part of a regular curriculum; Gunther Kress notes the way that school children are encouraged to illustrate their writing, yet their assignments are corrected for grammar and style and content while the art is not (16). Kress also notes that illustrations start to disappear from children's own work after about the second grade, and I would add that pictures progressively disappear from the books that they read as they get older. By the time children reach high school, their books tend to eschew illustrations, except (as Kress notes) in their textbooks that have specialized or functional images in the forms of maps or diagrams or photographs for particular purposes. Once readers have moved to so-called adult books, their fictional reading material is often devoid of illustrations—except in the case of certain genres, such as, for example, fantasy and science fiction, which often contain inside illustrations in the form of maps, and cover art with eye-catching otherworldly creatures or wizarding folk cavorting with magical beasts. Books with these sorts of covers, however, are often dismissed as "genre" by critics, with the implication that something that is "genre" is necessarily not "literature."[8] This sort of attitude perfectly sums up the implicit criticism of both audience and genre, that if one is silly enough to enjoy fantasy, or books with pictures, clearly one is not mature enough to be able to appreciate "real" literature and art.

Unfortunately, this blinkered attitude ignores not only the enormous delight and illumination to be gained from reading texts with their accompanying images, but also the aesthetic pleasure created from thinking and reading in a multidisciplinary way. W. J. T. Mitchell notes "that the interaction of pictures and texts is constitutive of representation as such: all media are mixed media, and all representations are heterogeneous; there are no 'purely' visual or verbal arts" (5), and Richard Howells adds that texts that include images "combine the visual with the verbal in order to get multilayered messages across" (5). This multi-layered effect is more complex than that achieved by stories told through a single medium. While a number of critics have written about the theory of visual semiotics,[9] one whose work is particularly useful for my purposes is picture book theorist Lawrence Sipe, who notes the necessity of invoking interdisciplinary approaches in considering visual literacy and draws on a combination of reader response theory, aesthetic criticism, linguistics and semiotics, and literacy theories to explicate what he sees as the way text and illustrations combine to create "synergy"—the combined effect of two or more agents that is greater than sum of separate efforts.[10] Sipe argues that when we read pictures and text, we use a kind of filling-in-the-gaps process, where the pictures fill in gaps left by the words and the words fill in gaps left by the pictures, creating fuller meaning than if either existed in an isolated state. He also uses Roman Jakobson's semiotic theory in relation to the distinctions between the text of written language and the image of visual art, where Jakobson distinguishes between the two, noting that the predominant nature of written language is sequential, while the predominant nature of visual art is simultaneous. Sipe clarifies this with his observation that the art of visual literacy for reading illustrated books, such as picture books, is both linear and temporal, and thus in order to "construct an integrated meaning" one must concurrently perceive the work both sequentially and simultaneously (101).[11]

These kernels of Sipe's theory, combined with a few other elements of reading pictures, serve as a springboard into my discussion of the phenomenology of Discworld illustrations and text. By breaking down the basic functions of illustrations in literature into five aspects—representation, decoration, clarification, elaboration, and extension—and applying these aspects to the various sorts of artwork that illustrates Discworld, we can participate in Sipe's process of filling in the gaps by reading the pictures to interpret the text and vice versa. Once we have completed that process, by considering all of the image-reading as a whole we can create a kind of synergistic interpretation that informs us about Discworld on a deeper level than a one-layered meaning might. In viewing the ways in which the text and illustrations work concurrently, in both sequential and simultaneous fashions, we can see that the fantasy art of Discworld, far from having the kind of parasitic nature that Perry Nodelman attributes to illustration,[12] instead reveals the artist's function as a kind of partner to the author "in shaping the reader's mental image and understanding of the text" (Shulevitz 129).

Cover Art

One of the first places readers might notice fantasy art is on the book jacket, where the first glimpses of some of the crucial elements of a story appear. For the Discworld series, the two most significant artists are Paul Kidby and the late Josh Kirby; their respective cover artwork has also appeared on numerous translations of the Discworld novels. As the series has grown in popularity, other artists' cover art has been used, occasionally in England as well as abroad, and the work of French artist Marc Simonetti has adorned the covers of several editions, but Kirby's and Kidby's names are still the most synonymous with Discworld covers.[13] Cover art, and especially fantasy cover art, plays an important role in marketing, being considered "the second most important marketing tool next to the author's name" (Frank 48); after all, covers are the first point of entry, and thus function as a kind of hook to grab the reader's attention and encourage her to pick the book up off the shelf and open it. Essentially, cover art is regarded by publishers as "a poster to sell the book" (Cherry). David Langford suggests that the function of book jacket is to tell readers what sort of book it is, invoke other books like it, and thus provide an indication as to whether it is the sort of thing a reader might enjoy (*Josh*), and certainly covers can do all of these things. At times, however, this effect can backfire: for instance, A. S. Byatt noted that her initial reaction to the Discworld novels was somewhat negative, since "Josh Kirby's covers with pink and bosomy cartoon women as well as energetic dragons did not seem to be my kind of thing" (11). Later, however, she came to appreciate Kirby's illustrations, noting that his "gleeful wild energy and intricacy—both brash and sophisticated—... is exactly right for these tales" (12). Her comment addresses an additional function for cover art: in addition to providing certain kinds of anticipatory indications for readers, cover art can also function as a kind of shorthand to enhance the sense of character, place, and overall impression of the world they are reading.

For many readers, and for many years, the Discworld covers by Josh Kirby were readers' first point of entry into Pratchett's world. Kirby illustrated over 400 published book covers between 1954 and 1999, twenty-eight of which were covers for Discworld and Discworld-related works.[14] His covers for *The Colour of Magic* and *The Light Fantastic* established him in the 1980s and 1990s "as *the* illustrator for Discworld" and Langford goes so far as to suggest that Kirby was as "inseparable" from the Discworld books as Sir John Tenniel was for *Alice in Wonderland* or Ernest Shepard was for Pooh (*Josh* 11). While some might argue with this claim, as Kirby was but one of several artists who contributed to Discworld's visual aspect, his work certainly is a major piece that creates the octarine shades of Discworld illustration. His cover for the Corgi paperback edition of *The Colour of Magic*, his first Discworld commission, was his only watercolor cover; his preferred medium was oil paint, and Langford has described him as "a cartoonist in oils" (*Josh* 6). Certainly his illustrations have a certain cartoonish and often carnivalesque style, containing exaggerated proportions like those appearing on *The Colour of Magic* cover, with rats the size of terriers and a toad bigger than one of them.[15] His covers always show plenty of action and color, and embody a kind of exuberant style which takes a central image and then surrounds it with anything (and everything) else from the story that takes his fancy. Kirby once described the Discworld books as "'Bruegel in literary form'" ("Out of"),[16] and Bruegel's influence is evident throughout Kirby's Discworld covers, particularly in the way they capture the flavor of an "abundance of bustling, imperfect humanity" (Langford *Josh* 6). Kirby also cited the artistic influences of the work of Titian and Rubens, as well as William Hogarth, Hieronymus Bosch, and Frank Brangwyn.[17] His delight in painting the human, and particularly female, form echoes the work of Rubens and Titian, while he shares Bosch's sense of colorful complexity, Hogarth's elements of visual storytelling and detail, and Brangwyn's grandeur of scale and design.

One of the main aspects of any of Kirby's illustrations is the sense of hectic activity: there is always so much going on it is difficult to know where to look first. For example, his cover for *Wyrd Sisters* depicts Nanny Ogg (*sans* red boots) in the stocks looking up at the ghost of King Verence; Duke Felmet and the Duchess are looking appropriately startled, while Granny Weatherwax, the Fool, and Magrat crash into the frame from above. Our attention alternates between the main characters and setting to Death and his lifetimers on the far left (on the back cover of the paperback), back to the image of the Fool and Granny Weatherwax at the top center, where our attention is arrested by her hugely exaggerated chin and nose. Similarly, Kirby's cover for the omnibus edition of *The Colour of Magic* and *The Light Fantastic* highlights Rincewind and Twoflower[18] racing through the air atop the Luggage, attended by Hrun the Barbarian and Liessa Wyrmbidder, the dragon maiden, giving Kirby ample opportunity to draw his trademark scantily-clad shapely heroine, complete with flowing long tresses and brandishing a sword. His cover here parodies typical pulp fantasy covers of the Hildebrandt brothers' variety and adds comic elements through not only the absurdity of the Luggage's appearance but also his pastel color choices of light blues, whites, and pinks. There is plenty of detail, including four apocalyptic figures in pursuit—Death appears second from the right, riding Binky—and numerous fantastic creatures glaring at them from the ground, including a small dragon and a large troll.

Kirby's covers also often combine several scenes, particularly when, as he observed, "'I can't find a single incident that represents the whole book'" (Langford *Josh* 13). Good examples of this tendency appear on the covers for *Witches Abroad, Hogfather,* and *The Truth*, all of which include numerous characters from different parts of the action brought together in a montage. The cover of *Hogfather*, for example, foregrounds Death and Albert riding on a sled being towed through the sky by the four Hogswatch Night hogs; the sled also carries Susan, Banjo, and Mr. Sideney, the wizard student (see Image 1). The lower right corner shows the assassin Teatime, apparently preparing to climb down a chimney, and in the bottom center the King and his footmen appear in the snow. Other details include the Death of Rats, snow-covered turrets, and bats flying in the night sky. The color palette is relatively restrained—for Kirby—with blues, whites, and yellows/oranges dominating. His cover for *The Truth*, in contrast, is more typical, with its cheerful jumble of characters piled together around the printing press in a scene that does not occur in the book, but that nevertheless invites close speculation as to the identities of each of the multitude of characters. While it is relatively easy to pick out the dwarf Gunilla Goodmountain, Gaspode the wonder dog, the "nuns" (one of them looking remarkably like a potato), and Sacharissa Crisplock,

1. *Hogfather*, by Josh Kirby (by permission of Colin Smythe on behalf of the Josh Kirby Estate).

Lord Vetinari looks more like a wicked priest than the former-assassin-turned-city-dictator, with his pronounced hunchback and pointed boots, neither of which is mentioned in any of the novels.

Two of Kirby's covers are especially interesting for more than just their eye-catching energy or representative aspects. His cover for *Reaper Man* has been referred to as "one of his most memorable Discworld paintings" since it shows the influence of Dutch seventeenth century "memento mori paintings" ("Out of"), paintings that were intended to be symbolic reminders of death's inevitability and that conveyed their messages through images conventionally associated with death, such as skulls or bones (see Image 2). Kirby's *Reaper Man* succeeds brilliantly here, combining images from the book—the field workers stopping for lunch, the threshing machine, the child Sal playing with Death's own small golden lifetimer, Death's overalls—with others that typically refer to mortality, such as the skeletal figure of Death holding his scythe and a setting crescent moon, along with imagery specifically associated with death in the Discworld, including the tree festooned with lifetimers and the Death of Rats. Kirby also invokes Van Gogh: echoes of *Starry Night* appear in not only in his use of color, with the midnight blue sky and bright yellow moon, but also in the pattern of stars leading to the crescent moon, though Kirby's moon is reversed and lower in the sky than Van Gogh's; similarly, Van Gogh's paintings of harvests and threshers, particularly *Harvest in Provence* and *Wheatfield with Crows*, are referenced in Kirby's composition, style, and color. The harvest background creates a pastoral scene, and the gentleness with which Death's hand sits on the small girl's hair is comforting, despite the surrounding iconography. Kirby's cover for *Soul Music* is similarly intertextual, but this time in relation to a record album cover. Fittingly, given its subject matter as a satire on rock music and musicians in general, Kirby's cover alludes to the iconic image from Meat Loaf's 1977 album, *Bat Out of Hell*.[19] While the album cover features a motorcycle erupting out of a graveyard, Kirby's cover shows Death doing a wheelie on a motorcycle; though the two images are facing opposite ways, the motorcycles themselves and the angles at which they are presented are nearly identical. Kirby was unhappy with the original hardcover version, feeling that its white background was too toned down for the effect he hoped to create, and so he completely redid the cover for Corgi's paperback, adding the flourishes so paramount in most of his paintings with extra stylization on the motorcycle, more stars in the sky, and the crowded landscape of Ankh-Morpork's many bridges and buildings below.

Kirby began illustrating Discworld covers for the Corgi paperback edition of *The Colour of Magic*, and he subsequently was asked to create the hardcover image for *The Light Fantastic*. When Pratchett changed publishers to Gollancz

2. *Reaper Man*, by Josh Kirby (by permission of Colin Smythe on behalf of the Josh Kirby Estate).

for the hardcovers, he asked that Kirby continue to do the cover illustrations, and at this point they started discussing the cover designs over the phone. However, according to Suckling, it was a "loose collaboration" and Kirby was "left pretty much to his own interpretations" (Suckling 92).[20] Usually his illustrations for the hardcover and paperback books are, if not exactly the same, very similar, with the same design but slightly different colors or more details, as for the *Soul Music* cover discussed earlier. Occasionally, however, Kirby would create a new painting for the paperback, as happened with *Lords and Ladies* "after a bad time with requested revisions to the hardback version" (Langford *Josh* 17). This is understandable, as the hardcover illustration includes figures not transparently related to the characters in the book. His revised cover for the paperback is much easier to follow, showing an easily recognizable Nanny Ogg, wearing her trademark red boots, along with the dwarf Casanunda as they confront the King in his lair.

Kirby's policy was "'not to do a Discworld cover that does not have a frameable painting at the end of it'" (Langford *Josh* 99),[21] which resulted also in two publications featuring the complete paintings: *The Josh Kirby Poster Book* and *The Josh Kirby Discworld Portfolio*. Though Pratchett did not agree with all of Kirby's interpretations of the Discworld, he did famously comment,

"I ... only invented the Discworld. Josh created it," and continued, "Many writers are unhappy about their jacket design, others like them. I'm one of the very few who wait anxiously to see what new delights the book cover will bring" (*Poster* n. pag.). That said, Pratchett has noted that sometimes Kirby gets it wrong, as with the witches: "Whatever the book says, he likes witches to look like crones 'otherwise how will anyone know they're witches?'" (*Poster* n. pag.). This of course misses the point: while Pratchett's witches might, at times, dress like witches and act like witches, they are first and foremost people, with complex personality traits and distinctive personalities—no one who has encountered Nanny Ogg in print is likely to forget her immoderate love of alcohol, her many husbands, or the Hedgehog Song. Indeed, Pratchett's creation of Nanny Ogg and Granny Weatherwax has undermined, or at the very least expanded, the archetype of what witches can be. Though Kirby attempted to justify his decision, noting that "'witches and wizards have their place in far more ancient folklore and I follow that convention—a sort of communal consciousness'" (Langford *Josh* 92), his disregard of specific textual descriptions in favor of archetypes can at times be annoying. His default presentation of female non-witches is also noteworthy: Pratchett has observed that even "if I take pains to dress young heroines from neck to ankle in Mother Hubbards, then Josh strips them down to their underwear because that's a fantasy convention hallowed by time" (*Poster* n. pag.). This tendency appears on Kirby's Discworld covers from the beginning: although the scene he paints from *The Colour of Magic* does not appear to include any female characters, a closer examination reveals a miniature bare-breasted woman posing on top of the toad—a minor detail that can easily go unnoticed except under the closest scrutiny.

It is in just these details, though, that the strength of Kirby's illustrations rests. Every time one returns to his covers, more details surface and impel the imaginative eye to curiosity and speculation, just as Pratchett's prose nudges one to suspend disbelief and become immersed in the Discworld and the lives of its inhabitants. Despite the interpretive differences between author and artist, Kirby's covers succeed in reflecting the frenetic energy of life on the Discworld: they communicate the incredible variation of both people and ideas that populate the books, and they also reflect the layers of meaning one finds throughout Pratchett's prose. Kirby's gallimaufry of colors and places and actions reflects the jumble of activity readers encounter in the books' pages, and the complexity of his cover illustrations allows readers to return to them with a better sense of understanding after having finished the book. In the end, Kirby's covers definitely succeed in catching attention, but they then take readers several steps further and continue to spark their imagination along their visual journey.[22]

The other artist whose Discworld covers succeed at catching readers' attention and enticing them into Pratchett's world is Paul Kidby, Pratchett's "illustrator of choice" (*Art*).[23] When he read *The Color of Magic* a number of years ago, Kidby felt "compelled to draw" its images, and after showing his sketches to Pratchett—who was immediately interested in them—at a book-signing, Kidby began working on illustrating the Discworld, drawing maps, postcards, chapter art, and other images ("Entrevista"). He began working exclusively with Pratchett in 1995, and upon the sudden death of Josh Kirby in 2001 he was asked to create the cover artwork for *Night Watch* (Lee). Kidby has commented that he and Josh Kirby knew each other, and that Kirby felt that their interpretations of Discworld "were so different that there was room enough for us both to explore and visually 'mine' its rich seams with our sketch-books" (Lee). Kidby has proven himself an adept and, indeed, gifted miner: in addition to the covers for thirteen Discworld novels, the four *Science of Discworld* books, *Nanny Ogg's Cookbook*, *The New Discworld Companion*, and *The Folklore of Discworld*, he has produced cover designs and images for Disc-world diaries, games, calendars, two full-length art books featuring his Disc-world art, and *The Last Hero*, a profusely illustrated novella on which he collaborated with Pratchett.[24] Kidby views his role as artist as someone who strives "to represent all the characters and try to capture [their] essence to marry Terry's words. It's a very exciting challenge for me and I love my job" ("Entrevista").

In creating the Discworld book covers, Kidby works closely with Pratchett and the marketing team. At the start of the process, he receives a specific brief whose details are agreed upon by the marketing, editorial and art teams at the publishers, in addition to having been approved by Pratchett. He then works with a designer for the duration of project, first doing preliminary sketches and sending those in for approval, and then submitting second drawings show-ing any changes, before starting to paint (Harvey). His vision and Pratchett's generally mesh, as Pratchett has noted:

> Paul sees things my way about seventy-five per cent of the time, which suggests either mind-reading is happening or that my vision of my characters is really rather vague until I see his drawings. And he remembers the history of the char-acters in a way that's almost frightening, so that a simple illustration will contain little details mentioned in half a dozen books [*Art* n. pag].

In the few instances where Kidby's interpretations have not corresponded with Pratchett's, Kidby has "changed the illustration to allow images to be what [Pratchett's] imagination has created" since he feels that they are, ultimately, Pratchett's characters and that his job as illustrator is "to give them life" (Vladimirova). It is perhaps this flexibility or at least willingness to submit his own artistry to that of the author's vision that has allowed Kidby to capture the essence of Pratchett's world and characters, and create images that make Pratchett's fantasy world seem even more accessible.

Kidby's covers are far less frenzied than Kirby's, although he still packs in plenty of information and detail. He tends to work "in a muted earth colour palette and tr[ies] to capture a historical feel whilst Josh used a bright palette and filled his page with a myriad of fantastical figures in his own unique and distinctive fantasy genre" (Lee). This historical style appears most prominently in Kidby's covers for *Night Watch* and *Monstrous Regiment*.[25] Both images are parodies of famous works, but are set in Discworld and contain a number of easily recognizable characters. *Night Watch* mirrors Rembrandt's famous paint- ing commonly known as *De Nachtwacht (The Night Watch)*,[26] with the original appearing on the back cover. Kidby utilizes the technique of chiaroscuro— the play of light and shadow—in a more restrained manner than Rembrandt, but it still appears in the way the light highlights young Vimes' face and the two other most important characters, the original Sam Vimes (impersonating John Keel) and the sweeper/history monk Lu-Tze, along with the cobblestones they stand on, against the arch of darkness behind them and the shadows around the picture's edges, most noticeably on the right in young Vetinari's black assassin's garb. A sense of edginess, both literal and metaphoric, is created by the way the light draws attention to the edges of the various spears and pikestaffs, while the generally muted colors not only create a kind of historical mood but also add a layer of realism. In the place of the small girl carrying the militia's goblet in Rembrandt's original, Nobby appears carrying the spoon given to him by Sergeant Keel, and there are lilac sprigs at the sweeper's feet, representing the participants in the People's Republic of Treacle Mine Road revolution. At the back, barely noticeable, is a smallish man standing beside Reg Shoe and peering over the shoulder of Waddy; this is the spot where Rem- brandt painted himself in the original, but where Kidby painted Josh Kirby as a tribute to him.[27]

The cover for *Monstrous Regiment*, rather than being straightforward parody, is more of an homage to a contemporary source, that of Joe Rosenthal's iconic photograph "Raising the Flag on Iwo Jima." Taken on February 23, 1945, during World War II's Battle of Iwo Jima, this photograph shows five U.S. Marines and a U.S. Navy corpsman raising the American flag on the top of Mount Suribachi. The photograph was reprinted in thousands of publica- tions, and was the only photograph to win the Pulitzer Prize for Photography in the same year as its publication; it "remains one of the abiding images of World War Two" (Howells 3–4). In contrast to the black-and-white image of 1945, Kidby's illustration is in color, but the angle of the flag is the same, the cloud cover has a similar pattern, and the overall composition of the illustration echoes Rosenthal's photograph. However, instead of carrying the national flag of Borogravia, the five figures in Kidby's image—Polly, Maladict, Jade, Shufti, and Tonker (Wazzer having collapsed from the effort of channeling the Duchess)—are carrying a white flag (which upon close inspection appears to be made of bloomers), a traditional indicator of surrender that in this case signifies the truce between Borogravia and Ankh-Morpork. Kidby's image portrays the soldiers looking directly at the audience, rather than at the ground, suggesting an element of illustrative metanarrative: in addition to playing with the raising-the-flag subtextual (and sometimes super-textual) narrative parody of Pratchett's novel, Kidby's characters demonstrate their awareness of their action's significance in the sense of being conscious of the audience's attention and, perhaps, the audience's recognition of the iconic original's significance.

This element of audience awareness occurs throughout Kidby's covers, and it is one of the many aspects that distinguish his covers from Josh Kirby's. Kirby's covers portray their characters thoroughly caught up in the action, intently focusing on whatever scenario they are embroiled in. In contrast, Kidby's covers initially appear to be more static—a moment caught in time— often featuring a group shot or a single instant caught for posterity. *Unseen Academicals*, for example, presents a group portrait of the Ankh-Morpork football team, with the Librarian looking predictably fierce and Vetinari (also predictably) unmoved by the young cheerleader standing next to him; all of the characters wear team portrait expressions and gaze directly at the audience. Similarly, the cover of *The Wee Free Men* features the somewhat daunting prospect of a large group of Feegles, weapons in hand, clustered together in various threatening stances and glowering at the audience, while the portrait of Commander Vimes on the cover of *Snuff* shows him standing at the tiller of the *Wonderful Fanny*, the goblin Stinky at his shoulder, glaring directly at the reader and ignoring the chaos of squawking chickens and tempestuous waters surrounding him. The cover image of *Thud!*, on the other hand, one of Kidby's most successful book jackets to date (Harvey), features Vimes standing in the centre of a Thud board flanked by troll pieces, holding a torch and looking up at someone out of the reader's view, with a dwarf piece bleeding from its head lying at Vimes' feet. This illustration is especially effective both in terms of design and color use: the black and white squares of the board, along with the stone and granite tones of the troll and dwarf pieces, work to draw our attention to the reds and golds and browns of Vimes in the center, and though the image appears to be in a freeze frame, Vimes' stance makes him look ready to run or spring at someone.

Kidby's illustrations possess a kind of realistic overlay that makes Pratchett's characters, who already seem fairly real due to their vivid textual depictions, become flesh-and-blood people, albeit of all different species, in a way that Kirby's illustrations never do. This is not to say that Kirby's illustrations and covers do not serve an important function; on the contrary, they do, but theirs is a function more connected with reinforcing the generic aspect of Pratchett's books as comic fantasies than with introducing readers to the characters or the locations of Discworld. In contrast, Kidby's illustrations have the effect of reminding readers about various aspects of what they already, perhaps subconsciously, know in relation to human nature, and then providing a platform for readers to plug that knowledge into their expectations about certain aspects of characters and places throughout the Discworld and apply it, so to speak, as they read. In a sense, then, Kidby's illustrations can provide a kind of recognition for readers, which allows them to suspend their disbelief in Pratchett's world perhaps a little more easily, and thus concentrate on aspects of the story that particularly grab them without having to reach after an image that might be elusive. Much of this effect has to do with Kidby's drawing style, which utilizes clean lines, generally accurate proportions and perspective, and that "truthfulness to life" that Maurice Sendak notes is the basis of all great art ("Caldecott" 149). In some ways, perhaps it is better that Kidby has been creating the later cover illustrations, as Pratchett's writing over the years has been acquiring a deeper level of sophistication, which has also contributed to our being able to see the people and spaces of the Discworld more clearly. Kidby's illustrations thus have the effect of allowing readers to imagine the Discworld as being somehow more real, which blurs the boundaries between reality and fantasy in pleasant ways.

Decorative Art

This blurring of boundaries has likely been exacerbated by the decorative art that abounds throughout many of the novels. This art appears not only in the form of chapter art and frontispieces, but also in desk diaries and calendars, greeting cards, posters, and essentially on anything that might be able to sport a visual image (mouse pads, tote bags, and a myriad of other items).[28] Books featuring the artwork of Discworld have also appeared, notably Paul Kidby's *The Pratchett Portfolio* and *The Art of Discworld*. Indeed, the vast majority of these images have been drawn by Kidby, although in a few of the books other artists fill in for particular purposes. Unlike a film, which, despite leaving a bit of room for interpretation, generally directs the viewer's imagination in particular ways (how an actor moves, for instance, or what the sounds of the night are), an illustration arguably leaves a bit more up to the imagination: it is a still shot, which allows the imagination to be nudged rather than specifically directed to flesh out the world it represents. Smaller illustrations often do this even better than the full scale scenes that appear on covers, since they provide a close-up of the larger whole that exists in the text of the books and on the canvas of readers' imaginations. Taken together, these images help to solidify those already there, and fill in some of the spaces that have not already been imagined, thus acting as a kind of springboard to encourage even more active visualization.

Paul Kidby's *The Pratchett Portfolio* and *The Art of Discworld* showcase a number of his Discworld character images alongside Pratchett's commentary. In his introduction to *The Pratchett Portfolio*, Pratchett comments on Kidby's realistic vision, noting "the feeling that he'd just strolled into the books with a sketchpad" (n. pag). More importantly, though, Pratchett comments on his sense that he does not provide a lot of physical description in the novels, because "character does not lie in two pages of dense depiction, but in modes of speech, the things people say and do not say. Character is the shape they leave in the world" (*Portfolio* n. pag.). Kidby renders this shape exceptionally well, especially (and in contrast to Kirby) with the witches. His Granny Weatherwax, "the witch with a personality like granite and a whim of chromium steel" (Langford "Pratchett" 487), appears to be the quintessential image of a stern and imposing lady whose power is conveyed in the pictures through her body language—ramrod posture, chin up, arms crossed—and steady gaze (see Image 3). One of his best images for capturing her essence appears in the small

3. *Granny Weatherwax Standing*, by **Paul Kidby (artwork copyright © 2013 by Paul Kidby, www.paulkidby. net).**

headshot of Granny with the bees converging on her head; here, lacking her customary scowl, she looks perhaps the closest we imagine to being happy or, at least, satisfied (see Image 4). Pratchett also likes Kidby's Rincewind, commenting, "He's one of the characters that Paul gets spot-on; Rincewind in Fourecks is exactly right" (*Art*). This image shows Rincewind running, sporting a sheep over one shoulder and a disgruntled expression, with the Luggage, its little feet wearing red high heels in a nod to the "girls" Rincewind meets who take a liking to "Trunkie," trailing behind him (see Image 5). This image exemplifies Roland Penrose's notion that "art has the unique quality of being able to halt the march of time while still giving the illusion of movement" (Nodelman 159)—something that would surely appeal to Rincewind.

Other characters that Pratchett feels Kidby captures well include Captain Carrot, Tiffany Aching, Death and his granddaughter Susan, Cohen the Barbarian, and the Feegles. Carrot and Cohen feature heavily in *The Last Hero*, discussed below, as does the Librarian, the Wizards at Unseen University, and the dragons. Tiffany and the Feegles appear in the frontispiece to *The Wee Free Men*—depicting Tiffany in a pose very similar to that of Granny Weatherwax, complete

4. *Granny Weatherwax with Bees*, by Paul Kidby (artwork copyright © 2013 by Paul Kidby, www.paulkidby. net).

with the ramrod posture and the glare, with Rob Anybody at her feet, brandishing a sword—and in many of the chapter headings of the four Tiffany Aching books. The Feegles, who appear in color images with electric blue skin and bright red hair, also show up in the page number decorations throughout *The Wee Free Men* and *A Hat Full of Sky* in Rackham-like silhouette images of Feegles rushing to battle and assuming fighting stances. Kidby's version of Death is also compelling: like Pratchett's prose creation, Kidby's artistic rendition of Death takes a figure that elicits fear in a number of cultures and translates it to a humanized individual who, despite his preternaturally sharp scythe,

Opposite: 5. *Rincewind in XXXX*, by Paul Kidby (artwork copyright © 2013 by Paul Kidby, www.paulkidby.net).

appears somewhat friendly, albeit not cuddly. He appears in such very human poses as riding a motorbike (wearing the Dean's "Born to Rune" black leather jacket over his robe), playing an electric guitar, stroking a kitten, and dressed up in a Hogfather costume. In all of the color images, Kidby shows Death with glowing blue eyes and outlined in a thin line of fluorescent blue, reflecting his otherworldly nature as well as Pratchett's descriptions of his scythe with its transparent blade's "edge glittering blue as air molecules were sliced into their component atoms" (*Maskerade* 349). This same glow is suggested in the non-color images through Kirby's use of chiaroscuro. One of his most intriguing paintings featuring Death is "Check Mort," painted for the cover of the French *Fun2Fantasy* "Homage to Sir Terry," showing Pratchett playing chess with Death in a parody of the scene from Ingmar Bergman's film, *The Seventh Seal* (*Discworld and Beyond*).

Kidby uses paper, pencil, and board along with oils or acrylics to create his pictures and "favours a subdued colour palette," a somewhat contentious choice in the fantasy industry since fantasy editors tend to prefer bold colors that are bright and eye-catching, but he nevertheless aims for a balance that works for both himself and publishers (*Discworld and Beyond*). This inclination can be seen especially well in Kidby's images of the Shamble as well as his version of Igor and Scraps (*Art*). Both are rendered in shades of dark blues and grays and whites, which works well to call attention to the fine detail in both pictures. With Igor and Scraps, we are immediately drawn to Igor's face with its many stitches running across his forehead, down both eyebrows, and around his nose and mouth—indicating places he has been "repaired" or stitched—and to his fingers, which are numerous and appear to include multiple thumbs. Scraps, on the other hand, has eyes of two different colors and an unusually long tongue and large nose for a dog his size; this is perhaps explained by the more subtle stitching around his face (his two tails are sadly not in evidence). Similarly, the subdued color palette of the Shamble allows readers to focus on its contents, which include not only a doorknob and feathers and a pencil but also buttons, a tuft of sheep's wool, a fossil, beads, Tiffany's necklace, and a bee. Kidby has commented that the Discworld characters "were so fully realised in Terry's writing that I felt drawing them was merely translating word to line ... I strive to achieve a realism that complements the text" (*Art* n. pag). This realism shows up particularly well in the images he created for *The Folklore of Discworld*. Each of its chapters includes a pencil illustration as a chapter frontispiece and feature most of the mythical, or at least folkloric, creatures of the Discworld, including dwarfs, elves, trolls, werewolves and vampires, Igors, golems and zombies, fantastic beasts, and Death, in addition to various landscapes including the Chalk and Lancre. Kidby portrays all of them convincingly enough that they seem not only believable but instantly recognizable. Even in his smallest illustrations, such as those that appear in the various Diaries, Kidby's illustrations project a kind of veracity that helps solidify the Discworld in a way that makes reading the stories even more enjoyable.

Other illustrations also appear in the Discworld books, including the frontispieces of *Night Watch* and *Monstrous Regiment* as well as the chapter illustrations for *Going Postal* and *Making Money*. The *Night Watch* frontispiece is a small cutaway drawn by Stephen Briggs[29] for *The Streets of Ankh-Morpork* map in 1993 (discussed below). The selected area focuses on where the main action of the rebellion, "The Glorious People's Republic of Treacle Mine Road," occurs. *Night Watch* is the first Discworld novel to include a frontispiece, and the novel suggests the shift in tone of the series from this book onwards, where Pratchett's writing style and focus seem to have more serious overtones than they had previously.[30] The map lends a sense of veracity to the novel, and by extension the series, in the sense of providing the illusion of reality while at the same time invoking the fantasy convention of having a map,[31] and thus works in much the same way as Pratchett's prose works, by making a joke about something, undercutting it to demonstrate its satiric point, and then overturning that satire to highlight the joke. Its detail reinforces the meandering nature and sheer disorder of the city's roads and districts that the characters navigate during the revolution. Similarly, the frontispiece for *Monstrous Regiment*, drawn by Paul Kidby, also evokes the sense of realism, this time though a cartoon satirizing the political situation between Borogravia and Ankh-Morpork and intended to convey the feisty nature of Borogravia as it stands up to the bigger bully of Ankh-Morpork. As the fictional journalist William de Worde points out in the novel, "In politics ... pictures like this are powerful" and asks Polly's unit to make a plea "for a little common sense" in an attempt to bring the war to an end (178). The cartoon does here just what political cartoons do in real life, namely to make something, usually a political leader or situation, appear ridiculous in order to call for some sort of reform. Although we obviously cannot call for real change to the political situation between Borogravia and Ankh-Morpork, the cartoon nevertheless has the effect of adding humor as well as the momentary illusion of realism. Curiously, the cartoon is unattributed on the copyright page, and it is simply signed "Fizz"—a nod to cartoonist Hablot Knight Browne (1815–1882), who used the pseudonym "Phiz" and drew illustrations (reproduced as copperplate engravings) for a number of Victorian works, including the novels of Charles Dickens.[32]

A number of illustrations in the form of headings, tailpieces, and occasional small insets enhance the pages of *Going Postal*, *Making Money*, and *Turtle*

Recall: The Discworld Companion ... So Far. The first two contain drawings designed by Pratchett and Bernard Pearson,[33] which in *Going Postal* are cancelled stamps showing minute images of the Ankh-Morpork Post Office, the cabbages of the Sto Plains, Lord Vetinari, Morporkia, and the Ankh-Morpork coat-of-arms, which consists of four hippos, two bags of money, and the motto "*Quanti Canicula Ille in Fenestra.*"[34] A particularly nice touch is Vetinari's face adorning the one penny stamp, perhaps on the grounds that this is the most commonly used stamp and so people are reminded of his presence constantly. The drawings in *Making Money* show coins featuring the Royal Bank of Ankh-Morpork (complete with its motto, "Integrity, Probity, Trust"), Morporkia, the coat-of-arms, the seal of the bank, a ship, a dog's paw print, and once again Lord Vetinari's head, this time on the one penny coin. *Turtle Recall*, the latest encyclopedic companion to the Discworld,[35] also includes numerous black-and-white illustrations, drawn by Stephen Briggs. In addition to decorated letters at the beginning of each section—for example, the entries under "L" are prefaced by a line drawing of the Librarian's teeth—there are full-page illustrations of places such as a street in the Shades (see Image 6), a view across the Ankh River, and a map of the Circle Sea area; detailed illustrations of a variety of coats-of-arms; small pictures of creatures such as the Quantum Weather Butterfly, an armored raven (see Image 7), and a hedgehog (not surprisingly with the entry for Nanny Ogg); illustrations of buildings, including the Assassins' Guild, Sybil Vimes' house, and the Hubward Gate; and depictions of items like Death's lifetimers, a Dried Frog Pills tin, Unseen University's pipe organ, and Granny Weatherwax's hat with its sign "I Aten't Dead." All of these images serve to reinforce the sense of Ankh-Morpork, and by extension the Discworld, as a quasi-real (albeit imaginary) place. This sense of quasi-reality is further supported by the rousing real-world trade that has sprung up in relation to the stamps: from the Discworld Emporium, philatelists can now purchase stamps and cover sheets of Discworld stamps, including minisheets of the 2p Guild of Archaeologists or Guild of Armourers, 4p special issue stamps featuring Bloodaxe and Ironhammer, and Glorious twenty-fifth of May Lilac Patrician sheets, among others.[36]

Illustrated Novels

At times, illustrations in the novels are an important and even integral part of the story. In *The Amazing Maurice and His Educated Rodents*, in addition to illustrated chapter headings with excerpts from *Mr. Bunnsy Has an Adventure* (the rats' metaphorical book of life), pictograms drawn by David

6. *A View in the Shades*, by Stephen Briggs (© Stephen Briggs 1994. From *Turtle Recall: The Discworld Companion ... So Far* by Terry Pratchett and Stephen Briggs, illustrations by Stephen Briggs, published by The Orion Publishing Group, London).

Wyatt appear that show the rats' development of a written language.[37] Their iconography is explicated by Peaches, the creator of the writing system, who must explain it to the other rats since using written language is a new concept for them. For "No Rat Shall Kill Another Rat" (see Image 8), the thick line means "no" while the trap is the sign for death, to which "she'd added the dead rat to make it all more *serious*" (*Maurice* 46; original italics). After reading

Peaches' explanation the picture makes sense; however, without the image we would be left with an insufficiently-constrained mass of options, most (if not all) of them anthropocentric. By including the image as (supposedly) drawn by a rat, the otherness of the rats is reinforced in a way that stresses one of the main themes of the book: that of coming to terms with a culture that is truly different from our own.

Nodelman has suggested that placing words and pictures in conjunction with each other "inevitably changes the meaning of both, so that good picture books as a whole are a richer experience than just the simple sum of their parts" (199). This is certainly true for the three fully illustrated

7. *Armoured Raven*, by Stephen Briggs (© Stephen Briggs 1994. From *Turtle Recall: The Discworld Companion ... So Far* by Terry Pratchett and Stephen Briggs, illustrations by Stephen Briggs, published by The Orion Publishing Group, London).

8. *No Rat Shall Kill Another Rat* from *The Amazing Maurice and His Educated Rodents*, by David Wyatt (illustration copyright © 2001 by David Wyatt; used by permission of HarperCollins Publishers).

Discworld novels: ~~Faust~~ *Eric, The Last Hero,* and *The Illustrated Wee Free Men.* All three contain significantly more illustrations than typical fantasy novels, and although Pratchett wrote the texts before Josh Kirby, Paul Kidby, and Steven Player (respectively) illustrated them, their images add another layer to reading a Discworld story. For Josh Kirby's illustrations for *Eric,* David Langford claims that Pratchett wrote a storyline "that deliberately whizzed wildly around in time and space, providing Kirby with opportunities for lavish illustration" (*Josh* 93). Kirby painted sixteen double-page color illustrations for the book, fourteen of which are interspersed with the text and the other two of which appear on the title page and the cover. These illustrations maintain his exuberant style, though at times they seem more streamlined than his Discworld covers, perhaps because rather than incorporating a number of different moments they are able to focus on a single scene. For example, the illustration of Death in his study contains plenty of detail, such as the giant scythe and lifetimers stretching up the wall behind him, but the lines are cleaner and the overall feeling of the scene is not as busy as a typical Kirby cover. Another excellent illustration, and one which perfectly demonstrates Kirby's cartoon-like style, depicts the Universe coming into being. The placement for this illustration is ideal, for it appears on a double-page spread free of any text, immediately following the sentence, "Seen from close by, though, it had a certain gaudy attraction" (89). The image shows Death whirling about in the center, well above the Great A'Tuin and the Discworld perched on top of the elephants, with Rincewind flying off, feet first, towards the bottom left of the page while Eric and, upwards to the right, Astfgl, look as though they have somehow exploded out of nothingness into existence. The colors are dominated by purples, yellows, reds, and blues and are surrounded by a clean white page, adding to the effect of something having just appeared out of nothing. Although this illustration, like the others throughout the book, provides more of a sense of representation than an extension of the text, it nevertheless adds much to the imagination, particularly in terms of reinforcing the chaotic element of the Discworld that so often appears in stories involving Rincewind.

Stephen Player's *The Illustrated Wee Free Men* also does an excellent job of representation, but moves a step further and adds a fair bit of clarification to the text as well.[38] For instance, his illustration of the shamble (1), while much simpler than the one Kidby imagines, nevertheless shows the important bits of it, like the egg, the stone, the twigs, and the pencil mentioned in the text. In addition to a number of watercolor decorations, often taking up a small space on a page otherwise filled with text, the book includes images that extend the story, such as a poster advertisement for the witches' school (named "Hovering Grange"), complete with a list of lessons Tiffany imagines (40).

Other kinds of textual complements show images of what Tiffany might find in some of her books, from the small inset image of the stages of the moon (43) to the full-page color illustration of a cacophony of faerie creatures, complete with a Feegle in the lower left corner making "a gesture with his hand ... a rude one" (45). Some of the literally in-text sketches illustrate things like a small Feegle standing on one word of the text and climbing up a couple of lines—the letters being stepped on and grabbed are misaligned (107)—or traces of water droplets or footprints with the text super-imposed over them (50–51). Occasionally, significant words appear beneath the printed text in the same sort of way—susurrus, mutter, patronizing, incursion, guzunder, for example—looking like watermarks. While these all have amusing as well as decorative functions, other illustrations more pointedly clarify the action, as in the fold-out pages that illustrate precisely how the landscape changes when Tiffany steps through the standing stone arch and moves from summer to winter (131). Another image shows the virtual witch's hat that Granny Weatherwax places on Tiffany's head, and though this is a simple line drawing it still conjures the sense of exactly what Granny has drawn in the air. Overall, the sheer variety of illustrations and illustration types engages readers' imaginations and extends the text in very satisfying ways.

Of the illustrated books, however, it is Paul Kidby's *The Last Hero* that most fully realizes the functions of not only representation and clarification but, more significantly, extension and occasional elaboration of Pratchett's text. As Pratchett noted, the book "was *planned* as an illustrated story right from the start," and he regarded the illustrations as a kind of shorthand: "if you have maybe 40,000 words to play with it's not a great idea to waste a hundred of them telling the reader what a character looks like when, hey, here's a picture of him, right here on the next page. Describing the colors of a rainbow is a fool's job if the man he's working with has a palette in his hand" (Pratchett "A Note"; original italics). In many places Kidby's illustrations do just what Tolkien intended his own illustrations to do for *The Hobbit*: they save the author time providing background information and characterization, and allow him to get on with his main job of telling the story. Cohen the Barbarian's heroic language—"stop talking like that and *follow me*!" (*Hero* 76; original italics) and "Behold!" (134)—is perfectly reflected in the images of his heroic charges and stances (see pages 48 and 136, among others). Ponder Stibbons, the wizard who serves as a nice parody of a research scientist, has a glum expression and shirt with the slogan "Actually I Am a Rocket Wizard" (123) that perfectly expresses his fussy brand of self-conscious intellectualism, which Pratchett hints at through Ponder's conversation. Kidby also does an excellent job with places, providing a double-page spread of Ankh-Morpork in sepia tones, with mist swirling around the wizards' Tower of Art and the streets crowded with buildings; the color choice allows readers not only to perceive the city's sense of history but also smell some of its fog. In contrast, his images of Dunmanifestin, the mountain where the Discworld gods reside, are often rendered in whites and blues, and have sharp lines and edges that convey its height, its remoteness, and its danger. Kidby has an equally good eye for minute details, many of which appear in his meticulous diagrams of Leonard of Quirm's inventions. These include the frying pan for use in gravity-free environments, with burrs on the bottom to keep it in place (Discworld's equivalent of Velcro), as well as blueprints of the Kite, the dragon-powered airship modeled (according to Leonard's notes) on an eagle clutching a salmon in its talons. The sketches here include a view of the bridge, complete with carefully labeled parts such as "Dragon Pod Separation," the "Device for Looking Behind You," and "Prince Haran's Tiller" (the autopilot). While these titles are pure Leonard, Kidby's intertextual leanings creep in, with the "No handball playing allowed" note mirroring the sign that John Glenn allegedly attached to the instrument panel of the Mercury flight saying "No Handball Playing in this Area," a reference that also appears in the 1983 film *The Right Stuff.*

Representations of heroic masculinity appear brilliantly with Kidby's versions of Carrot and Cohen, though in somewhat different ways. While his visual portrayal closely reflects Pratchett's verbal description, Kidby's images arguably work even better than words to emphasize Carrot as the type of "virile, spectacular masculinity" (Adams 10) that was one of the main components of early science fiction illustration. His stance throughout the book, seen perfectly when he is shown saluting and placing the flag of Ankh-Morpork on the moon (*Hero* 128) and again when he faces Cohen and the Horde to arrest them (159), is one of stereotypical heroic masculinity, which meshes with his character in this and the other books in which he appears. His "godlike proportions" (*Thud* 90) are accentuated by his strong jaw, direct gaze, and sincere demeanor very fitting for the supposedly rightful yet undeclared heir to Ankh-Morpork's throne. Cohen, in a satiric way, also reinforces this fantasy hero model. As Adams suggests, "When we peruse the contours of a spectacularly muscled warrior on a fantasy novel, in many ways we are encouraged to number him among the ranks of other pseudo-classical heroes to whom he is kin" (27). This is exactly Cohen's stance, both physically and mentally (see Image 9): from his perspective, at least, he belongs at the top of their ranks because he exists in the "bold unequivocal milieus ... where moral absolutes give way to 'higher' truths: namely, a kind of manifest destiny where one can and does continually iterate the superiority of one's being and cause simply by being victorious" (Adams 168). While in a number of ways we are invited to view

9. *Cohen the Barbarian,* **by Paul Kidby (artwork copyright © 2013 by Paul Kidby, www.paulkidby.net).**

Cohen as being a parody of the hero, this gets undercut by the story, since he continues to be victorious even at the end. However, even the undercutting gets undercut—in true Pratchettian fashion—as parody (re-)enters the picture through Kidby's illustrations of Cohen and his Horde as wiry old geezers with false teeth, thinning (or absent) hair, wizened and wrinkled faces, and needing canes or wheelchairs for balance as they wield their swords. Despite their geri-atric status, Cohen and the Silver Horde are still dangerous, precisely because they are successful at being "very old *heroes* … they've had a lot of *experience* in doing what they want to do" (*Hero* 19; original italics). As Pratchett has commented about the Horde, "somehow they always win because they're so *good* at it!" ("Discworld & Beyond" 75; original italics).

Kidby's artwork also reflects Pratchett's intertextual style, and both include elements of pastiche in the way that they draw on different genres and sources. A variety of "sketches & notes in the style of Leonardo" appear throughout *The Last Hero* (*The Illustrator*), including Rincewind as the Vit-ruvian Man and Leonard's drawing of a perfect circle.[39] The tapestry on the title page and at the end of the story is modeled after the Bayeux Tapestry, which depicts the story of the Battle of Hastings; here it illustrates many of Cohen's and the Silver Horde's adventures, beginning with their departure from the Agatean Empire through fighting sea monsters, slaying warriors, trav-elling to Cor Celesti with the bomb, being greeted by the Valkyrie warriors at the end, and then riding off into the sky. Pairing these images with those on the Bayeux Tapestry suggests that the kinds of adventures that Cohen and his Horde have experienced hold a similar historical stature to those of William the Conqueror, which contradicts Nodelman's argument that pictures do not require as much prior knowledge as words to understand the information being conveyed. For Kidby's art, at least, recognizing the layers of historical and artistic riffs adds an additional dimension of understanding and meaning to the story. Cohen's finger gesture to Blind Io in the parody of Michelangelo's *Creation of Adam* (painted on the ceiling of the Sistine Chapel, from about 1509–1512) and Rincewind's posture emulating that in Edvard Munch's paint-ing *The Scream* are much funnier when one is familiar with the originals, and no one who has read *Hamlet* can miss the connections between the image of the minstrel and the skull at the end with the grave-digger in *Hamlet* and his "Alas, poor Yorick!" speech (*Hamlet* V:1). The way that Kidby's illustrations provide a kind of historical counterpoint to Pratchett's fantasy adds not only a layer of humor but also elements of social commentary and satire that make *The Last Hero* resonant on multiple levels of meaning.

Hypotrochoidal Texts

According to the *OED*, a hypotrochoid is "the curve described by a point rigidly connected with the centre of a circle which rolls on the inside of another circle" (see Figure 1 below). I have borrowed this concept to serve as a

metaphor for the types of works discussed in this final section, publications that have been generated from
and appear within the Discworld
multiverse and have a kind of simultaneous resonance. These are items
to which characters make specific
references, as in the cases of *Where's
My Cow?*, *The World of Poo*, *Nanny
Ogg's Cookbook*, and *The Discworld
Almanak*, as well as works that characters are either shown consulting or
could conceivably consult, as in the
case of the maps and *The Compleat
Ankh-Morpork City Guide*. These
publications are also items that Discworld fans might (and, from all evidence, do) enjoy as supplemental

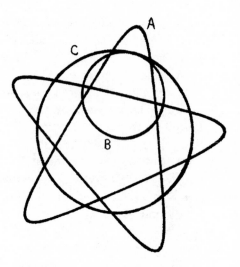

Figure 1. The curve [A] is a hypotrochoid drawn as the smaller circle [B]
rolls around inside the larger circle [C].

materials to the novels. The term seems especially appropriate: the curve
(labeled A in the diagram) is traced with a line pinned to the centre of
the small circle (labeled B in the diagram) that extends outside of both circles
to a point; the small circle moves counterclockwise around the inside of the
large circle (labeled C in the diagram) while the trace moves clockwise to
create the curve, which intersects and overlaps with both circles as well as
itself. If the large circle represents the Discworld multiverse, the small circle
represents the Discworld novels, and the trace represents the other texts generated from within the novels, their trajectory diagrammatically represents
the concurrent incarnations of those texts within the Discworld novels, the
Discworld multiverse, and in our mundane world—for example, the recipes
in *Nanny Ogg's Cookbook* are (for the most part) palatable in all worlds
involved.[40]

To date, several works have been published in the real world that originated from within the Discworld novels, two of which are ostensibly for children and are read by or to young Sam. Like all good children's literature, the
first—Pratchett's picture book[41] *Where's My Cow?*, illustrated by Melvyn
Grant[42]—has depths of meaning and significance beyond its apparently simple
storyline and pictures. Mentioned in *Thud!* as the reason that Vimes rushes
home at precisely 6:00 p.m. every evening to read to young Sam, *Where's My
Cow?* is a book with "rounded and soft [pages] where Young Sam had chewed
them" (*Thud* 120) and follows the very basic events of the narrator seeing and

hearing a number of typical (sheep, horses, pigs) and a few not-so-typical (hippopotamus) animals as s/he searches for a lost cow. In the end, not surprisingly, the cow is found—"Hooray, hooray, it's a wonderful day, for I have found my cow!'" (*Thud* 336)—and everyone lives (presumably) happily ever after. Snippets of the text, along with descriptions of both the pictures and young Sam's and Vimes' reaction to them, appear throughout *Thud!*, and the way these are delivered appears to gently mock not only the kinds of drivel that many adults seem to think small children must like to hear, but also the kinds of repetitive narrative and storyline that many parents have read to their children through the ages as comforting bedtime stories. However, like all of Pratchett's works, larger points are being made here, both with the book's significance within *Thud!* and with the picture book itself. Near the end of the novel, Vimes terrifies the deep-down dwarfs with his insanity-tinged recitation of parts of the book while trapped in the Koom Valley caves, the words of the story "boom-[ing] under Koom Valley, shaking the rock of ages and making the stalactites hum in sympathy" (341). Miraculously, as Vimes bellows the words, young Sam sits up in his nursery miles away, "happy but puzzled" (334), and responds. This incident exemplifies Vimes' love for his son, but more significantly allows readers to witness the utter inseparability of Vimes' identity from his rigid dedication to the law and his notion of what is right: to uphold the light in the face of the gathering (or Summoning) dark.

Where's My Cow? has far more multiple layers than a cursory reading might suggest, and most of these are indicated through the pictures rather than the words. The words are assembled from the bits in *Thud!*, with a few additions, and every page has illustrations that appear in conjunction with the words. The book opens with images of young Sam, Vimes, Lady Sybil, and some dwarfs in their "real" world, and the second page spread shows Vimes taking the *Where's My Cow?* story book off the shelf while young Sam clamors to have it read to him. Over the next several pages, the illustrations have a kind of dual layering: in addition to showing Sam and his father reading and acting out various parts of the story, they also show images from the story book itself. The separation between the two layers is clearly demarcated, with young Sam's and Vimes' reality being portrayed with realistic colors and proportions—even the pet dragon is believably real within their world—while the story book's pictures have soft pastel illustrations, wide lines and unrealistic proportions. When Vimes' awareness of the absurdity of the narrative becomes too much for him, the illustrations suddenly become unbalanced and disproportional, with various objects in the room flying about and fantastic images invading this primary layer of illustration. When Vimes shifts to a more realistic kind of story—one that begins, "Where's my daddy? Where's my daddy?

It goes, 'Bugrit! Millennium Hand and Shrimp!' It is Foul Ole Ron! That's not my daddy!" (*Cow* n. pag)—the majority of the picture returns to darker and more realistic hues, and Foul Ole Ron appears as a more credible character than the pig and goose from the story. This technique continues as Vimes' revised narrative progresses, and the story book images shrink in size as well. By the end of the picture book, which concludes, "Sam Vimes leaned over the cot and whispered, 'Where's my daddy? Is that my daddy? It goes: 'I arrest you in the name of the Law!' *That's* my daddy!'" (*Cow* n. pag; original italics), the pastel colors have largely disappeared, the room's proportions and angles are nearly back to normal, and the image of Vimes arresting someone morphs into the final picture of him smiling down at his sleeping son, with a framed portrait of Pratchett on the wall in the shadows adding a nod to their creator. The unrealistic illustrations of the story book layer have the effect of reinforcing the authority of the picture book layer, which in turn adds to the sense of realism of the story as a whole.

The other work that young Sam becomes fascinated with is *The World of Poo*, a juvenile novel written by fictional author Miss Felicity Beedle intended to instruct young readers about everything there is to know about dung. It is first mentioned in *Snuff*, where Vimes notes that in addition to its humor, "interspersed with the scatology was actually quite interesting stuff about septic tanks and dunnakin divers and gongfermors and how dog muck helped make the very best leather, and other things that you never thought you would need to know, but once heard somehow lodged in your mind" (*Snuff* 60). The text is embellished with illustrations by Peter Dennis[43] in the form of chapter headings as well as quarter-, half- and full-page pen-and-ink drawings reminiscent of Gordon Browne's illustrations for E. Nesbit's children's books (this is at least in part due to the somewhat Edwardian flavor and setting of the story). Each of the chapter headings has a picture of a jar with a specimen in it, and the number of jars correspond to the chapter number (three jars for the third chapter, six jars for the sixth chapter, and so on). The rest of the illustrations generally have either representative or decorative functions, as when they show images of Geoffrey's grand-mama greeting him, the toy-filled nursery, or the fancy table setting at the luncheon he attends at the Guild of Plumbers and Dunnakin Divers. In a few places they provide humorous spoilers by showing readers what is happening before the text tells them. For example, after Geoffrey's visit to the Sunshine Sanctuary for Sick Dragons, he takes away with him "a small glowing ember" that was deposited on his glove while he was holding a baby dragon and that he surreptitiously transfers to his jacket pocket (*Poo* 47); the image shows him walking away with his pocket leaking smoke. It is not until two pages later that his grand-mama notes the smoking jacket pocket and "extracted the charred ember with the sugar tongs and transferred the hot little nodule to an empty snuff tin" (49). Overall, the illustrations do here what they do in juvenile novels of this ilk, which is to provide interesting images that complement what is happening in the text.

Similarly, the illustrations in *Nanny Ogg's Cookbook* (see Image 10) serve both representative and decorative functions, while those in *The Discworld Almanak* are primarily decorative. Nanny Ogg appears in a number of Paul Kidby's smaller illustrations in his Discworld art books, but the *Cookbook* showcases the tone of her wicked sense of humor, often delivered through the sort of innuendo that appears in recipe titles like "Nanny Ogg's Perfectly Innocent Porridge with completely Inoffensive Honey Mixture Which Shouldn't Make Anyone's Wife Laugh," which is followed by Nanny's commentary: "... 'cos they made me take out a couple of what you might call the more active ingredients" (70). "They" refers to Nanny's publishers, Mr. Goatberger and Mr. Cropper, whose fascinated reaction to and subsequent publication of the *Cookbook* in *Maskerade* provides the excuse for Nanny's and Granny Weatherwax's trip to Ankh-Morpork. Kidby's portrayal of Nanny perfectly indicates her big grin and raucous laugh, her ample proportions indicating her love of life's many pleasures (many, though not all, of them involving food), her face "like a small dried raisin" (*Wyrd* 43), and his images convey in her twinkling eyes the sense of her as a woman who has had many husbands, three of them her own.[44] Throughout the book Kidby also presents numerous portraits of other Discworld inhabitants, including especially good ones of Leonard of Quirm and the dwarf Casanunda. The book parodies not only Mrs. Isabella Beeton's famous *Beeton's Book of Household Management* (1861) but also modern cookbooks, with their occasionally unusual dishes and experimental cooking techniques, and includes images of some of the more interesting ingredients for the recipes, such as for Deep-Sea Blowfish (lethal unless you discard the blowfish). *The Discworld Almanak*, illustrated by Kidby, Bernard Pearson, and Sheila Watkins, is also mentioned in passing in *Maskerade*: "'Everyone I knows buys the Almanack,' said Granny. 'I reckon everyone in Lancre buys your Almanack. Everyone in the whole Ramtops buys the Almanack, even the dwarfs.... Your Almanack will last a household all winter, with care.... Providing no one's ill and the paper's nice and thin'" (187). Its numerous and varied ornaments include advertisements, pithy sayings, notes on astrology, and other useful and not-so-useful information, such as "Interesting Cabbage Fact No 324" (87).[45]

These were not Pratchett's initial ventures into the area of hypotrochoidal works; instead, this distinction belongs to the Discworld maps. Pratchett's novels since their first inception have included numerous references to maps

10. *Nanny Ogg's Cookbook*, by Paul Kidby (artwork copyright © 2013 by Paul Kidby, www.paulkidby.net).

in both literal and metaphoric senses, and the dedication line to *Sourcery* includes Pratchett's invitation: "This book does not contain a map. Please feel free to draw your own." The most frequent references to physical maps occur for maps of the Discworld as a whole (in twelve novels) and to the city of Ankh-Morpork (in six novels). Other places that are either mentioned as having maps or shown via characters consulting their maps include the Ramtops and the village of Bad Ass, Überwald, Bonk, Klatch, Borogravia, Fourecks (XXXX or EcksEcksEcksEcks), and the Counterweight Continent. Pratchett's visual sense of the Discworld's fictional geography first appears in *The Color of Magic* with a gaming board made of "a carefully carved map of the Discworld, over-printed with squares" (65). In *Sourcery*, Carding, Spelter, and Coin get a aerial view of first Ankh-Morpork and then the greater world:

> Ankh-Morpork spread out like a map, the river a trapped snake, the plains a misty blur.... The Discworld appeared below them, and from up here you could see that it was indeed a disc, pinned to the sky by the central mountain of Cori Celesti, where the gods lived. There was the Circle Sea ... there was the vast continent of Klatch, squashed by perspective. The Rimfall around the edge of the world was a sparkling curve [108–109].

Despite Pratchett's now much-quoted comment that "the Discworld is not a coherent fantasy world. Its geography is fuzzy, its chronology unreliable.... There are no maps. You can't map a sense of humor" (Pratchett "Foreword"),[46] he has collaborated in the creation of four maps of Discworld and its environs, along with a city guide and map of Ankh-Morpork, in the form of an old-fashioned gazetteer, and the Discworld map electronic application. The first three maps—*The Streets of Ankh-Morpork, The Discworld Mapp,* and *A Tourist Guide to Lancre*—were created in conjunction with Stephen Briggs, with artwork by Stephen Player (for the first two) and Paul Kidby (for the third), while the fourth—*Death's Domain*—was created in conjunction with Paul Kidby, who also did the artwork. In addition to consulting with Briggs, Player, and Kidby as to details and locations, Pratchett wrote most of the material for the booklets that accompany the earlier maps, and added details and other material to the Ankh-Morpork gazetteer and the electronic version. This written material might suggest that the maps have a kind of weight that many other fantasy maps do not, and in some ways that might be true; however, as Pratchett notes in his introduction to *The Discworld Mapp*, "I said there would never be a map of the Discworld. This is it.... This map possibly isn't the way things are. But it is one of the ways they could be" (Pratchett "I Needed").[47] Their function as hypotrochoidal texts appears in the way that they have been engendered by the details of the novels and yet have also influenced the novels in turn: in addition to being shaped by the diegetic outline of the landscape and geography of Discworld, they have in turn shaped Pratchett's creation of it.

When Stephen Briggs first approached Pratchett about creating a map for Ankh-Morpork, Pratchett's reaction was somewhat negative, commenting that he considered it "unmappable because I'd made it up as I went along," and he noted that he preferred to leave it vague (Pratchett "The Streets"). However, after giving the matter some thought, he soon realized that "most ancient cities got made up as people went along" and that, furthermore, certain things have to stay in the shape that he has already described them throughout the novels in order to reinforce the sense that readers have of the city's geographic validity ("The Streets"). To create the map, Briggs went through the books and made notes on paper and file cards, and then began to plan it, consulting with Pratchett throughout this drafting process, and he comments that Pratchett took "a *lot* of constructive interest in the map. This is a polite way of saying that before long the master copy had so much Tipp-ex on it that it was hard to lift" (Briggs "Mapping"; original italics). At times the details Pratchett mentioned referred to novels that were not yet published, and a kind of fantasy architectural history started to emerge. The map's full title—*The Streets of Ankh-Morpork Being a concise and possibly even accurate Mapp of the Great City of the Discworld*—suggests a sense of history, which is reinforced by its sepia color and Stephen Player's fantastic ancillary decorations with gargoyle-adorned plinths, a turtle compass marking the Hubwards direction, and coats-of-arms for various families and guilds (including the Vetinari and Ramkin families, and the guilds for Fools and Joculators, Alchemists, and Assassins, among others). The map's details include a rabbit's warren of streets and areas, showing such locations as Sator Square and Unseen University, the Shades, Treacle Mine Road, and the cemetery in Small Gods, along with the walls around the city and the eight city gates. The booklet accompanying the map contains small pen-and-ink drawings of various places and Tudor-style buildings in the city, as well as map grids and the map key. The map itself is a thing of beauty: single-sided, it folds out to about 28 inches by 29 inches (the same size as the other three maps) and is printed in sepia tones with shades of aqua, ultramarine, rose, and moss. As a work of art, it is something that map lovers of all sorts might enjoy hanging on a wall; as a map, Discworld characters could consult it to determine possible routes of travel within the city, while both characters and readers can study it to help solidify their sense of spatial relationships within the city as well as get a sense of the city's vast and complex layout (see Image 11).

The other maps function in similar ways, as a kind of inside/outside view of the Discworld's places. Briggs used references from all of the books up to *Interesting Times* to create *The Discworld Mapp: Being the Onlie True & Mostlie Accurate Mappe of the Fantastyk Magical Dyscworlde*, and also did some reading in geography, at Pratchett's suggestion, thus avoiding such potential errors as placing the Great Nef Desert where a swamp would be (Briggs "Many Miles"); a sense of history is reinforced by not only the map's subtitle, but also its archaic

11. *The Streets of Ankh-Morpork* (detail), by Stephen Player (reproduced by permission of Stephen Player, playergallery.com).

spelling conventions. The introductory material, in addition to brief notes by Pratchett and Briggs, includes character sketches of some of Discworld's most famous explorers, garnished by a map showing the first three "epic voyages" of General Sir Roderick Purdeigh around the Widdershins Ocean, "on which he proved conclusively that the Counterweight Continent and the continent of XXXX could not possibly exist" (Pratchett "Here Be Dragons"). It concludes with a section on the history of the Discworld, providing its dimensions—20,000 miles across and thirty miles thick at the Rim, though considerably thicker towards the Hub—and an interesting note about the way it changes its direction of spin every 100,000 years. As with his artwork for *The Streets of Ankh-Morpork*, Steven Player uses muted colors, this time in mostly blues and greens, and the decorations around the map have a winged motif that echo the Great A'Tuin's stately flight though space: an owl carries the map's scale, flying eyeballs (with tails) as well as a grouchy-looking aged male angel ornament the perimeter, and two winged hippos bear the title as well as the acknowledgement: "the Result of intents Research by Our Skilled Teem of Surveyors, Skillfully Drawn with Great Skill by Skilled Dwarf Crafts-men." The layout, rather than being a road map, instead has topographical overtones and thus does not indicate the boundaries between the various nations. Like *The Streets of Ankh-Morpork*, it is aesthetically pleasing, and is the kind of map that people (both in and outside of the Discworld) could believably hang on their walls, or, in the case of Discworld characters, use to gain a broad sense of the shape of their world, not to mention reinforcing the belief that their Disc sits atop a gigantic chelonian. However, it is not the sort of "workman's map" like the one Vetinari consults in *The Truth* (30), but instead an artistic rendering of the Disc.

Like the first two Discworld maps, *A Tourist Guide to Lancre: A Discworld Mapp* includes prefatory material written by Pratchett and Briggs, along with short essays serving as introductions to the area by the fictional champion walker, Eric Wheelbrace, and Gytha Ogg, as well as a lengthier extract from Wheelbrace's *A Pictorial Guide to the Lancre Fells* and a concluding note by Nanny Ogg on Folk Lore of Lancre. Their essays are decorated with a few small illustrations of items such as a compass and a set of wire-cutters—indicating Wheelbrace's habits and attitudes towards the thorny issue of right-of-way in the countryside—as well as a stone footbridge, a well, and a view (subtly presented from the side) of the Long Man. The map is designed with numbers corresponding to such locations as Granny Weatherwax's cottage, the town of Lancre, the Castle, some of the mountain peaks, and the village of Bad Ass which, despite being described in *Equal Rites* as a village that "wouldn't have shown up on a map of the mountains. It barely showed up on a map of the village" (11), nevertheless shows up here. It also includes detailed inset maps of both Lancre Town and Lancre Castle, along with a portrait of Granny Weatherwax and Nanny Ogg as well as ones of the Queen of the Elves and the King of the Elves. Kidby's border includes more natural elements than Player's, which works for a map of a rural area, and the entire view is framed by intertwined branches of trees, roots, and leaves. The Lancre map provides an excellent sense of the sheer verticality of the Kingdom, as well as presenting a better awareness than the novels do of the distance between Granny's cottage and Nanny's house in town. Like the other maps, by indicating a sense of geographic proportions it reinforces the idea of the geographic space of the Discworld, however imaginary.

Death's Domain: A Discworld Mapp depicts a setting outside of the Discworld and indeed outside any level of reality, even that contained within an imaginative place. Described as "a landscape, hanging in space" (*Music* 68), Death's home appears "on no map, [and] existed only in those far reaches of the multiplexed cosmos known to the few astrophysicists who have taken really bad acid" (*Mort* 32). The prefatory material is more extensive than for the other maps, and much of it corresponds more directly to places on the map. Pratchett's description of Albert's attempts to grow pineapples "in a deep warm pineapple pit" corresponds with map location 21 showing the site of the pit, while Death's hobby of golf is reflected not only on the map, where there appears a small golf course containing both a miniature windmill and a sand trap complete with a skeleton (location 28), but also in the booklet with an illustration of Death assuming a golfer's stance with a driver in his grasp, the Death of Rats on his shoulder, and Albert as his caddy balancing a golf cart that holds other golf clubs along with Death's scythe. Moreover, the text notes that though the colors of Death's domain "tend towards the black" this still has its own spectrum, and Kidby's illustrations mirror that spectrum with shades of deep purples and gently marbled grays, providing a sense of dreaminess that obviates the potentially fearsome notion of this being Death's abode. The map's border is created with sculpted and intertwining bones that frame images of Albert, Susan, and the Death of Rats as well as scenes from the house, such as the front entrance with its double stairway, Death's wall of lifetimers, flowers in both black and white, and Death himself. The edges of the map are traced with the thin line of electric blue that Kidby characteristically uses to outline Death throughout his illustrations. His attention to the very smallest details appears throughout as well, perhaps most strikingly in the peacock that ornaments the border, whose tail-feather pattern is made up of tiny skulls. All of these details add elements to Death that help flesh out (so to speak) his character, just as the illustrations throughout the novels help expand our imaginative concepts of the Discworld and its inhabitants.

The most recent additions to Discworld maps appear with *The Compleat Ankh-Morpork* City Guide and map, and the corresponding *Ankh-Morpork Map for iPad*, both of which were created by Pratchett with the assistance of the Discworld Emporium—Bernard Pearson, Reb Voyce, Isobel Pearson, and Ian Mitchell—and with additional illustrations by Peter Dennis.[48] The City Guide comes with an oversize, double-sided pull-out map, measuring 38.5 inches by 35 inches, with an extremely detailed street map on one side and an aerial view of the city on the other. The street map looks like many other street maps, with every street having a name and the Legend distinguishing between major thoroughfares, minor roads and lanes, and waterways, and the map points out significant places of interest including principal buildings and landmarks such as the Patrician's Palace, the Dysk, Small Gods cemetery, and numerous other spots. Its borders are intricately decorated with stylized flowers and toadstools, and its sepia tones support the illusion of this being an aged map of an even older city. The map is divided into grids corresponding to entries in the City Guide's street directory, which also includes enlarged maps for The Shades and the Cattle Market Districts. The other side of the map provides a more realistic representation of the city, as if painted by someone looking down on it. This view gives an excellent sense of the circular sprawl of the city and the way the buildings are clustered together along with sections of green parkland, bridges, fields, the great brown river Ankh that bisects the city, and the wizard's Tower of Art looming near the Hubwards end (or, for those of us outside the Discworld's multiverse, the north end). The detail here is remarkable, with sails and even oars being visible on the boats, people of various shapes and sizes going about their daily business, and the occasional seagull (or perhaps pointless albatross) flying below. The City Guide reads like a typical travel guide, with information about what to do during accidents or emergencies, details for walking tours, and innumerable advertisements in the style of those that appeared in Victorian serial publications such as *David Copperfield*. These list just about anything readers could imagine, along with many things they might not—mousetraps, spirits and wine importers, tattoo parlors, "Verdant Spring—Cosmetics for the Troll of Today," Jolly Sailor tobacco, Wee Mad Arthur's service, humorous vegetables—and provide plenty of reading as well as decoding in relation to the habits and culture of Ankh-Morpork. The City Guide is heavily illustrated, not only with the decorations for advertisements but also with illustrations for various places, such as the one for Twilight Canyons, "A residential home.... Famed for the care of elderly trolls and dwarfs, united against young people," which includes a half-page image of an aging dwarf sitting next to an aging troll, the latter of whom is wearing bunny slippers (see Image 12).

The electronic *Discworld: The Ankh-Morpork Map for iPad* mirrors the paper copy in that it provides both the street directory and the aerial view; however, the electronic version has the additional benefit of being interactive. Readers can zoom in on any detail and tap an icon on the map to get more information.[49] For example, the City Watch Headquarters has two pop-up icons, one for the Headquarters itself, which provides more information about the Watch, and another with information about the City's legal system. The aerial view, referred to as a "Living Map," contains a three-dimensional city landscape and the same informational pop-up boxes along with the added dimensions of sound and movement. When opened, the bird's-eye view of the city is married with birdsong and by the muted sounds of a city. As readers zoom closer, the sounds focus on those of the areas being viewed, such as the squeaks and creaks of the Clacks Tower, the river's slow burbling and bubbling, sizzles of fuses being lit and their subsequent small explosions outside the Guild of Alchemists, the noises of animals squealing and clucking, and near the Opera House the notes of a musical rehearsal, complete with

12. *Twilight Canyons* **from** *The Compleat Ankh-Morpork*, **by Discworld Emporium (reproduced by permission of the Discworld Emporium).**

fragments of songs and the stage director's voice in the background. Movements appear in smoking chimneys and a huge number of people of all species purposefully wandering about the city. Many of these are familiar Discworld characters who, when tapped, say something and have pop-up information cards that can be read. Commander Vimes, for instance, is accompanied by the whistle sounds of the watch, and the voice-over, "We're a bit short-staffed, so if I give you a cigarette would you mind kicking yourself in the teeth?" Granny Weatherwax's comment is similarly typical: "Now you be quiet, Gytha Ogg, and don't you criticize nobody unless you can walk a mile in her shoes!" Pratchett himself makes a couple of unattributed appearances, first in a character named Silas T. Firefly, who looks remarkably like Pratchett, and also in the voice of C.M.O.T. Dibbler, whose "Sausage inna bun. Sausage inna bun. Both ends meet—don't ask me which *kind* of meat, both ends meet" (my transcription) sounds remarkably like Pratchett's voice.

The maps and the illustrations in the City Guide all have a sepia wash with yellow and green overtones, and the artwork is done in acrylic inks on illustrators board; this conveys the mood of the maps perfectly, providing just enough detail to be interesting while still conveying a slightly older look that suits Discworld's time period. From the perspective of a character within Discworld, all of the maps could be useful for finding one's way around the city, and the electronic version would have the added bonus of working by magic. They also provide a sense of proportional relationships—how far away one street is from another, for instance—as well as information about where various places are located. This could be interesting for Discworld readers, who might be curious as to these locations, as well as potentially useful for Discworld inhabitants, although here at least one Discworld character might disagree: Granny Weatherwax, who "didn't like maps. She felt instinctively that they sold the landscape short" (*Abroad* 28). Her comment is accurate, as this is certainly what maps do if one assumes they are expected to provide a literal representation of the landscape. However, most maps are not intended to be an exact replica, albeit in miniature, or even scale models of a place, but instead tend to serve as merely sketches or indications, beginning thoughts to help form one's sense of a place. The existence of a map, of either a real or a fantasy place, can reinforce a sense of the landscape being structured, or organized, in much the same way as other real places that the readers' experience has structured. Nicholas Tam addresses the negative aspects of this effect specifically in relation to the Discworld maps:

> There is something completely bounded about maps. We all know that the data they present is highly selective, as is also true for prose, with strategic omissions and gaps left for future exploration. Yet the boundedness of maps commits to an illusion of having reached a roughly finished state, as if everything inside has already been fixed and everything outside is still untouched and malleable [25].

Tam goes further, suggesting that "from the perspective of someone involved in creating a world, particularly in a series that continues to emerge over time, a map intended to serve as an aid may also be a suffocating constraint" (26). He raises some sound points here, particularly since we tend to give maps of real places a certain authority, perhaps because they give us the illusion that we are in control of where we are and where we are going. It is important to remember, though, that this authority is an illusion: maps cannot actually directly give control, but instead can be used as one of many tools that provide information and, at times, suggest possible journeys or potential routings for excursions. In the end, we must take charge of our travel. By using them as a jumping-off point, or suggestion of something that might influence the imaginative conception of a place but not necessarily lock it into being, the Discworld maps are useful as a springboard. Maps of imaginary places are fun to look at for that very reason: they pique our curiosity and excite in us a sense of wonder. Pratchett, not surprisingly, addressed this point as well in relation to *The Discworld Mapp*, noting, "It's not *completely* accurate. It can't be. The only accurate map is the one inside my head, and yours" ("I Needed"; original bold-face).

*****

The nature of fantasy arguably lends itself more to visual interpretation than many other genres—novels of manners, for instance—in part because of its strangeness. In fantasy, authors often create places that no one has ever seen and that do not exist, and must do so in a tangible enough way that readers can suspend their disbelief and enter the story without being unceremoniously bumped back into reality when the first three-headed dragon or talking rock appears. As Maurice Sendak has noted, "fantasy makes sense only if it's rooted ten feet deep in reality" (Hautala), and this comment is particularly apt in relation to illustration. Fantasy illustration is most effective when it portrays its fantastic scene in a way that makes it seem both real and recognizable. One of the ways in which fantasy artists create this verisimilitude is by relying on "the pictorial conventions associated with realism: gesture and human expression, spatial depth and natural light, the inclusion of detail, logical scale relationships, and so on" (Hackford 172). We see this sort of realism demonstrated in both Paul Kidby's and Stephen Player's illustrations, with their realistically proportioned characters whose facial expressions make them look like real people, and with their incredible attention to even the very smallest details (see Image 13). Similarly, Stephen Briggs' sketches of Ankh-Morpork buildings and scenery, as well as such minute items as the Bursar's Dried Frog Pills tin, and Bernard Pearson's designs for coins and stamps have the effect of creating a sense of authenticity, while the Discworld Emporium's use of scale in their maps and the realistic details of the City Guide provide representations that encumber doubt. In addition to this sense of realism, though, George Landow argues that artists of fantasy also need to emphasize "the element of whimsy" (109) to evoke in the reader a sense of wonder. Certainly the art of Josh Kirby induces this sense of wonder, his illustrations jam-packed with fantastic creatures of all sizes and shapes accentuating more elements of whimsy—in its original meaning of a feeling of dizziness, giddiness, or vertigo—per square inch than any other fantasy artist may have achieved. Kidby's and Player's art, in contrast, tends to contain more whimsical overtones than actual whimsy; in other words, their art tends to be fanciful rather than whimsical, particularly in the ways in which they include creatures such as dragons, trolls, or the Feegles alongside their more realistic human counterparts, rendering them in ways that make them seem believable and, indeed, realistic. As Hackford observes, "it is this fusion of the familiar and the magical ... that animates the best fantasy

13. *Feegles*, **by Stephen Player (reproduced by permission of Stephen Player, playergallery.com).**

art" (172), and certainly when fantastic creatures look the way they are supposed to, or the way we expect them to, it adds to our pleasure in the texts.

Ultimately, good fantasy illustration enlightens readers by bringing images to life in an instantly familiar way, which allows us to see something for the first time but with a strong sense of recognition. The art of Discworld, in all of its incarnations, has exactly this effect, especially when the various artists' images are considered together. One excellent place to view these images is in the Discworld Calendars, particularly those that are compilations of various artists' Discworld illustrations.[50] These calendars indicate that Pratchett's Discworld has now evolved to a point where it can appear in illustrations without the accompanying texts: there are enough people cognizant of the Discworld to enjoy the images not just for their own sake, but because they recognize the place and people they evoke. The wide variety of visual types reinforce this point: the cover art, the decorations, the lavishly illustrated novels, the hypotrochoidal texts such as picture books and maps all provide different kinds of images which, when viewed with Pratchett's words on the page in mind, combine into a synergy that creates a greater whole. Naturally when we first start reading and looking, there are gaps in our imaginative visions and we inevitably interpolate among the texts we read and the pictures we see and the images we create in our minds to approximate a coherent representation, but as we progress further into the Discworld multiverse we have an ever-expanding body of mental images, both imagined and remembered, that we might consciously or unconsciously summon to produce a kind of higher synergistic experience. In this way, while each of the artist's images add something different to our own vision of Discworld, when taken collectively the art they have produced creates in our imaginations the color of octarine.

NOTES

1. This, incidentally, is one of the concerns every time a film version (to choose one of the most typical types of adaptation for any popular work) is created: so many millions of people all over the world have such a strong sense of how they envision the Discworld, and who the people are who inhabit it, that re-envisioning it in any way is a risky business at best.

2. Including *The Unseen University Cut-Out Book*, an amazingly detailed cardboard model needing assembly, along the lines of the well-known paper model of the Globe Theatre.

3. The illustrations for *The Colour of Magic* and *The Light Fantastic* graphic novels illustrate Scott Rockwell's adaptation of Pratchett's prose, just as Graham Higgins' illustrations for *Guards! Guards! A Discworld Big Comic* illustrate Stephen Briggs' adaptation. While *Mort: A Discworld Big Comic* was adapted by Pratchett himself, Higgins' illustrations were still created for the adaptation rather than for the original novel.

4. Josh Kirby provided some of the artwork for computer games including *Discworld I* (TWG/Perfect 10 Production, Psygnosis Games, 1995); *Missing Presumed...* (Perfect Entertainment/Psygnosis, 1997); and *Discworld Noir* (Perfect/TWG, 1999). Paul Kidby produced the art and illustrations for the GURPS *Discworld Roleplaying Game* (Steve Jackson Games, 2002). Paul Kidby, Bernard Pearson, Peter Dennis, and Ian Mitchell provided cover artwork and game card images for the *Discworld: Ankh-Morpork* board game (Treefrog Games, 2011).

5. This ignores the question of whether all reading is, at some level, a visual semiotic process.

6. It is worth noting that while fantasy art has its roots in the illuminated manuscripts of the Middle Ages, it did not really take off again until the *beaux-arts* movement in mid- to late–Victorian Britain with the art of the Pre-Raphaelites, along with William Morris and the English Arts and Crafts Movement, when the connections between images and the texts they illuminated had a resurgence in the popular imagination. Though early twentieth century fantasy artists "were primarily employed creating science fiction illustrations for pulps" (Layne 65), today the field has broadened to encompass fantasy art "involving dungeons, dragons, star warriors, and alien worlds of every imaginable ilk" (Layne 65). The 1970s was a "critical decade" in the history

of fantasy art, with films like *2001: A Space Odyssey* (1968) and *Star Wars* (1977) having an influence not only on the genres of science fiction and fantasy as a whole but also on its illustration and how we thought about it (Frank). Moreover, the 1970s were important because that was when artists started becoming more recognized: they began receiving contracts for work, getting their art back from the publishers, and signing their works in ways that made it harder to crop out their signatures (Frank). The Hugo Award for Best Artist was established in 1953, and other awards followed, including the World Fantasy Award for Art in 1975, awards for art from the British Science Fiction Association and the British Fantasy Society in the 1970s, and the Chesley Award in 1985, named for science fiction artist Chesley Bonestell and given in several categories, including Best Cover Illustration awards for hardcover and paperback books as well as magazines, Best Gaming Related Work, Best Three Dimensional Work, Best Interior Art, and others.

7. This particular attitude towards the genres of both fantasy and children's literature, while common enough in not only everyday conversation but also the circles of literary criticism, is perhaps best expressed in Jonathan Myerson's short piece, "Harry Potter and the Sad Grownups," which appeared in *The Independent* in 2001. Myerson maintains that, as an adult, he reads novels for the moral, psychological, political, or sexual truths that he can gain from reading them and that he "cannot hope to come closer to any of these truths through a children's novel, where nice clean white lines are painted between the good guys and the evil ones, where magic exists, and where there are adults on hand to delineate rules" and that, furthermore, adult readers need to "get real, please, there is so much good fiction out there, written specifically for your adult age group, written with you in mind. Please, next time, choose that. Don't keep running away from life" (Myerson).

8. It is worth noting that cover artists earn a one-time fee for a cover, while authors get royalties for each book sold; thus, the more copies sold, the more profit an author makes, but the artist's profits remain static. This lack of financial recognition also implies the kind of second-rate status, or devaluation, that at least certain forms of artwork suffer in relation to the text.

9. The list of names in the field is quite lengthy, depending on the field in which the theorists locate themselves (semiotics, children's literature, narratology, and visual media, to name but a few). That said, the theorists' works I have found the most useful in influencing my thinking for this essay include Perry Nodelman's *The Pleasures of the Text*, W. J. T. Mitchell's *Picture Theory*, Maria Nikolajeva and Carole Scott's *How Picturebooks Work*, Uri Shulevitz's *Writing with Pictures*, and Maurice Sendak's *Caldecott & Co.: Notes on Books & Pictures*.

10. According to Sipe, Philip Pullman uses the musical term "counterpoint" to explore the process of reading and interpreting text and illustrations, while Allan Ahlberg uses "antiphonal" effect to mean music that is sung alternately in a kind of call-and-response pattern. Other theorists invoke terms from science: Miller uses "interference" (from wave theory) to refer to the way two different wave patterns may combine to form a complex new pattern, while Moebius draws a parallel to "plate tectonics." Semioticians like Lewis call it "polysystemy," which means piecing together text from different kinds of signifying systems, "relaying" (Barthes), "irony" (Nodelman), and "congruency [and] deviation" (Schwarcz), the latter of which considers the way pictures can present images that either are harmonious and complementary or

that veer away from the text to oppose it, or telling a different story in the two media (Sipe 98–101).

11. He also references other theorists who expand on Jakobson's ideas, suggesting that both Perry Nodelman and German Romantic philosopher G. E. Lessing distinguish between arts that are perceived simultaneously (such as painting and sculpture) and thus experienced concurrently, and those perceived successively (such as music and literature) and thus experienced linearly.

12. Nodelman's exact phrase is "Illustrators are subsidiary artists, their work a parasite on work that already exists" (79).

13. This essay focuses on the book covers for the first editions of hardcovers and paperbacks published in England. Although some of the earlier American covers were done by other artists, these are more difficult to trace and not only less interesting but also, I would argue, less influential, than the covers by Kirby and Kidby. Covers for the audio books tend to vary, depending on whether they are published in England or the United States and whether they are abridged or unabridged. Older audio CDs tended to include images from either Kirby's or (for books published after 2001) Kidby's covers, while some of the most recent ones have updated covers by a variety of artists.

14. Kirby (1928–2001) studied at the Liverpool City School of Art before moving to London and working in advertising; early in his career he also created images for jigsaw puzzles, before moving on to illustrating covers for pulp fiction and science fiction novels and anthologies, including cover images for works by Ray Bradbury and Ron Goulart ("Out of"). In addition to the Discworld illustrations, he created a series of paintings entitled *Voyage of the Ayeguy*, regarded as his *tour de force*, which tackled the challenges and emotions experienced by a spaceman protagonist during his mission across a strange planet ("Out of"). Kirby won the British Fantasy Award for Professional Artist in 1996.

15. *Carnival* is a term usually associated with the work of Russian scholar Mikhail Bakhtin and his theory of laughter; his seminal work on the topic, *Rabelais and His World*, focused on the medieval carnival, which was marked by a kind of chaotic excess in terms of the way one experiences the world, and embodied the drive towards liberation and subversion. Linda Hutcheon notes that Bakhtin reveals the paradox of carnival in its "authorized transgression of norms" (Lacombe 517), and other critics have commented on its patriarchal attitudes, especially in the ways the female body and voice are represented. Modern carnival employs ritual language and gesture, and often focuses on the grotesque; it consciously celebrates the resistance of "order, closure and the sacrosanct" (517). Visual carnival examples appear throughout the works of Hieronymus Bosch, Pieter Bruegel and Marc Chagall—all artists whose influence over Kirby was profound.

16. Pieter Bruegel the Elder's (1525–1569) paintings of the Tower of Babel perhaps best illustrate this sense of bustling human life.

17. The Italian painter Tiziano Vecelli, known as Titian (?1488–1576) and the Flemish Baroque painter Paul Rubens (1577–1640) were both recognized during their lifetimes for their portrait painting, and both were especially highly regarded for their use of color. The English painter William Hogarth (1697–1764) also painted portraits, and was considered tremendously influential on satirical political illustration due to his rendering of contemporary moral subjects. Hieronymus Bosch (1450–1516) was

known for his complex and dense paintings that used fantastic imagery and portrayed complicated inventions; his triptych entitled *The Garden of Earthly Delights* (probably dating to about 1504, though it could have been painted any time between 1490 and 1510) was one of his masterpieces. The Anglo-Welsh artist and illustrator Frank Brangwyn (1867–1956) was also a muralist, designer, and engraver.

18. For both *The Colour of Magic* and *The Light Fantastic*, Kirby shows Twoflower having literally four eyes, which was apparently a misinterpretation of Pratchett's reference to spectacles. When Twoflower first appears, the beggar Blind Hugh "found himself looking up into a face with four eyes in it" (*Color* 10)—one wonders, of course, how Blind Hugh can see this in any case—and Twoflower is shortly thereafter referred to as "the four-eyed man" (*Color* 11); later, in *Interesting Times*, Rincewind refers to Twoflower as "you four-eyed little git!" (108). By the time he painted the cover for *Interesting Times*, Kirby had started reading the novels (rather than relying on a short digest of them), and corrected his image of Twoflower to appear wearing glasses, as he does on the covers of *Interesting Times* as well as the omnibus edition of *The Colour of Magic & The Light Fantastic*.

19. The album is also mirrored in Pratchett's text, initially in a reference to "one out of three ain't bad" (2)—a nod to the song on the album "Two Out of Three Ain't Bad"—and later with "The flower-bed erupted. Modo had a brief vision of flames and something arcing into the sky before his vision was blotted out by a rain of beads, feathers, and soft black petals" (344), corresponding to much of the cover image of Meat Loaf's album.

20. When Kirby created the cover for *Equal Rites* he had not yet met Pratchett personally and did not realize they had a completely different perception of witches until after the painting was finished; however, "[a]lthough they debated the point, no changes were called for" (Suckling 102).

21. The sizes of paintings for the covers were usually four times the width and height of the paperback cover. The process took Kirby about eight weeks from start to finish, including the time to read (or scan) the novel and create the design; typically it took him four weeks to complete the illustration itself.

22. Kirby also painted three paintings to be used for Dave Greenslade's musical interpretation, *From the Discworld*. Containing fourteen tracks of music, inspired by passages, characters, and settings, the CD's cover image is Kirby's *Eric IV: Discworld I*, from *Eric*, which shows Rincewind and Eric riding on the Luggage far above the Disc, while the back cover features an image from Kirby's *Unseen University*. A painting titled *When Will We Three Meet Again?* appears in the booklet, showing the opening scene from *Wyrd Sisters* with Nanny Ogg, Granny Weatherwax, and Magrat. A third painting, titled *Ankh-Morpork*, was commissioned for the CD but not used, and appears in *A Blink of the Screen*.

23. Kidby is self-taught and always focused on his goal of becoming a self-employed artist. After graduating from high school, he worked making false teeth, painting blinds in a factory, and designing greeting cards and packaging before moving on to magazine covers and then to illustrating for Pratchett. His artistic influences are wide-ranging, though he specifically notes Arthur Rackham, the Pre-Raphaelites, Alphonse Mucha, Norman Rockwell, Gustave Doré, Albrecht Dürer, and Maxfield Parrish as inspirations (Kidby "RE: Enquiry"). In addition to his Discworld art, he also paints faerie art (much of which can be seen in his *Le Royaume Enchanté*), and

creates sculptures of fantastic creatures such as dragons, winged horses, griffins, and mermaids, among others.

24. Kidby also created the cover and chapter headings for Pratchett's *Dodger*, a non–Discworld novel set in the same world as *Nation*.

25. Though *Night Watch* is often referred to as Kidby's first Discworld cover, he actually painted a number of Discworld-related covers before 2002, including those for *The Science of Discworld*, *Nanny Ogg's Cookbook*, and *The Last Hero*. In addition, his covers for many of the diaries, maps, and *The Pratchett Portfolio* appeared well before *Night Watch*.

26. The painting's full title is "The Company of Captain Frans Banning Cocq and Lieutenant Willem van Ruytenburch Preparing to March Out"; painted in 1642 by Rembrandt van Rijn, it is displayed in the Rijksmuseum in Amsterdam.

27. The painting for the *Night Watch* cover exemplifies Howells' comment that "art as history and art as commodity appear ... to be inextricably linked" (Howells 75). During Rembrandt's time, it was not uncommon for wealthy patrons to pay to have themselves included in his paintings, and this happened for his painting of *The Night Watch*. Kidby was aware of this tradition, and when it transpired that "there had been a charity auction at a Discworld event whilst the book was being written and three fans had paid to be written into the 'Night Watch' story.... It therefore seemed creatively fitting that the Discworld auction winners should also have their portraits painted into the cover. The original artwork is now owned by one of those featured on the cover" (Lee).

28. In 1998, Terry Pratchett and Stephen Briggs released *Discworld's Unseen University Diary 1998* with illustrations by Paul Kidby; this was followed by several more diaries in the same format, with illustrated front and back covers pertaining to their topic. For instance, *Lu-Tze's Yearbook* has a picture of Lu-Tze and his broom on the front, with an image of two monks being chased by Mrs. Cosmopilite on the back, while *Discworld's Ankh-Morpork City Watch Diary 1999* has front images of Carrot, framed by a badge shape, and a back image of the badge sporting the letters AMCW and the motto, "Fabricati Diem, Pvnc." Other diaries include *Discworld Assassins' Guild Yearbook and Diary 2000*, *Discworld Fools' Guild Yearbook Diary 2001*, *Discworld Thieves' Guild Yearbook & Diary 2002*, *Discworld (Reformed) Vampyre's Diary 2003*, and the *Ankh-Morpork Post Office Handbook Discworld Diary 2007*. In addition to being handy marketing tools that increase Discworld visibility (and revenue), these are also fun for readers who enjoy suspending belief in the Discworld in a way that exceeds merely reading the books.

29. Stephen Briggs is a British thespian and civil servant, and has recorded a number of Pratchett's Discworld novels for audio book editions. He is the author/updater of the *Discworld Companion*, and also created a number of Discworld merchandise items, such as the Unseen University scarf (Smythe "Terry Pratchett").

30. While in some ways the series had been building towards heavier overtones of social and political criticism for awhile, and hit a kind of stride in *The Fifth Elephant* as well as *The Amazing Maurice*, I would still argue that *Night Watch* is the novel where that tone was sustained throughout the entire book.

31. See Ekman's *Here Be Dragons: Exploring Fantasy Maps and Settings* for an extensive discussion of this convention.

32. Paul Kidby and Colin Smythe have both confirmed that Kidby was the artist

here (Kidby "RE: Enquiry" and Smythe "Re: Query"). In some ways, the lack of attribution adds to the verisimilitude of the ubiquitous presence of Victorian political cartoonists.

33.   Bernard and Isobel Pearson, the founders of the Discworld Emporium, have worked with Pratchett for nearly thirty years, "creating numerous Discworld artefacts, sculptures and games as well as collaborating with Terry on books such as *The Unseen University Cut Out Book, The Discworld Almanack, The World of Poo* and *The Compleat Ankh-Morpork*" (Mitchell "RE: Discworld Emporium").

34.   This translates roughly as "How much is that dog in the window?"

35.   Two other versions of Discworld Companions were published before *Turtle Recall*, both written by Pratchett and Briggs and illustrated by Briggs: these were *The Discworld Companion* and *The New Discworld Companion*. This third version includes all of the text and illustrations from the second, and was expanded to include some of the material from the first that had been deleted from the second for reasons of space.

36.   The Discworld Emporium also publishes *A History of Discworld Stamps,* "an illustrated history of how the stamps began on an A3 double-sided poster presented in a near-facsimile copy of the very first cover created for Waterstone's Booksellers in conjunction with Transworld publishers for the launch of *Going Postal*. The cover bears some of the very first stamps, as described in *Going Postal* and seen in the Sky1 film adaptation. This item is a fabulous introduction to the world of Discworld Stamps and contains never before seen material for the hardened collector" (Discworld Emporium "Description").

37.   In the American edition, these chapter headings are simply printed in a different font; in the British edition, the *Mr. Bunnsy* text is inset into a scrap of parchment with decorations such as butterflies, flowers, brambles, or mushrooms. Artist David Wyatt attended art college in Reading, and is an acclaimed children's book illustrator and cover artist. He has created illustrations for a number of fantasy works including books by Alan Garner, Diana Wynne Jones, J. R. R. Tolkien, Brian Jacques, Megan Whalen Turner, and Ursula Le Guin.

38.   Stephen Player has created illustrations for a number of science fiction and fantasy works, including covers for the dramatic adaptations of *Wyrd Sisters, Mort,* and *Guards! Guards!,* among others. While studying illustration at the Camberwell School of Arts and Crafts in London he met horror writer Clive Barker, and after graduating began publishing artwork for science fiction, fantasy, horror, and children's literature. He has also illustrated graphic novels and video game covers, and has created artwork for film, television, and electronic games. He has won a number of awards for his artwork, including the British Science Fiction and Fantasy Association award in 1994 for *The Streets of Ankh-Morpork*.

39.   Leonard's perfect circle is connected with the story of Leonardo da Vinci being asked by the Pope to "submit some of his work for a competition for a new commission. Leonardo kept putting him off, saying he was too busy, as the requests grew more and more insistent. In the end, to avoid the Pope having him arrested, he drew, freehand, at arms length, a perfect circle on a sheet of paper and sent it to the Pope, who promptly gave him the commission. The reason for this is that to draw a perfect circle, freehand and unsupported is one of the hardest things possible to draw, achieved by few artists, usually only after much practice and was for a long time considered to be the pinnacle of artistic achievement" (Breebaart).

40. The metaphor seems doubly apt when one sees the image in motion, with the curves being created from start to finish in a repeating loop. The involuntary "It does move!" elicited from this sight echoes Om's faithful followers in *Small Gods* and their watch-phrase "The turtle moves!" (31). Moreover, the shape serendipitously approximates an aerial view of the Great A'Tuin with the Discworld perched on top of its back. The closest theory I am aware of that relates to this idea appears in Gérard Genette's *Paratexts*, where the term *paratexts* refers to liminal texts that serve as a kind of a threshold "between the inside and the outside" or on the fringes of other texts (2). In contrast, the term *hypotrochoidal texts* refers to texts that are generated from within another text but that exist both inside and outside it, for characters and readers concurrently. I am indebted to Bill Spruiell for listening to my convoluted thoughts about this concept and then finding the perfect image with which to express it.

41. I will refer to Pratchett's *Where's My Cow?* as a picture book, which is a book whose story relies on both words and pictures to tell the story, and the same-titled book that young Sam and Vimes read as a story book, a book that contains both words and pictures but whose pictures serve to decorate rather than extend the text and thus do not serve the same sort of interdependent function as those in a true picture book.

42. Grant began studying at the Brassey Institute of Fine Arts in Hastings, Sussex at the early age of twelve, and describes himself as "a nonconformist with a Bohemian attitude" ("Grant" 245). While his approach is rooted in traditional fine art, he favors fantasy and horror genres, and his illustrations have also appeared in children's books and posters, romance, historical literature, and general fiction.

43. The title page also credits Bernard and Isobel Pearson for assistance, but much of the turn of phrase seems very Pratchettian. Artist Peter Dennis studied illustration at Liverpool Art College and has worked as an illustrator for over forty years. In addition to creating the illustrations for *The World of Poo,* he contributed illustrations for the *Discworld: Ankh-Morpork* board game and has worked with the Discworld Emporium on *The Compleat Ankh-Morpork* (Mitchell "RE: Discworld Emporium").

44. "Nanny had nothing against witches being married. It wasn't as if there were rules. She herself had had many husbands, and had even been married to three of them" (Pratchett, "The Sea and Little Fishes" 224).

45. This consists of an anecdote about a group of Pseudopolitan soldiers who hid beneath cabbage leaves in a trench and ended up being planted by the Sto Militia (*Almanak* 87). The alternate spelling of the word *Almanack* mirrors the variable spelling of the Discworld population in general.

46. Pratchett continues, "Anyway, what is a fantasy but a space beyond which There Be Dragons? On the Discworld we know that There Be Dragons Everywhere. They might not all have scales and forked tongues, but they Be Here all right, grinning and jostling and trying to sell you souvenirs" ("Foreword" n. pag).

47. The area of fictional cartography is relatively new in relation to literary theory as a whole, having really only emerged in the last twenty or so years as a burgeoning area of study. That said, as a field it is far too vast to do justice to here, and so my attention is focused primarily on the illustrative, or aesthetic, aspect of the Discworld maps. For an extensive and detailed introduction to the fictional cartography of fantasy, see Stefan Ekman's *Here Be Dragons: Exploring Fantasy Maps and Settings*; for a shorter but excellent overview, see Nicholas Tam's essay "Here Be Cartographers: Reading the Fantasy Map."

48. "Ian Mitchell & Reb Voyce joined the Discworld Emporium in 2006 after training at the Falmouth College of Arts. They have been lucky enough to collaborate with Terry on the *Compleat Ankh-Morpork* and are currently working on *The Compleat Discworld* as well as *A Compleat Discworld Bestiary*" (Mitchell "RE: Discworld Emporium"). See earlier notes for biographical information on Bernard Pearson, Isobel Pearson, and Peter Dennis.

49. Readers can also take guided tours of the city, zooming in on various places and tapping the screen to get a pop-up information card and sometimes a picture, in addition to collecting points for their various achievements.

50. There have been annual Discworld calendars since at least 1999. Some have featured the artwork of a single artist—Josh Kirby (1999, 2002, 2011), Paul Kidby (2003 and 2012), and Marc Simonetti (2013); others have featured a selection of artists, and have included artwork by Stephen Player, Angelo Rinaldi, Chris Riddell, David Frankland, David Wyatt, Dominic Harman, Edward Miller, Gino D'Achille, Graham Higgins, Jackie Morris, James Mayhew, Jon Sullivan, Les Edwards, Mark Edwards, Melvyn Grant, Paul Kidby, Sandy Nightingale, and Stuart Williams.

Works Cited

Adams, Tamla Ebony. "Icon: Masculine Myths and the Visual Culture of Fantastic Art Illustration." Diss. University of Minnesota, 2006. *ProQuest*. 29 June 2012.

Beeton, Mrs. [Isabella Mary]. *The Book of Household Management*. London: S.O. Beeton, 1861.

Breebaart, Leo, ed. "The Last Hero." *The Annotated Pratchett File, v.9.0*. L-Space. 2 Feb. 2008. Web. 20 Oct. 2012.

Briggs, Stephen. *Armoured Raven*. Ink drawing. 1994. *Turtle Recall: The Discworld Companion ... So Far*. By Terry Pratchett and Stephen Briggs. London: Gollancz, 2012. 137.

———. "Many Miles Across Tortuous Terrain...." *The Discworld Mapp*. By Terry Pratchett and Stephen Briggs. Illus. Stephen Player. London: Corgi, 1995. N. pag.

———. "Mapping the City." *The Streets of Ankh-Morpork*. By Terry Pratchett and Stephen Briggs. Illus. Stephen Player. London: Corgi, 1993. N. pag.

———. *A View in the Shades*. Ink drawing. 1994. *Turtle Recall: The Discworld Companion ... So Far*. By Terry Pratchett and Stephen Briggs. London: Gollancz, 2012. 100.

Byatt, A. S. "Foreword." *A Blink of the Screen: Collected Shorter Fiction*. By Terry Pratchett. London: Doubleday, 2012. 11–15.

Cherry, David A. "An Appreciation of Michael Whelan." *Bucconeer: The 56th World Science Fiction Convention*. Baltimore. Aug. 1998. Address. Web. 21 June 2012.

The Discworld Emporium. "Description of *A History of Discworld Stamps*." Discworld Emporium. N.d. Web. 15 June 2013.

———. "Twilight Canyons." Ink drawing on board. *The Compleat Ankh-Morpork*. By Terry Pratchett and The Discworld Emporium. London: Doubleday, 2012. 19.

Ekman, Stefan. *Here Be Dragons: Exploring Fantasy Maps and Settings*. Middletown, CT: Wesleyan University Press, 2013.

Eliot, T.S. "Tradition and the Individual Talent." *The Egoist* 4:6 (Sept. 1919): 54–55.

"Entrevista a Paul Kibdy [sic], magia con las manos y mucho cuteness 'Interview with

Paul Kibdy [sic], magic hands and much cuteness.'" *Be Literature*. 4 Mar. 2013. Web. 15 Apr. 2013.

Frank, Jane. "Historical Overview, from the 1970s to 2000." *Science Fiction and Fantasy Artists of the Twentieth Century*. Ed. Jane Frank. Jefferson, NC: McFarland, 2009. 35–68. *MyLibrary*. 21 June 2012.

Genette, Gérard. *Paratexts*. Cambridge: Cambridge University Press, 1997.

Grant, Melvyn, illus. *Where's My Cow?* By Terry Pratchett. New York: HarperCollins, 2005.

"Grant, Melvin." *Science Fiction and Fantasy Artists of the Twentieth Century*. Ed. Jane Frank. Jefferson, NC: McFarland, 2009. 245–46. *MyLibrary*. 21 June 2012.

Hackford, Terry Reece. "Fantastic Visions: Illustration of the *Arabian Nights*." *The Aesthetics of Fantasy Literature and Art*. Ed. Roger C. Schlobin. Notre Dame, IN: University of Notre Dame Press, 1982. 143–75.

Harvey, Lloyd. "Paul Kidby Interview." *Inside the Artist's Studio*. http://artistinsight. blogspot.com/2010/01/paul-kidby-inrerview.html 4 Mar. 2010. Web. 30 May 2012.

Hautala, Laura. "CJM's Sendak On Sendak: Where the Child Things Are Rather Grown Up." *The San Francisco Appeal*. 9 Sept. 2009. Web. 29 July 2013.

Heller, Steven, and Marshall Arisman, eds. *The Education of an Illustrator*. New York: Allsworth, 2000.

Howells, Richard, and Joaquim Negreiros. *Visual Culture*. 2003. 2d ed. Cambridge: Polity, 2012.

"Hypotrochoid." Def. *The Oxford English Dictionary*. 15 Apr. 2013.

The Illustrator Who Makes Terry Pratchett's Characters Come Alive!—Paul Kidby and His Magical Creations. By Ms. Z. *The Genius Salon*. 27 Nov. 2012. Web. 30 Nov. 2012.

Jean, Vadim, and Terry Pratchett. *Terry Pratchett's* The Colour of Magic: *The Illustrated Screenplay*. London: Gollancz, 2008.

Jean, Vadim, Terry Pratchett, Bill Kaye and Stephen Player. *Terry Pratchett's* Hogfather: *The Illustrated Screenplay*. London: Gollancz, 2006.

Kidby, Paul. *The Art of Discworld*. By Terry Pratchett and Paul Kidby. New York: HarperCollins, 2004. N. pag.

_____. *Cohen the Barbarian*. Oil on board. Private collection. *Discworld and Beyond: A Retrospective*. Hampshire, UK: St. Barbe Museum & Art Gallery, 2012. 10.

_____. *Discworld and Beyond: A Retrospective*. Hampshire, UK: St. Barbe Museum and Art Gallery, 2012. 10.

_____. *Granny Weatherwax Standing*. Pencil drawing. Private collection. *Discworld and Beyond: A Retrospective*. Hampshire, UK: St. Barbe Museum and Art Gallery, 2012. 36.

_____. *Granny Weatherwax with Bees*. Pencil drawing. Private collection. *The Pratchett Portfolio*. By Terry Pratchett and Paul Kidby. London: Gollancz, 1996. N. pag.

_____. *Nanny Ogg's Cookbook*. Cover image. Pencil drawing. Private collection.

_____. *The Pratchett Portfolio*. By Terry Pratchett and Paul Kidby. London: Gollancz, 1996.

_____. "RE: Enquiry." E-mail to the author. 13 July 2013.

_____. *Rincewind in XXXX*. Oil on board. Private collection. *The Art of Discworld*. By Terry Pratchett and Paul Kidby. New York: HarperCollins, 2004. N. pag.

_____, illus. *The Folklore of Discworld*. By Terry Pratchett and Jacqueline Simpson. London: Corgi, 2009.

_____, illus. *A Hat Full of Sky*. By Terry Pratchett. 2004. London: Corgi, 2005.

_____, illus. *The Last Hero*. By Terry Pratchett. 2001. New York: HarperCollins, 2002.

_____, illus. *Nanny Ogg's Cookbook*. By Terry Pratchett and Stephen Briggs. London: Transworld, 1999.

_____, illus. *A Tourist Guide to Lancre*. By Terry Pratchett and Stephen Briggs. London: Corgi, 1998.

_____, illus. *The Wee Free Men*. By Terry Pratchett. London: Corgi, 2003.

Kidby, Paul, and Vanessa Kidby. *Le Royaume Enchanté*. Paris: Daniel Maghen, 2009.

Kirby, Josh. *Hogfather*. 1996. Oil painting. Private collection.

_____. *The Josh Kirby Discworld Portfolio*. 1993. Intro. Nigel Suckling. London: Paper Tiger, 2001.

_____. *Josh Kirby Poster Book*. Intro. Terry Pratchett. London: Corgi, 1989.

_____. *Reaper Man*. 1991. Oil painting. Private collection.

_____, illus. *From the Discworld*. By Dave Greenslade. London: Virgin, 1994. CD.

Kress, Gunther, and Theo van Leeuwen. *Reading Images: The Grammar of Visual Design*. 1996. 2d ed. New York: Routledge, 2006.

Lacombe, Michéle. "Carnival." *Encyclopedia of Contemporary Literary Theory: Approaches, Scholars, Terms*. Ed. Irena R. Makaryk. Toronto: University of Toronto Press, 1993. 516–18.

Landow, George P. "And the World Became Strange: Realms of Literary Fantasy." *The Aesthetics of Fantasy Literature and Art*. Ed. Roger C. Schlobin. Notre Dame, IN: University of Notre Dame Press, 1982. 105–42.

Langford, David. *Josh Kirby: A Cosmic Cornucopia*. Illus. Josh Kirby. Foreword by Tom Holt. London: Paper Tiger, 1999.

_____. "Pratchett, Terry (David John). *St. James Guide to Fantasy Writers*. Ed. David Pringle. New York: St. James, 1996. 486–88.

Layne, Gwendolyn. "Mum's the Word: Sexuality in Victorian Fantasy Illustration (and Beyond)." *Eros in the Mind's Eye: Sexuality and the Fantastic in Art and Film*. Ed. Donald Palumbo. New York: Greenwood, 1986. 59–74.

Lee. "Fantastic Fantasy Artwork #2: Night Watch (Discworld: Book 29) by Paul Kidby." *Fantasy Book Review*. 11 Oct. 2011. Web. 27 Oct. 2011.

Le Guin, Ursula K. "The Despised Genres: Women Writers and the Canon." University of Calgary. 24 Sept. 1996. Lecture.

Meat Loaf. *Bat Out of Hell*. Sony, 1977. LP.

Mitchell, Ian. "RE: Discworld Emporium." E-mail to the author. 18 July 2013.

Mitchell, W. J. T. *Picture Theory: Essays on Verbal and Visual Representation*. Chicago: University of Chicago Press, 1994.

Myerson, Jonathan. "Harry Potter and the Sad Grown-Ups." *Independent* 14 Nov. 2001: N. pag. 2 Mar. 2007.

Nikolajeva, Maria, and Carole Scott. *How Picturebooks Work*. New York: Routledge, 2001.

Nodelman, Perry. *Words about Pictures: The Narrative Art of Children's Picture Books*. Athens: University of Georgia Press, 1988.

"Out of This World: The Art of Josh Kirby." 15 June–30 Sept. 2007. *Walker Art Gallery Exhibition* 2007. Liverpool, UK. 10 Oct. 2012.

Player, Stephen. *Feegles*. Watercolor painting. Private collection. *Terry Pratchett's Discworld Collectors' Edition Calendar 2008*. London: Gollancz, 2007. N. pag.

_____. *The Streets of Ankh-Morpork*. Watercolor painting. Cover image. *The Streets of Ankh-Morpork*. By Terry Pratchett and Stephen Briggs. London: Corgi, 1993.

_____, illus. *The Discworld Mapp*. By Terry Pratchett and Stephen Briggs. London: Corgi, 1995.

_____, illus. *The Illustrated Wee Free Men*. By Terry Pratchett. London: Doubleday, 2008.

_____, illus. *The Streets of Ankh-Morpork*. By Terry Pratchett and Stephen Briggs. London: Corgi, 1993.

Pratchett, Terry. *The Colour of Magic*. 1983. Illus. Josh Kirby. London: Corgi, 1985.

_____. "Discworld & Beyond." *Locus* (Dec. 1999): 4, 73–76.

_____. *Equal Rites*. Illus. Josh Kirby. London: Corgi, 1987.

_____. ~~Faust~~ *Eric*. Illus. Josh Kirby. London: Gollancz, 1990.

_____. *The First Discworld Novels: The Colour of Magic & The Light Fantastic*. Illus. Josh Kirby. London: Colin Smythe, 1999.

_____. "Foreword." 1999. *The Colour of Magic*. 1983. Illus. Josh Kirby. London: Corgi, 2012.

_____. *Going Postal*. Illus. Paul Kidby. London: Doubleday, 2004.

_____. "Here Be Dragons ... and Here ... and Here...." *The Discworld Mapp*. By Terry Pratchett and Stephen Briggs. Illus. Stephen Player. London: Corgi, 1995. N. pag.

_____. *Hogfather*. Illus. Josh Kirby. London: Corgi, 1996.

_____. "I Needed a Map." *The Discworld Mapp*. By Terry Pratchett and Stephen Briggs. Illus. Stephen Player. London: Corgi, 1995. N. pag.

_____. *Interesting Times*. 1994. Illus. Josh Kirby. London: Corgi, 1995.

_____. *Making Money*. Illus. Paul Kidby. London: Doubleday, 2007.

_____. *Maskerade*. 1995. Illus. Josh Kirby. London: Corgi, 1996.

_____. *Monstrous Regiment*. Illus. Paul Kidby. London: Doubleday, 2003.

_____. *Mort*. 1987. Illus. Josh Kirby. London: Corgi, 1988.

_____. *Night Watch*. Illus. Paul Kidby. London: Doubleday, 2002.

_____. "A Note to Readers of This Text-Only Version of THE LAST HERO." E-mail from Colin Smythe. 19 July 2012.

_____. *Reaper Man*. 1991. Illus. Josh Kirby. London: Corgi, 1992.

_____. "The Sea and Little Fishes." 1998. *A Blink of the Screen: Collected Shorter Fiction*. London: Doubleday, 2012. 218–67.

_____. *Small Gods*. 1992. Illus. Josh Kirby. London: Corgi, 1993.

_____. *Snuff*. Illus. Paul Kidby. New York: HarperCollins, 2011.

_____. *Soul Music*. 1994. Illus. Josh Kirby. London: Corgi, 1995.

_____. *Sourcery*. 1988. Illus. Josh Kirby. London: Corgi, 1989.

_____. "The Streets of Ankh-Morpork." *The Streets of Ankh-Morpork*. By Terry Pratchett and Stephen Briggs. Illus. Stephen Player. London: Corgi, 1993. N. pag.

_____. *Thud!* Illus. Paul Kidby. London: Doubleday, 2005.

_____. *The Truth*. 2000. Illus. Josh Kirby. London: Corgi, 2001.

_____. *Unseen Academicals*. Illus. Paul Kidby. London: Doubleday, 2009.

_____. *Witches Abroad*. 1991. Illus. Josh Kirby. London: Corgi, 1992.

_____. *The World of Poo*. By Miss Felicity Beedle. Assisted by Bernard and Isobel Pearson. Illus. Peter Dennis. London: Transworld, 2012.

_____. *Wyrd Sisters*. 1988. Illus. Josh Kirby. London: Corgi, 1989.

Pratchett, Terry, and Stephen Briggs. *The Discworld Companion*. London: Gollancz, 1994.

_____. *The Discworld Mapp*. Illus. Stephen Player. London: Corgi, 1995.

_____. *The New Discworld Companion*. London: Gollancz, 2004.

_____. *The Streets of Ankh-Morpork*. Illus. Stephen Player. London: Corgi, 1993.

_____. *A Tourist Guide to Lancre*. Illus. Paul Kidby. London: Corgi, 1998.

_____. *Turtle Recall: The Discworld Companion ... So Far*. London: Gollancz, 2012.

Pratchett, Terry, and The Discworld Emporium. *The Complete Ankh-Morpork*. London: Doubleday, 2012.

_____. *Discworld: The Ankh-Morpork Map*. London: Transworld, 2013. App.

Pratchett, Terry, and Paul Kidby. *The Art of Discworld*. New York: HarperCollins, 2004.

Pratchett, Terry, and Bernard Pearson. *The Discworld Almanak*. Illus. Paul Kidby, Bernard Pearson, and Sheila Watkins. London: Transworld, 2004.

_____. *Death's Domain: A Discworld Mapp*. London: Corgi, 1999.

The Right Stuff. Dir. Philip Kaufman. Warner Bros., 1983.

Rosenthal, Joe. "Raising the Flag on Iwo Jima." 23 Feb. 1945. *Wikimedia Commons*. Creative Commons. 23 Feb. 1945. 3 Nov. 2012.

Sendak, Maurice. "Caldecott Medal Acceptance." 1964. *Caldecott & Co.: Notes on Books & Pictures*. 1988. New York: Noonday Press, 1990. 145–55.

Shakespeare, William. *Hamlet*. 1600. New York: Simon & Schuster, 2003.

Shulevitz, Uri. *Writing with Pictures: How to Write and Illustrate Children's Books*. New York: Watson-Guptill, 1985.

Sipe, Lawrence R. "How Picture Books Work: A Semiotically Framed Theory of Text-Picture Relationships." *Children's Literature in Education* 29:2 (1998): 97–108.

Smythe, Colin. "Re: Query Regarding On-Line Pratchett Bibliography." E-mail to the author. 1 July 2013.

_____. "Terry Pratchett: The 2012 Convention—the Past Two Years." *Terry Pratchett*. Colin Smythe Limited. N.d. 18 July 2013.

Suckling, Nigel. *In the Garden of Unearthly Delights: The Paintings of Josh Kirby*. 1991. London: Paper Tiger, 1995.

Tam, Nicholas. "Here Be Cartographers: Reading the Fantasy Map." *Nick's Café Canadien*. 18 Apr. 2011. Web. 30 May 2013.

Van Gogh, Vincent. *Harvest in Provence*. 1888. Oil on canvas. Israel Museum, Jerusalem, Israel. *Vincent: The Vincent Van Gogh Gallery*. 5 Aug. 2013.

_____. *The Starry Night*. 1890. Oil on canvas. Museum of Modern Art, New York, USA. *Wiki paintings*. 5 Aug. 2013.

_____. *Wheatfield with Crows*. 1890. Oil on canvas. Van Gogh Museum, Amsterdam. *Van Gogh Museum*. 5 Aug. 2013.

Vladimirova, Asia. "Как се рисува светът на Тери Пратчет 'How to Paint the World of Terry Pratchett.'" *Dneven Trud 'Labour.'* Culture section. 2 Feb. 2013. Web. 15 May 2013.

Wyatt, David. *No Rat Shall Kill Another Rat*. Ink drawing. *The Amazing Maurice and His Educated Rodents*. By Terry Pratchett. 2001. New York: HarperCollins, 2001.

_____, illus. *The Amazing Maurice and His Educated Rodents*. By Terry Pratchett. 2001. London: Corgi, 2011.

Tell It Slant
Of Gods, Philosophy and Politics in Terry Pratchett's Discworld
GRAY KOCHHAR-LINDGREN

Trickery with words is where *humans* live.—Terry Pratchett

Terry Pratchett is a first-class comic, a wit *par excellence*, and, as such, his writing is both profound and whimsical. Its very lightness—of touch, of style—enables all apparently weighty matters such as philosophy, religion, and politics to leave the ground and float in the airy medium of writing. His Discworld novels act to snip off the ideological roots of old gods, patriarchies, and worn-out narratives and then to re-graft them so that they take on a new form, an occurrence that liberates the reader from her static set-up and opens, in a dialectic of the fantastic, a different positionality. This is the miracle concocted by reading.

Pratchett's fantasy world is supersaturated in religion and philosophy, with their necessary connections to politics, but it requires not adherence to an ideology—a stale habit of perception—but, rather, a quirky kind of faith, a belief, we might say, in the possibility of belief by one, at least, in the magic of language. His writing demonstrates the power of fictionalizing, an enterprise that, emphatically, is *not* opposed to the real. Without fictionalizing, in fact, there would be no real. The truth can be told but it must, as Emily Dickinson has reminded us, be told "slant" if we are to know the "Truth's superb surprise" (507). Pratchett, a master punster, enacts these qualities at the level of the word, the sentence, the theme, and the genre of the fantasy novel. These terms are both a giver of possibilities and a limit, since everything has a limit. But, since every limit has a limit—how could it not?—then every limit is opened up within itself to that which undoes the limit, leaving it limitless. It looks as if Discworld is a coherent world-unto-itself, self-contained, but, instead, it constantly opens to other worlds of history, myth, religion, anthropology, philosophy, literature, the contingencies of each idiosyncratic reader, and to the unpredictable future. Is Pratchett, then, a fantasist or a philosopher? What is the difference? Who cares?

Hogfather opens itself with that most profound of questions, that of origins. "Everything starts somewhere," the narrator says, "although many physicists disagree. / But people have always been dimly aware of the problem with the start of things ... there is the constant desire to find some point in which the twisting, knotting, raveling nets of space-time on which a metaphorical finger can be put to indicate that here, *here*, is the point where it all began..." (1; original italics). There is, really, no need to read another passage from Pratchett's *oeuvre*: it's all here. Everything is a knotted net. The "here," however, is not quite as here as we might expect, so we might as well continue reading.

Giving the finger the task of pointing at the *here* is an essential gesture of understanding, indicating as it does a function of indexical referentiality as the word replaces, or augments, the silent expressivity of the finger. "Here it is! The beginning! Look, right here! Over there! There it is right in front of you!" This action is called, by the wags at Unseen University, no doubt, as well as by the linguists at various Seen Universities, *deixis*, a term that refers to the simple act of pointing, of referring to a "this" or a "that" in sentences in which the context is required to understand the meaning of a word (such as pronouns). And, as Pratchett indicates, the finger is always "metaphorical," a figure that is always moving the pieces of the cosmic and novelistic text-puzzle around and that can never, as much as we might wish it, be "direct." Metaphors are playfully whimsical creatures and tend to create a slight sense of epistemological dizziness in the pit of the stomach. It's like riding a whirligig.

This metaphoricity, this literariness, is another name for the "twisting, knotting, raveling nets of space-time" (1), a series of images of rhizomatic networks whose origin can never be identified, since everything implicates everything else. (The Buddhists have a leg-up on this discussion of dependent co-origination, but the quantum physicists and the philosophers of difference are making progress.) This is also, precisely, the image of textuality that has dominated the discussion of literature and its theories since at least the 1960s. As Roland Barthes, representing a complex ensemble of writers, has famously said: "*Text* means *Tissue*: but whereas we have always taken this tissue as a product, a ready-made veil, behind which lies, more or less hidden, meaning (truth), we are now emphasizing, in the tissue, the generative idea that the text is made, is worked out in a perpetual interweaving" (62). We all actively weave the fabric of the tissue of stories that we call "life."

The idea of "here"—and, again, we are simply tracing the opening pages of *Hogfather* and its question of origins, as we head toward the primordial past of the Ur-Turtle—is undone, rewoven, by the groundless metaphoricity of textuality, but there is another avenue into the question of the "here" that takes us back to the "Sense-Certainty" section of G. W. F. Hegel's *Phenomenology of Spirit* (1807). In this section, Hegel is considering the fact that we all naturally take sense-certainty as assured self-evidence—"Look! Here!"—but that, in fact, it is always a complex of "mediated simplicities" (61), his provisional definition of the "universal." Here we are now, we say to ourselves. This is the sunlight of morning falling across my desk. But, Hegel avows, the very fact that we *say* this to ourselves *means* that what we thought we were trying to capture—the slant of sunlight on the desk—has vanished and a new perception has taken its place. What looks to be the simplest of all things—the perception of the here-and-now—turns out to be an exceedingly complex structure.

Language, in other words, radically intervenes in sense-certainty: "we do not strictly say what in this sense-certainty we *mean* to say," Hegel argues, for "in [language] we ourselves directly refute what we *mean* to say, and since the universal is the true [content] of sense-certainty and language expresses this true [content] alone, *it is just not possible for us ever to say, or express in words, a sensuous being that we* mean" (60; my italics). We can never say what we mean and we cannot, strictly speaking, mean what we say. Therefore, there is a need for fantasy novels, which incorporate this (un)truth into their very structure of composition. The Hogfather may not be real—I'll say just for the sake of argument—but he expresses truth. But not straight on, not face-to-face.

Hegel continues this line of thinking with an example of the piece of paper upon which he writes, or was writing upon several centuries ago: "If they actually wanted to say 'this' bit of paper which they mean, if they wanted to *say* it, then this is impossible, because the sensuous This that is meant *cannot be reached by language*, which belongs to consciousness, i.e., to that which is inherently universal" (66; original italics). And, finally, having already passed through the examples of the "open Mysteries of Ceres and Bacchus" (65)—and these mythical allusions to divinities that have supposedly died, passed on, have everything to do with Pratchett's recuperative fantasies—Hegel concludes the section by remarking that "if I want to help out language—which has the divine nature of directly reversing the meaning of what is said, of making it into something else, and thus not letting what is meant *get into words at all*—by *pointing out* this bit of paper, experience teaches me what the truth of sense-certainty in fact is: I point it out as a 'Here,' which is a Here of other Heres, or is in its own self a 'simple togetherness of many Heres,' i.e., it is a universal" (66). (It's all quite bracing, isn't it?)

Object, consciousness, and language are "twisting, raveling, knotting nets" (1) that are all in constant motion, and, therefore, there can be no adequate answer to the question of origins. Following a long detour through Kant, Hegel, Husserl, and Heidegger that cannot be recapitulated here, Jacques Derrida, that deconstructive punster, can eventually argue that

> traces thus produce the space of their inscription only by acceding to the period of their erasure. From the beginning, in the "present" of their first impression, they are constituted by the double force of repetition and erasure, legibility and illegibility ... [and] "perception," the first relation of life with its other, the origin of life, had always already prepared representation ["Freud" 226].

Hogfather, then, gets it right. There is no *here* of the origin of origin that can be pointed to, origins arise only in their inscriptions, and there are therefore, and of necessity, stories, *fabula* of the fabulous.

Hegel's phenomenology as the key to the philosophical dimensions not only of *Hogfather*, but of Pratchett's Discworld cosmos as a whole? Please. (*Puh-leaze*, if you please). It is nonetheless indubitable, however, that, referring to the soul of the tube worm, the narrator of the novel remarks, "It had never bothered itself with questions like 'Why am I here?' because it had no concept at all of 'here' or, for that matter, of 'I'" (37). Clearly Pratchett, or perhaps the tube worm, is offering a critique of German philosophy between Kant, Hegel, Fichte, and the Romantics. In any case, between the introduction of the Guild of Assassins and Mister Teatime (*Teh-ah-tim-eh*, if you please) and the introduction of the Senior Wizards of Unseen University—the dialectic is already taking shape—Pratchett takes us back past the forgetting of the blood that seeps through all the old stories, through the sticky-string webs of space-time, and, finally, into the dark corners of primordial caves. Back to the womb of all hominization, perhaps? "Or, possibly not, of course. The philosopher Didactylos, Two-Fingers, has summed up an alternative hypothesis as 'Things just happen. What the hell'" (2). It is a statement, not a question.

There are, in *Hogfather*, assassins, wizards, universities, possibilities and unpossibilities, worldviews galore, the metaphorical compression of history, the belief of at least one as the minimal requirement for a god, and that curious philosopher, Didactylos, to whom we shall return. History has always already begun, even when we ask ourselves, as we all do, the question of origins, which is simultaneously a question about both ourselves and about the cosmos. Consciousness and world. Two, always two. At least two, but then more, many more. (The third always intervenes and who knows where the numbering stops?) Perhaps the Auditors know, for they "did not believe in anything, except possibly immortality. And the way to be immortal, they knew, was to avoid living. Most of all they did not believe in personality. To be a personality was to be a creature with a beginning and an end" (46). Discworld, in other words, offers a philosophy of finitude to stand against the desire for everlastingness. Words come, then they go, erasing traces that constitute "life" and the world. Sometimes, but not always, they come back around, but they are then different. Words are tricky little buggers.

The plot of *Hogfather* is a simple tale about the death of a god—or at least a rotund demigod of sparkling trees, ho-ho-hos, and gift-wrapped presents who has difficulty climbing in and out of chimneys on a certain day of the year—and about how Death, along with his granddaughter, Susan, and sundry other characters intervene for the good. It is quite a bit funnier than *Thus Spake Zarathustra* or *Die fröhliche Wissenschaft*, but laughter, after all, is the point of both philosophy and fantasy novels. It is not the "real" world and it is not the "not-real" world, but it is a "SPECIAL CONGRUENT REALITY CREATED FOR THE HOGFATHER. NORMAL RULES HAVE TO BE SUSPENDED" (79). This is the essence of the literary, which can—like any self-respecting thought-experiment in physics or in philosophy of that odd analytic sort—create whatever words can imagine. Pigs *can* fly. Or, for example, this might be a world in which some of the "characters [of books] hovered above the pages or moved in complicated little patterns as they read you while you read them" (90). This all makes perfectly good sense since we are all objects of each other's interpretive phantasmagorias.

Hogfather, then, accomplishes philosophical tasks, but in Pratchett's inimitable style. It addresses questions of origins, identity, symbolic representation, death, immortality, and ethics: how shall we then live? And, as with any good philosophy, it is self-reflective. Ponder Stibbons, a Reader in Invisible Writings, has constructed Hex, an oracular writing machine, in the Unseen University, a "magical university where the border between the real and the 'not real' was stretched so thin you could almost see through it" (171); and, as Death insists, "THE HOGFATHER CAN TEACH PEOPLE THE *UNREAL* MEANING OF HOGSWATCH" (181). Fiction questions the status of that dull division between the real and un-real, for these are not opposites but con-sanguinities, flowing in the same blood.

*****

Pratchett, in the Discworld novels, addresses philosophical and religious questions and responds to these through the concoction of an alternative world full of characters that are contextualized by traditional narratives, but reinvented for different purposes. This is also seen within the realm of a more overt politics of gender, exemplified by his novel *Monstrous Regiment*. The basic plot is straightforward as a group of young Borogravian recruits—as well as established officers—who initially disguise themselves as men come out, over the course of the novel, as a group of accomplished and courageous women. And the title itself is a remix, already accomplishing the ethical work of fiction, which is to re-imagine the real.

In his "The First Blast of the Trumpet Against the Monstrous Regiment of Women" (1558), John Knox, the famous Protestant Reformer, gets right to the point of his diatribe against the dominion of women, in general, and, more specifically, against the monarchy of Mary Tudor in England (just before she is deposed by Elizabeth):

> Wonder it is that amongst so many pregnant wits as the isle of Great Britain hath produced, so many godly and zealous preachers as England did sometime nourish, and amongst so many learned and men of grave judgment as this day by Jezebel are exiled, none is found so stout of courage, so faithful to God, nor loving to their native country, that they dare admonish the inhabitants of that isle how abominable before God is the empire or rule of a wicked woman, yea, of a traitoress and bastard [37].

Wit, apparently, can be "pregnant," but those who can literally become "pregnant" with political power are "abominable." Writing from Dieppe in 1557–58, Knox places himself in the symbolic position of courageous prophet—Ezekiel is the primary model—who is willing to address the abuses of the power of women in positions of governmental authority, who are cast, by analogy, as Jezebel. (Yawn.) The rhetorical structure of the "First Blast" is thoroughly predictable, since "prophet" and "Jezebel" are pre-established types within the biblical narrative and, as such, offer forms of address that can be (re)filled with whatever content is the most contentious at any given moment of history. In 1558, with the Reformation and the complexity of the political environment bearing down on him and on the green isle of Britain, Knox fulminates that it is this "monstriferous empire of women (which amongst all enormities that this day do abound upon the face of the whole earth is most detestable and damnable) be openly revealed and plainly declared to the world to the end that some may repent and be saved" (40). The *most* detestable and damnable.

Repetition is one of the typical strategies of rhetorical (and prophetic) force, so Knox keeps repeating that "to promote a woman to bear rule, superiority, dominion, or empire above any realm, nation, or city is repugnant to nature, contumely to God, a thing most contrarious to his revealed will and approved ordinance, and, finally, it is the subversion of good order, of all equity and justice" (42). This "good order" is what he will mean by "regiment" and any order imposed by the sovereign will of a woman will be "monstrous." It is important to underline this opposition between "order" and "monstrosity," both because it is an extraordinarily powerful and lasting philosophical-social trope and because it is precisely at this point that Pratchett's novel drives an explosive device into the bedrock of traditional religious and political narrative organized around gender.

Knox's argumentative strategies take on a familiar shape. Using an erudite list of the greats, including not only a host of biblical writers but also Aristotle, Tertullian, Origen, Augustine, St. Ambrose, Basilius Magnus, and others, Knox "establishes" that the entire Judeo-Christian tradition speaks with one blaring voice: women, and especially women rulers, are monstrous. They do not fit into their own proper shape; they exceed the regulative law of nature. Chrysostom, in the *Homilies on St. John*, gives Knox a particularly pertinent summary: "But woman can never be the best governor by reason that she, being *spoiled of the spirit of regiment*, can never attain to that degree to be called or judged a good governor; because in the nature of all woman lurketh such vices as in good governors are not tolerable" (54; my italics). The footnote tells us this is a reference to prostitutes, something not mentioned by Knox, but, given his general logic of gender and power, this is in any case irrelevant. All women are monstriferous, which is clearly proven by God's word, the indisputable law of nature, and a litany of erudite philosophers and righteous prophets.

> That God hath subjected womankind to man by the order of his creation and by the curse that he hath pronounced against her is before declared. Besides these, he hath set before our eyes two other mirrors and glasses, in which he will that we should behold the order which he hath appointed and established in nature. The one is the natural body of man; the other is the politic or civil body of that commonwealth in which God by his own word hath appointed an order [55].

Order, given by God, is established by the "natural body" of man—phallogocentrism at its most compressed—but also in the civil order of politics. Women disrupt this natural order and offer a kind of surrealist, or Cubist, body in place of the ordered one: "For who would not judge that body to be a monster where there was no head eminent above the rest, but that the eyes were in the hands, the tongue and mouth beneath the belly, and the ears in the feet?" (56).

The doubled and doubling mirror, for Knox, shows us the true order of the good, the just, and the real, while the body of woman is, as it were, reflected only in the broken shards of a perverse mirror of the representation of reality. In its most general form, this argument is based on a conviction of the givenness by God of both nature and of the polity, as well as on the assurance that

John Knox and other prophets can clearly read and reproduce this divine revelation. "As a prophet, Knox believed himself adept at reading the times: the past leading up to the present. He interpreted history exactly as he interpreted a book like the Bible, identifying simple narrative patterns such as the success of a faithful covenanted people and the demise of a people unfaithful to their covenant" (Schrock 89). England, and their damnable queen(s), could never fulfill the covenant of a people with their God.

Pratchett, in contradistinction to Knox, delightedly *invents* his world (though not, of course, *ex nihilo*) and thus, by the very act of writing fantasy disrupts the cosmos of putatively given "good order" for the sake of a more just order. *Justice depends, finally, not on law but on inventiveness.* He takes the world as mirrored by Knox's text (itself attempting to mirror a certain interpretation of Judeo-Christian tradition), folds it into a reflective origami (and of course in the Unseen University there is a Professor of Recondite Architecture and Origami Map Folding), and thereby opens space for a different political philosophy of gender. Derrida has clarified one of the essential functions of the monstrous:

> But the notion of the monster is rather difficult to deal with, to get a hold on, to stabilize. A monster may be obviously a composite figure of heterogeneous organisms that are grafted onto each other. This graft, this hybridization, this composition that puts heterogeneous bodies together may be called a monster. This in fact happens in certain kinds of writing. At that moment, monstrosity may reveal or make one aware of what normality is. Faced with a monster, one may become aware of what the norm is and when this norm has a history—which is the case with discursive norms, philosophical norms, socio-cultural norms, they have a history—any appearance of monstrosity in this domain allows an analysis of the history of the norms. But to do that, one must conduct not only a theoretical analysis; one must produce what in fact looks like a discursive monster so that the analysis will be a *practical* effect, so that people will be forced to become aware of the history of normality [*Points* 386; original italics].

This is precisely the function of Pratchett's narrative strategy in *Monstrous Regiment*. He re-regiments the "regiment" by re-ordering the word and the narrative. Fantasy has the power to reorder the order of ideology as women, disguised as men (complete with socks awkwardly bulging in their pants), move through a series of masques and costumes to take on their own names and their own power. The monstrous is a strategy of revelation as well as a transformation of the sedimented and rigidified social order.

*****

In a very complicated argument illuminating Martin Heidegger's concept of time as it relates to Aristotle's commentary in *Physics IV*, Derrida asks a pointed question: "Have not meaning, reason, and 'good sense' been produced within this right [of the present, of the now]?" ("*Ousia*" 38). *Good sense* is the naturalist attitude that the world, including thought and the now of presence, is apparently simply given by nature, which is the foundation of ideology and the good regiment of the social order (as we have seen with Knox's text). Derrida, in that micro-hermeneutic methodology from which we have learned such a great deal, focuses on *hama*, a single throw-away word in Aristotle's text. Aristotle himself makes nothing of it, never thematizes it, but Derrida shows that precisely because it "*goes* without saying, making discourse play itself out in its articulation" that it will, indeed, act as the "pivot of metaphysics" (56; original italics). *Hama* is what happens "at the same time" and it says the "complicity, the common origin of time and space, appearing together [*com-paraître*] as the condition for all appearing of Being. In a certain way, it says the dyad as the minimum" (56).

Didactylos of *Small Gods* knows the secret of thought: it takes two to tango. Two is the minimum; no word stands alone and a story takes at least a now-now and a here-here. These non-ones always multiply, for "We must be several," Derrida reminds us, "in order to write, and even to 'perceive'" ("Freud" 226). As the Discworld & Terry Pratchett Wiki, a source that members of the Seen University are often quite wary of, tells us:

> Didactylos' name literally mean "two fingers." He resembles various Roundworld philosophers, notably Diogenes, who also lived in a barrel and carried an oil-less lantern in his fruitless search for an honest man. [Pratchett] also alludes to aspects of the characters of, the philosophical ideas of, or events from the lives of Plato, Archimedes and Aristotle in his description of Didactylos.

Two-fingers, then, is a multiplier, and another example of Pratchett's ability to embody many figures from history into a newly invented, newly named figure who simultaneously (*hama*) does the assembling work of remembering, inventing, and projecting new possibilities. "All would be simple if the *physis* and each one of its others were one or two. As we have suspected for a long time, it is nothing of the sort, yet we are forever forgetting this. There is always more than one—and more or less than two" (Derrida "Archive" 9). Didactylos is many, and as Gilles Deleuze reminds us, "there is no true beginning in philosophy, or the true philosophical beginning, difference, is in-itself already repetition" (129). Didactylos; Dialectic; Didactic. Fantasy creates a delightful dizziness.

Any talk of fingers in philosophy brings to mind Socrates's disquisition in the *Republic* (VII 523–525) on fingers, perception, and understanding; on the one and the many; and on relative and absolute understanding (not bad for some fingers and a couple of pages). How does the unifying force of a definition of "finger" relate to the perceptual and conceptual plurality of fingers? How does the long and the short, the thick and the thin relate to that which numbers and calculates the real? The one cannot be thought; the two gives rise to distinctions and thus the possibilities of comparison: thinking can now begin, since the possibility of a question is based on the minimality of the two. In a lovely term, Plato says that such perceptual questions *summon* us to attempt to understand the perplexity.

Deleuze argues that there is a fundamental "image of thought" that has governed philosophy for as long, almost, as philosophy has been philosophy. He calls this image, much like Derrida, "Good Sense" or "Common Sense" and it is that which everyone, apparently, can agree upon.

> According to this image, thought has an affinity with the true; it formally possesses the true and materially wants the true. It is in terms of this image that everybody knows and is presumed to know what it means to think. Thereafter it matters little whether philosophy begins with the object or the subject, with Being or with beings, as long as thought remains subject to this Image which already prejudges everything... [131].

As we have seen, this is Pratchett's strategy as well. By *not* acceding to the given (of perception, tradition, or ideology), he enables us to experience the world anew by asking questions, even if not formally thematized ones, about the apparently *given*. He writes freshness. He writes against the Auditors of Discworld and the Auditors of Roundworld.

The Auditors, those who are disdainful of individuality and personality, "SEE TO IT THAT GRAVITY WORKS AND THE ATOMS SPIN, OR WHATEVER IT IS ATOMS DO. AND THEY HATE LIFE ... IT IS ... IRREGULAR. IT WAS NEVER SUPPOSED TO HAPPEN. THEY LIKE STONES, MOVING IN CURVES. AND THEY HATE HUMANS MOST OF ALL. Death sighed. IN MANY WAYS, THEY LACK A SENSE OF HUMOR" (*Hogfather* 289). The Auditors are the Spirits of Gravity, nihilists stuck in their ways. They are reductionists who despise the fuzzy fizz of life, its unpredictability and exposure to contingency. They believe, they think in naked facts, and if the Hogfather had vanished, "THE SUN WOULD NOT HAVE RISEN.... A MERE BALL OF FLAMING GAS WOULD HAVE ILLUMINATED THE WORLD ... TRICKERY WITH WORDS IS WHERE *HUMANS* LIVE" (*Hogfather* 335). Given our discussion of Hegel, it's not even the case that there could be a "mere ball" without significance, since perception itself, for us, always brings significance along with it since it is "stated" in language. Words are tricky, but that is precisely, and only, where we exist, within this space of the trick, the game, the throw of the dice. Terry Pratchett revels, with great lucidity, in this irreality and, through his stories, he is able to tell the truth, knowing he must "tell it slant" (Dickinson 506).

WORKS CITED

Barthes, Roland. *The Pleasure of the Text.* Trans. Richard Miller. New York: Hill and Wang, 1975.

Deleuze, Gilles. *Difference & Repetition.* Trans. Paul Patton. New York: Columbia University Press, 1994.

Derrida, Jacques. "Freud and the Scene of Writing." *Writing and Difference.* Trans. Alan Bass. Chicago: University of Chicago Press, 1978.

_____. "*Ousia* and *Grammē*: Note on a Note from *Being and Time.*" *Margins of Philosophy.* Trans. Alan Bass. Chicago: University of Chicago Press, 1982.

_____. *Points...: Interviews, 1974–1994.* Trans. Peggy Kamuf, et al. Stanford: Stanford University Press, 1995.

_____, and Eric Prenowitz. "Archive Fever: A Freudian Impression." *Diacritics* 25:2 (Summer 1995): 9–63.

Dickinson, Emily. *The Complete Poems of Emily Dickinson.* Ed. Thomas H. Johnson. Boston: Little, Brown, 1960.

Discworld and Terry Pratchett Wiki. 2012. Web. October 2013.

Hegel, G. W. F. *Phenomenology of Spirit.* Trans. A. V. Miller. Oxford: Oxford University Press, 1977.

Knox, John. *The Political Writings of John Knox. The First Blast of the Trumpet Against the Monstrous Regiment of Women and Other Selected Works.* Ed. Marvin A. Breslow. Washington, DC: Folger, 1985.

Levinson, Stephen C. "Deixis." *International Encyclopedia of Linguistics.* Ed. William J. Frawley. Oxford University Press, 2005. Oxford Reference Online. Oxford University Press. University of Washington. 6 September 2012.

Plato. *The Republic.* Trans. G. M. A. Grube; rev. C. D. C. Reeve. Indianapolis: Hackett, 1992.

Pratchett, Terry. *Hogfather.* New York: HarperTorch, 1996.

_____. *Monstrous Regiment.* New York: HarperCollins, 2003.

_____. *Small Gods.* New York: HarperTorch, 1992.

Schrock, Chad. "The Pragmatics of Prophecy in John Knox's *The First Blast of the Trumpet Against the Monstrous Regiment of Women.*" *Renaissance and Reformation* 30:2 (Spring 2006): 83–99.

The Watchman and
the Hippopotamus
Art, Play and Otherness in Thud!
CAROLINE WEBB

Comic novelist Terry Pratchett's concern with attitudes to race and human perceptions of the Other has been foregrounded especially in his Watch sequence of Discworld novels. In *Men at Arms*, for example, the Watchmen have to deal with hereditary prejudice as members of different species begin to enter the Ankh-Morpork City Watch, while in *Jingo* the notion of national identity and its apparently automatic correlation with rejection of the foreign is critiqued and ridiculed. In *The Fifth Elephant*, Pratchett's hero Commander Vimes becomes both a suspect in a crime in the dwarfs' kingdom and the prey in a ritualized hunt by atavistic werewolves, forcing him to confront his own understanding of cultural relativism. While Pratchett's ethical and humanist approach to the concept of race has always been clear, his fictions are significant in their insistence on engagement with the reality of interracial suspicion. If racism based on skin color has rarely been a problem in the Discworld, Pratchett makes clear that this is only because "black and white [have] lived together in perfect harmony and ganged up on green" (*Abroad* 167).

Meanwhile, Pratchett's Discworld writing is, arguably, preoccupied with its status as literary text. Though intertextual references abound, the Witches sequence of novels highlights particularly its own relationship to earlier literature, whether to Shakespeare in *Wyrd Sisters* or *Lords and Ladies* or to fairy tale in *Witches Abroad*, while Nickianne Moody has remarked that "it is narrative causality which structures the plots of the Death sequence," pointing to the literary self-consciousness visible in those novels (155). Andy Sawyer has discussed how *The Science of Discworld*, co-written by Pratchett and the scientists Jack Cohen and Ian Stewart, parodies the scientific method in its fictional passages while deploying story to explain science. As Sawyer argues, *The Science of Discworld* provides insight into "the roles both science and fiction have in making us human" (Sawyer 78). The Watch sequence itself is studded with references to detective stories, especially the "hardboiled American cop tradition," as Edward James puts it (197), noting how Pratchett in this sequence comments on "the conventions of popular entertainment in the late twentieth century: particularly those of heroic fantasy" (199).

Nevertheless, I would suggest that the prominence of explicit reference to, and discussion of, art both in general and in various forms (including the literary) in *Thud!* (2005) is striking even within the context of Pratchett's *oeuvre*. A list of the visual art-forms alone present or referred to in *Thud!* includes the following: landscape painting; portrait painting; representations of the nude; symbolic painting, as for example a picture of a goddess; abstract sculpture; pantograph; iconograph, i.e., photograph; picture book; wallpaper decoration; images on a child's clock and blanket; and graffiti, in the form of the mystic mine signs of the dwarfs. Further, the picture book, *Where's My Cow?*, is also a story, one in fact told within *Thud!* three times, and Death appears to Vimes reading a novel and pondering "the strangeness of written narrative" (*Thud!* 388), extending the novel's reflection on art to fiction itself.

In case the reader misses all this, long-familiar characters Sergeant Colon and Corporal Nobbs are early found musing at some length over what art is when they investigate the theft of a painting from the art museum:

> [Colon] knew in his heart that spinning around a pole wearing a costume you could floss with definitely was not Art, and being painted lying on a bed wearing nothing but a smile and a small bunch of grapes was good solid Art, but putting your finger on why this was the case was a little tricky.
> "No urns," he said at last.... "Nude women are only Art if there's an urn in it." This sounded a bit weak even to him, so he added, "or a plinth. Both is best, o' course" [*Thud!* 55].

In this essay I shall examine not only Pratchett's study in *Thud!* of the nature of racial conflict but his exploration of the power of art of all kinds—including, most particularly, games—in both perpetuating and resolving that conflict. Art—as story, as painting, as game—is depicted within the text as a potential means of engagement with the human, and offered as a site through which people, both individually and as racial groups, can confront and critique the notion of the Other and the tensions (within the individual, as well as between groups) that obscure the commonality of the human.

Race, Identity and Conflict

Before turning to the question of art I wish to review Pratchett's attitude to conflict, especially racial conflict, across his writing. Pratchett has always demonstrated a resistance to violence highly unusual among writers of heroic fantasy. It is at once a characteristic joke against generic convention and a marker of the values expressed in his fiction that the protagonist of the first and several subsequent Discworld novels, the failed wizard Rincewind, is a committed coward who specializes in running away from danger. In the children's book *Only You Can Save Mankind* (1992), set in our own world, the protagonist Johnny Maxwell learns to take seriously the suffering inflicted in warfare when the enemies he is happily destroying in a shoot-'em-up computer game identified as descended from Space Invaders attempt to surrender and he is forced to recognize them as entities with their own lives, fears, and desires, rather than simply as targets. It is clear that Pratchett recognizes the drive to conflict as originating in the definition of self against Other described by Andrew M. Butler ("We Has Found").

In the Watch series, Pratchett acknowledges the reality of prejudice and hatred. Even in the first of the series, *Guards! Guards!* (1989), the power-seeking villain is able to muster the petty resentments, mostly class-based, of his Mystical Brethren to summon the destructive energies of a dragon. But Pratchett depicts his central figures as endeavoring, not always successfully, to overcome such hatred. In the comparatively early *Men at Arms* (1993) this is not always too difficult: the dwarf Cuddy and the troll Detritus become buddies in the time-honored cop story way, by going on the beat together and assisting each other. But things are not always so simple. As James observes, "even [Pratchett's] most moral characters have problems in adhering to a tolerant attitude" (212). Thus in *Men at Arms* the dwarf-raised human Carrot acknowledges that he can respect humans as well as dwarfs and even trolls, but has trouble with the undead (100), of which there are many kinds on the Discworld. Vimes can cope with most of the undead as well as with the living, but in *Thud!* still wants to draw the line at vampires—and is never too happy about aristocrats of his own species either.

While it is the aristocrats who, in *Jingo,* manipulate the chance discovery of a newly risen island into a *casus belli* for conflict between Ankh-Morpork and the neighboring nation of Klatch, the ordinary populace of the city is revealed to be equally ready with unthinking prejudice against even those Klatchians who have lived and worked among them for years. As Farah Mendlesohn observes, "Pratchett's emphasis on the ability of the ordinary person ... to commit unimaginable acts of atrocity denies us the chance to separate the characters into the simply good and the simply bad or mad. It refuses us the binary shelter of the 'us' versus 'them'" (255). In *Jingo*, Vimes and the Patrician Lord Vetinari, ruler of the city, resort to unorthodox tactics to avoid violence. Vimes uses his rights as a knight to enlist citizens in an expanded Watch, works in an informal alliance with the dangerous Klatchian 71-hour Ahmed, who turns out to be a fellow policeman, and ends up arresting both armies for "behaviour likely to cause a breach of the peace" (*Jingo* 368). While the armies are waiting, Carrot, the Watch Captain, gets them playing a vast game of football (soccer); I shall return later to the implications of this.

The novel's identifiable villains are found on both sides: the Klatchian Caliph who turns out to be behind an assassination attempt on his own brother that is intended to provoke a war that will enable him to expand his empire, and the Ankh-Morporkian general Lord Rust, whose perception of war as a game of honor with rigid rules that involve sacrificing human lives—and even neglecting the ostensible goal of victory—is condemned as fatally destructive. Lord Vetinari's decision to surrender and give up the island seems unthinkably dishonorable to Rust, who threatens him with prosecution for treason; however, Vetinari's submarine study of the island has assured him that it will soon sink again, and the despicable ratification of the surrender he is due to perform there cannot therefore take place, voiding his concessions to Klatch. Vetinari's attention to detail—in this case the specific physical attributes of the island—rather than to the abstractions of the chivalric code thus enables political victory both over the enemy ruler, who loses face and therefore his post, and over Lord Rust, ensuring the continuity of the *Pax Morporkia*. As Mendlesohn remarks, "Vetinari's conclusion to the war emphasizes both the game like nature of the proceedings and its brutal reality" (254). In place of the values underlying Lord Rust's attitude to war, we are invited to admire instead Vetinari's superior intelligence and political gamesmanship. Thus Pratchett evokes an idea of patriotism dependent neither on hatred of the Other nor on death-or-glory zeal, but on the shared will to protect the people of the city that in different ways motivates both Vimes and Vetinari.

In *Thud!* the issue of race and how to engage with the Other, especially where that Other has been declared an enemy, governs the text, as the interspecies conflict between dwarfs and trolls is traced to its historical crisis point, the Battle of Koom Valley. As is characteristic in Pratchett's Watch sequence, the novel's structure begins with the detective story, recording the Watch's investigation of a crime. In this case the murder of the dwarf Hamcrusher, blamed by the dwarfs on the trolls, becomes the catalyst both for violence and for Vimes's investigation into the origins of the mutual hatred between the species. Pratchett makes plain, primarily through the dwarfs, how hatred is used to fuel pride in one's own identity: the city dwarfs, previously tolerant, are being incited to hatred by the "deep-downers," who represent their idea of what dwarfs should be.

> They were "grags." Vimes had just enough dwarfish to know that grag meant "renowned master of dwarfish lore." Hamcrusher, however, had mastered it in his own special way. He preached the superiority of dwarf over troll, and that the duty of every dwarf was to follow in the footsteps of their forefathers and remove trollkind from the face of the world.... Young dwarfs listened to him, because he talked about history and destiny and all the other words that always got trotted out to put a gloss on slaughter [*Thud!* 37].

In addition to Hamcrusher's use of heady rhetoric, his message resonates because the dwarfs' sense of identity is currently unstable:

> [S]omewhere in the head of every city dwarf there was a little voice that said: you should live in a mine, you should be in the mountains, you shouldn't walk under open skies, you should be a *real* dwarf. In other words you shouldn't really be working in your uncle's pigment and dye factory.... However, since you *are*, you could at least try to *think* like a proper dwarf. And part of that meant being guided by the deep-downers.... Somewhere down there in the dark was true dwarfishness. They had the knowing of it [*Thud!* 84; original italics].

Identification of self is simplest, and easiest, when it can be defined against the Other, as Hamcrusher offers the city dwarfs a way to do. The enmity that was readily overcome by Cuddy and Detritus in *Men at Arms* leads in *Thud!* to many dwarf and troll members of the now expanded Watch resigning in order to go home to protect their own families. And humans, nervous of both, are vulnerable too. Mr. Shine, the diamond troll born to be king, explains to Vimes that the dwarfs have exploited human ignorance of trolls: "You really know very little about us, Mister Vimes. You see us down on the plains, shambling around *talkin' like dis*.... You see the hunched troll, dragging his club. That's what the dwarfs did for us, long ago. They turned us, in your minds, into sad, brainless monsters" (*Thud!* 257; original italics). The parallels with European images of Africans, and the images' effects across the globe well into the twentieth century, are not far to seek.

Unsurprisingly, perhaps, given Pratchett's earlier fiction, it emerges that the murderer of Hamcrusher was not a troll but a dwarf (which one we never discover). Hamcrusher was attempting to destroy words, a serious crime to the deep-downers, who despise "Blackboard Monitor Vimes" (*Thud!* 94). But the murder is blamed on trolls by deep-downers who, like Hamcrusher, are desperate to conceal the words (which are recorded on an ancient Device), if not destroy them. The truth of the first Battle of Koom Valley, Vimes discovers, is that the dwarf and troll kings were seeking to make peace before erroneous cries of ambush went up (as in Malory's account of Arthur's final battle), as revealed by the recording made by the kings who fought there: "They fell to fighting and would not hear our commands. So troll fought troll, and dwarf fought dwarf, and fools made fools of all of us as we fought to stop a war, until the disgusted sky washed us away" (*Thud!* 419). Species hatred—which in this novel looks just like race hatred—is identified as a folly that resonates for centuries, but a folly that need not exist or persist. The current Low King of the dwarfs and Diamond King of the trolls are already, it emerges, secretly seeking to negotiate, and the discovery at the end of *Thud!* of the dead kings facing each other over a game board in the caverns below Koom Valley produces some prospect of a durable peace.

The Power of Games

Countering the forces of violence and hatred in *Thud!* are those who provide alternative ways to define identity. A key incident occurs when Angua, a member of the Watch known to be a werewolf, is looking for clues in the slimy mud of the dwarfs' exploratory tunnels below the city with the vampire Sally. As a werewolf, Angua is instinctively and ancestrally hostile to Sally, who radiates the confidence and stylish elegance of the vampire, and the situation is not improved by Angua's recognition that Sally is attracted to Captain Carrot, Angua's heroic human boyfriend. As Angua's fury rises, Sally stops her:

> "Hold it! ... We're both wearing nothing, we're standing in what, you may have noticed, is increasingly turning to mud, and we're squaring up to fight. Okay. But there's something missing, yes?"
> "And that is?"
> "A paying audience? We could make a *fortune!*" Sally winked. "Or we could do the job we came here to do?" [*Thud!* 207; original italics].

While Sally's appeal to Angua's sense of duty is certainly important, it is also significant that her comment on the potential spectacle of their situation is transformative. What has been another instance of the age-old conflict between vampire and werewolf, or of two females over the possession of a male, becomes a sport—and, crucially, one in which women are on one side of a barrier, watched by men on the other. In mud-wrestling, despite the ostensible conflict, the women are working together, defined by the spectator males. In any case Sally's observation shifts the reader's interpretation of the event, removing it to the level of spectacle or entertainment rather than the grim confrontation that Angua, and with her the reader, has been experiencing.

Sally's image of the game of mud-wrestling defuses violence and enables Angua to dissociate herself at least temporarily from her identification of herself as werewolf and Sally as vampire and focus instead on their joint concerns as members of the Watch. Later, Angua, Sally, the dwarf Cheery—who in *Feet of Clay* (1996) expressed strong prejudice against werewolves (127) before discovering that Angua was one—and the human Tawneee, a pole-dancer, go out drinking together; their shared identity as females, and particularly females in need of a drink, is of far greater importance than their species status, and does lead, despite Angua's protestations, to bonding.

While mud-wrestling may not be defined by all of us as an artform, it can be seen as one of many play-based activities that Pratchett deploys in opposition to the valuing of conflict. Sergeant Colon is not in fact so far off the mark in his recognition that the presence of urns (or plinths) in a painting of a nude distinguishes it from pole-dancing as Art. Although art has been defined in terms of aesthetics and creative expression, one of its key features, as demonstrated in twentieth-century practice following Marcel Duchamp's controversial 1917 artwork *Fountain* (a urinal submitted to the Society of Independent Artists exhibition, but rejected), is that it is framed as an object to be considered in terms other than the functional. In *Thud!* Corporal Nobbs scrutinizes the artist Daniella Pouterina's highly valued artwork *Don't Talk to Me About Mondays* and is informed that it has been transformed from what he first sees as "a load of stinking ol' rubbish" (*Thud!* 51) by its framing in the museum context. He then suggests that the museum curator deal with the embarrassing problem of the theft of Rascal's vast painting of the Battle of Koom Valley by renaming the space: "'Tell you what, then, sir,' said Nobby helpfully. 'Why don't you leave the ol' big frame where it is and give it a new name, like *Art Theft*?'" (*Thud!* 52). Although the curator rejects the suggestion as foolish, Nobby has recognized an important element in the contemporary understanding of art. In this sense art has close affinities with play, of which Huizinga has said,

> [W]e might call it a free activity standing quite consciously outside "ordinary" life as being "not serious," but at the same time absorbing the player intensely and utterly. It is an activity connected with no material interest, and no profit can be gained by it. It proceeds within its own proper boundaries of time and space according to fixed rules and in an orderly manner [32].

Like art, play can be imaginative and is frequently mimetic, imitating images and social practices while abstracting them from their real-world contexts and function.

This process of abstraction, or framing, is crucial to the transformative possibilities Pratchett identifies in both art and game within *Thud!* This is a different kind of abstraction from that exemplified by Lord Rust in *Jingo*. Instead of reducing real human beings to game pieces expendable in the name of honor, both games and (most) artworks substitute play for suffering: Pouterina's *Freedom* in effect "frames" the stake to which she had been nailed by her ear, an initially involuntary experience she plans to duplicate (*Thud!* 52). If the danger in *Only You Can Save Mankind* is that such elimination of suffering in shoot-'em-up games may risk blindness to real suffering produced by the bright streaks of bombers in the 1991 Gulf War,[1] in *Thud!* Pratchett suggests the obverse, that the abstraction of play represented both in games and in artworks may provide ways to see beyond the "us versus them" mentality of race/species hatred.

On the face of it, then, the game of Thud itself operates most strikingly in this novel to defuse conflict, although as I shall show other forms of art/play here may be read as similarly powerful in formation of a positively defined identity. According to the novel, Thud is a board game with affinities to the old game of Fox and Geese. One side consists of eight pieces designated as trolls, having the troll characteristics of near-immobility but great force, while the other consists of thirty-two pieces designated as dwarfs, able to move great distances in any direction but with little striking power (*Thud!* 259). As a strategy game it appears, as Vimes observes, to favor the dwarf side, though the troll king Mr. Shine assures Vimes that "among the best players the bias is slightly in favour of the trolls" (*Thud!* 259). Where it differs from similar strategy games, however, is that a complete game consists of two battles; players must switch sides after the first. As Mr. Shine notes, "to *win* you must play both sides. You must, in fact, be able to think like your ancient enemy.... When you're under his skin you start to see the world through his eyes" (*Thud!* 260; original italics). The ingenuity of Thud is that it formalizes the species differences by which dwarfs and trolls define themselves against the Other: dwarfs are small and fast, trolls slow-moving and ponderous. In this way it at once emphasizes and reduces to play what elsewhere have been archetypes generating deadly conflict—as human warfare is tamed to and by football in *Jingo*, as female possessiveness is reduced in mud-wrestling, or as traditional feudal warfare is formalized in chess, a game Vimes despises because of its aristocratic conservatism: "If only the pawns united, maybe talked the rooks round, the whole board could've been a republic in a dozen moves" (*Thud!* 86).

At the same time, however, the game of Thud compels empathy: every player of Thud must learn to think in terms of the abilities and strategies appropriate to at least one species other than his or her own. In particular, the hereditary enemies troll and dwarf must learn the ways of the Other. Not only does the game, as game, remove them to a different space from direct violence, as with Sally's joke about mud-wrestling, but this game promotes a deep understanding that refuses the simple rejection enabled by defining identity through difference. It is no surprise then that at the novel's resolution the long-dead dwarf and troll kings discovered beneath the floor of Koom Valley having attempted to make peace are found facing each other over a makeshift Thud board.

The educational value of Thud, which as Vimes can see in Mr. Shine's games room is being played by young people of various species including dwarfs and trolls (*Thud!* 254–55), may provide an indication of how Pratchett views the potential value of games. In *Only You Can Save Mankind* the reduction of warfare to streaks of light was seen as dangerous. Johnny, the more bloodthirsty Kirsty, and indeed the contemporary West have been conditioned by the computer games to see warfare as just another game, especially through the film footage of the attacks on Baghdad in the 1991 Gulf War, which Johnny watches on television (and critiques as film) early in the novel. However, in *Thud!* the power to transform war to game can be seen as potentially constructive. Whereas Johnny was disturbed by the conceptual reduction of warfare—"We turn it into games and it's not games" (*Only You Can Save Mankind* 161)— Pratchett suggests through Thud that there can be games that (to be speciesist) humanize rather than dehumanize. In Space Invaders and its myriad descendants the player's enemies are fictional and faceless: we have not met the enemy and therefore he is not us, to misquote Pogo. Like Lord Rust in *Jingo*, the computer game-players see an abstraction in which the enemy is simplified to a set of missiles. In the game of Thud, by contrast, the whole point of the double game is to see and even become the enemy. Thud allows the hereditary enemies dwarfs and trolls to sublimate enmity within the game and use their will to win to expand empathy instead of violence.

Carrot's use of the football games in *Jingo* is similar: warring street gangs and national enemies can both be persuaded to transform violent conflict into game-playing in which all are collaborators in the activity, bound by the same rules. Although it is not clear that any of them have actually learned the values that Carrot insists they always already share, what they do in fact share is the reluctant recognition of how both sides have in fact been dominated by Carrot's own charismatic personality. Carrot thus creates a new kind of commonality in which both sides are on the same side in relation to the rest of the world—they are players in the game, and subject to Carrot's arbitration—similar to Sally's location of her battle with Angua as the spectacle of mud-wrestling. As Vimes suggests, this is "sport as a substitute for war" (*Jingo* 382)—and as Carrot points out, it works.

Art, Story and Identity

In both *Thud!* and *Jingo*, then, games may be seen as alternatives to species-based conflict, enabling collaboration in the activity of playing even as they reduce conflict itself to play. But I would argue that *Thud!* extends Pratchett's commentary on the power of abstract play to forms more generally recognized as art. A clue to this may be found in the stolen painting of the original Battle of Koom Valley; seen by many as a map concealing a clue to treasure, *Da Vinci Code*–style, the painting turns out indeed to be a map to the truth when framed in a new way. When it is displayed in the round, instead of flat on the wall, it pinpoints the location at which its painter, the mad Methodia Rascal, picked up the Device later found by the deep-downers that carries the words of the famous dwarf king B'hrian Bloodaxe and the then Diamond King of the trolls after they were trapped by a flood during the battle. Both the deep-downers and Vimes can use the painting to seek out the truth, holding it (or a pantograph of it) around themselves and matching the mountains on its circular horizon to what they see. Perspective is thus crucial to the interpretation of the painting, and truth, as is to be expected in Pratchett, is not two-dimensional.

Perspective is an important element within narrative, as well, and Pratchett's deployment of narrative techniques highlights his concern with art in this novel. It is noteworthy that, unusually in Pratchett's writing, several episodes within *Thud!* have been presented in flashback, drawing the reader's attention to narrative process. For instance, when the dwarf Ardent leads Vimes through the labyrinthine tunnels of the dwarf workings underground, he responds to Vimes's increasing impatience by saying "We are nearly there, commander.... Nearly there!'" (*Thud!* 101). But instead of proceeding to the expected encounter with the deep-down dwarfs, Pratchett interrupts the story with an apparent digression to the wandering of a troll called Brick, whose thoughts are represented in near stream-of-consciousness style: "Dat mine wi' dem dwarfs, was *dat* real? You go an' find a place to lie down and watch der pretty pitchers, suddenly you're in dis dwarf hole? That couldn'a bin real!" (*Thud!* 102; original italics). And this passage is followed by the statement "When Vimes stepped out into the brilliant daylight the first thing he did was draw a deep breath" (*Thud!* 103). The shock of this vision of sudden emergence from darkness is notable; there is also a suggestive evocation of the novel's prefatory passage, "The first thing Tak did, he wrote himself.... The first Brother walked towards the light, and stood under the open sky. Thus he became too tall. He was the first Man. He found no Laws, and he was enlightened" (*Thud!* np). Vimes may have been enlightened (not, to the dwarfs, a compliment), but the reader remains in the dark as to what he has learned underground: the passage about the previously unknown Brick substitutes for Vimes's meeting with the dwarfs, offering the reader, but not yet Vimes, an alternative line of investigation into the murder of Hamcrusher. The substitution of troll for dwarfs, of light for darkness, in the reader's expectations highlights the importance of narrative art in shaping our understanding. It demonstrates how in the act of reading we engage continually with substitution, especially through metaphor, as well as how we depend on expectations based on the past to form a meaningful future. Substitution is the stuff not only of games like Thud but also of art.

This is made explicit in perhaps the most important of the artworks mentioned in *Thud!*: the picture book *Where's My Cow?* According to the novel,[2] this picture book, read every evening by Sam Vimes to his infant son, Young Sam, follows the quest of the unnamed narrator to find his or her cow through investigation of alternative candidates for the role, such as a sheep, a horse, and a hippopotamus. As noted above, the story of the picture book is not merely mentioned or mentioned as being read but is actually told, at least in part, on three occasions within *Thud!*, to different effect in each case. It is made very clear that this book is crucial not only in Vimes's understanding of the mystery he confronts as a detective (itself interestingly symbolized by Vimes as a jigsaw puzzle on a number of occasions) but even in his construction of his identity.

The first reading of *Where's My Cow?* amusingly takes place after the Ankh-Morpork equivalent of a car chase. We are shown Sam Vimes running desperately across the city, hijacking coaches, running across boats, and even taking advantage of major streets especially closed for the purpose by Carrot, in order, as it turns out, to reach home by six o'clock and read to his young son. "It was important that no one else was here. This moment in time was just for the Sams.... There was The Reading of the Picture Book to be undertaken. That was the *meaning* of six o'clock" (*Thud!* 149; original italics). Vimes's desperate, city-stopping run makes clear the importance of the six o'clock reading: this is Vimes's very newly self-imposed personal limit to concessions to the demands of his job. Both in *Thud!* and earlier, Vimes has had on many occasions to apologize to his wife, Sybil, for abandoning her in order to deal with some actual or imminent crime; the overruling authority of six o'clock therefore marks a powerful change in Vimes's apprehension of himself. Potentially, he has become something other or at least more than the Watchman; however, as Pratchett demonstrates, his identity as Watchman is never more important to events than in *Thud!*. Yet the resolution of this apparent conflict itself significantly depends on the role of the picture book in Vimes's sense of identity.

On its first reading in the text, Pratchett quotes the early part of the story and provides what is presumably Vimes's own commentary on its absurdity. The first observation has overtones of the police report: "The unidentified complainant had lost their cow" (*Thud!* 150). But this brief summary of the story's situation is followed by a critical review not yet of the story but of the creative process:

> Then the author began to get to grips with their material:
> Where's my cow?
> Is that my cow?
> It goes, "Neigh!"
> It is a horse!
> That's not my cow!
> At this point the author had reached an agony of creation and was writing from the racked depths of their soul [*Thud!* 150].

As in game and art, the narrative comment here again shifts us to the level of abstraction. Rather than engage with the story, the narrator provides what seems an empathetic response to the inferred travails of the artist as Romantic creator. The comic disjunction between this emotional and emotive description and the banal repetition of the picture book extracts invites readers to question their conception of art and literature: must the production of art involve the "agony of creation?"

But the repetition also highlights the minimal variation within the picture book—only the name of the animal and the noise it makes changes from section to section—and thus demonstrates its emphasis on similarity and substitution. The horse is not a cow, not because of its appearance, but because it goes "Neigh!" *Thud!*'s narrator observes that

> some suspense was lent by the fact that all other animals were presented in some way that could have confused a kitten, who perhaps had been raised in a darkened room. The horse was standing in front of a hat-stand, as they so often did, and the hippo was eating at a trough against which was an upturned pitch-fork. Seen from the wrong direction, the tableau might look for just one second like a cow ... [*Thud!* 150–51; original ellipsis].

Like other picture books for very young audiences, this one shapes learning into discovery and quest, teaching not just about animals and the noises they make but about similarity and difference, self and other.

It is the quest element that dominates the second reading, in which the quotations from the story are interpolated with Vimes's thoughts not, this time, about the story itself, but about his case. Following hints provided by Mr. Shine, he is able to put together clues to the dwarfs' behavior:

Where did I see one of those Thud boards recently?
    It goes, "Neigh!"
Oh, yes, Helmclever. He was very worried, wasn't he? ... That was a dwarf under
pressure if ever I saw one; he looked as if he were dying to tell me something...
    Where's my cow?
That look in his eyes...
    Is that my cow?
I was so *angry*. Don't tell the Watch? What did they expect? You'd have thought
he would have known...
    It goes, "Hruuugh!"
He *knew* I'd go spare!
    It is a hippopotamus!
He wanted me to be angry! [*Thud!* 267–68; original ellipses and italics].

As the process of the quest for the cow requires interrogation of suspicious
resemblances, so Vimes's assessment of Helmclever's behavior changes once
he focuses on the dwarf's expression and considers him as a person desiring
to communicate rather than simply as an enemy. Helmclever is not merely the
agent of the deep-downers; he has his own agenda that is at odds with theirs.
Vimes's recognition of Helmclever's motivation reclassifies him, in effect, as
a hippopotamus rather than as a recalcitrant cow, and his dealing with Helmclever can shift to that of an ally helping Helmclever (appropriately, through
a game of Thud) to articulate his concerns with the actions of the deep-
downers he serves. This second reading of *Where's My Cow?* thus underscores
the process of connection and differentiation essential to Vimes's unraveling
of the mystery.

However, although the picture-book's story ends, inevitably in Vimes's
view, with the discovery of the cow—"It was that much of a page turner"
(*Thud!* 150)—the point for the nascent reader after the first reading is not
mystery, but the process of repetition and confirmation of what he already
knows. A horse, even if standing behind a hat stand, goes "Neigh!"; only a
cow goes "Moo!" Every reading after the first one is a game. The two readings
provided thus far, which are both already for Vimes and Young Sam re-
readings, dramatize the pleasure of play formalized in Thud: individuality is
simplified to stereotype, a structure is established, rules are followed, and the
reader achieves narrative satisfaction.

The picture book is read by characters within the novel on a further occa-
sion, in a communal reading, not quoted in the text, in which Vimes's most
trusted members of the Watch assist with the production of the animal noises,
underlining the reading as collaborative play. But the final "reading" of *Where's
My Cow?* provided within the text is quite different from any of these. It is
Vimes's recital of the story when, at six o'clock, far from sitting in his child's

bedroom, he is charging through the caverns under Koom Valley possessed by the Summoning Dark (a murderous entity known to the dwarfs that has been evoked by a dying curse). The dwarfs are horrified by the sight of the berserk figure approaching them:

> Vimes crouched and whirled the sword around in a circle. A little lamb rocked in front of his eyes.... He had found what he was seeking.
> "Is that my cow? It goes 'Mooooo!'"
> Picking up another fallen axe, Vimes started to run.
> "Yes! That's my cow!"
> The grags were behind a ring of guards in a frantic huddle, but Vimes's eyes were on fire and there were flames streaming from his helmet. A dwarf holding a flame-thrower threw it down and fled.
> "Hooray, hooray, it's a wonderful day, for I have found my cow!" [*Thud!* 395].

The Summoning Dark has attempted to harness Vimes's fury at the deep-downers' attack on his family in its pursuit of the cursed grags, and the images from Young Sam's bedroom (including the rocking lamb from his clock) support his vengeful rage against the Other. "And then the screaming started. His son, screaming. It filled his mind. *They will burn*" (*Thud!* 392; original italics). However, at this crucial moment when Vimes's own sanity as well as his ethical code is at stake, the quest for the criminals—by now revealed as the deep-downers themselves—and Vimes's own moral conscience are alike sustained by the picture book around which he has shaped his life since the birth of Young Sam. His identification of the grags as the criminal/cow he has been seeking does not after all lead to his slaughtering them. Instead he is revealed to be guarded from within:

> *"They would have killed his family!"* The darkness lunged, and met resistance. *"Think of the deaths they would have caused! Who are you to stop me?"*
> He created me. Quis custodiet ipsos custodes? *Who watches the watchman? Me. I watch him. Always. You will not force him to murder for you"* [*Thud!* 397; original italics].

As a cow may be cursorily if misleadingly represented as an animal with horns (and an identifying moo), Vimes has symbolized himself as the Watchman, a game figure who guards the streets of his own mind. This identity, with the identification of himself as the civilized father who reads to his child so successfully that Young Sam coos along with the story though twenty miles away, overcomes the power of the Summoning Dark.

Not only the process of learning, the play with formula and substitution, and the narrative quest found in the picture book have assisted Vimes across this novel. Rather, his response to ultimate stress is founded on his new identification of himself as the father whose "day [goes] soft and pink" at six o'clock

(*Thud!* 265), and whose job is always to protect the vulnerable. As the young Thud-playing grag Bashfulsson explains, "You wouldn't strike the helpless, you see. You resisted [the Summoning Dark].... I was frightened that the struggle inside would rip the tendons from your bones" (*Thud!* 404). The deepdowners are arrested, the secret of the dead kings revealed, and the dwarfs and trolls prepare to make peace. As demonstrated through Vimes's reading of the picture book, art as well as games can be identified as a means through which the respondents can define their values and produce a positive identity based on these rather than, as Hamcrusher has advocated to the dwarfs, simply on rejection of the Other.

It is therefore no accident that when Death appears to Vimes near the climax of *Thud!* he is reading a detective story, and invites the half-crazed Vimes to contemplate the strangeness of doing so given that "ALL ONE NEEDS TO DO IS TURN TO THE LAST PAGE AND THE ANSWER IS THERE. WHAT, THEREFORE, IS THE POINT OF DELIBERATELY NOT KNOWING?" (*Thud!* 388). This postmodern moment removes the reader from the action just as it appears at last to have become heroic adventure in Vimes's rush through the cavern after the deep-downers, instead focusing our attention on the fact that Pratchett's *Thud!* is itself an artwork. We are invited to see how even "genre writing"—heroic fantasy, police procedural, detective story, thriller—can be deployed, and is here being deployed, not (or not only) to assist in our escape from the difficulties of our lives, nor to promote the easy acceptance of stereotype that can be fostered by fantasies (and games) that reductively assign immutable sets of characteristics to groups, but to enlighten—or, as the dwarfs would say, to endarken. Death's question goes to the heart of our humanity: we are, as Huizinga suggests, the species that plays, that makes art, and that revels in the experience not merely of reading but, as for Young Sam, even of re-reading. We engage in the activity of play for its own sake rather than functionally to resolve a mystery or conquer an enemy. Like other human activities, this one can have powerful effects, which may not always be positive, as Johnny observed in *Only You Can Save Mankind*. In *Thud!*, however, Pratchett focuses on the positive value of play. He demonstrates how we may learn from art, even picture books like *Where's My Cow?*, about the importance of similarity and difference, or from games like Thud about the power of empathy. Encouraged by our reading of *Thud!*, we can engage with our own potential for civilization and, like Vimes, create our own internal Watchman to guard an identity constructed in terms of tolerance and cultural openness rather than by definition through hatred.

NOTES

1. As Cherith Baldry observes, "The influence [of the shoot-'em-up game] may be practical and direct.... Or it may be more insidious, in creating a society which believes that war is acceptable and that those who wage it enjoy what they do" (47).

2. Pratchett simultaneously published a picture book entitled *Where's My Cow?* (2005) that frames the narrative described in *Thud!* with an account of Vimes's reading and re-writing of it, in a *mise en abyme*.

WORKS CITED

Baldry, Cherith. "The Children's Books." Butler, James, and Mendlesohn 41–65.

Butler, Andrew M. "'We Has Found the Enemy and They Is Us': Virtual War and Empathy in Four Children's Science Fiction Novels." *The Lion and the Unicorn* 28 (2004): 171–86.

Butler, Andrew M., Edward James, and Farah Mendlesohn, eds. *Terry Pratchett: Guilty of Literature.* 2d ed. Baltimore: Old Earth, 2004.

Huizinga, Johan. *Homo Ludens: A Study of the Play-Element in Culture.* 1949. London: Granada, 1970.

James, Edward. "The City Watch." Butler, James, and Mendlesohn 193–216.

Mendlesohn, Farah. "Faith and Ethics." Butler, James, and Mendlesohn 239–60.

Moody, Nickianne. "Death and Work." Butler, James, and Mendlesohn 153–70.

Pratchett, Terry. *Feet of Clay.* 1996. London: Corgi, 1997.

_____. *The Fifth Elephant.* 1999. London: Corgi, 2000.

_____. *Guards! Guards!* 1989. London: Corgi, 1990.

_____. *Jingo.* 1997. London: Corgi, 1998.

_____. *Lords and Ladies.* 1991. London: Corgi, 1992.

_____. *Men at Arms.* 1993. London: Corgi, 1994.

_____. *Only You Can Save Mankind.* 1992. London: Corgi, 2004.

_____. *Thud!* 2005. London: Corgi, 2006.

_____. *Where's My Cow?* Illus. Melvyn Grant. New York: HarperCollins, 2005.

_____. *Witches Abroad.* 1991. London: Corgi, 1992.

_____. *Wyrd Sisters.* 1988. London: Corgi, 1989.

Pratchett, Terry, Ian Stewart and Jack Cohen. *The Science of Discworld.* London: Ebury, 1999.

Sawyer, Andy. "Narrativium and Lies-to-Children: Palatable Science in *The Science of Discworld.*" *Journal of the Fantastic in the Arts* 13.1 (2002): 62–81.

Counting Dangerous Beans
Pratchett, Style and the Utility of Premodified Bits
WILLIAM C. SPRUIELL

"A poet removes all signs from their places. An artist always incites insurrections among things."—Viktor Borisovitch Shklovsky, trans. Robinson [127–8]

"Devices that attract attention to words, sounds, or other embellishments instead of to ideas are inappropriate in scientific writing."—*American Psychological Association Style Manual*, 6th ed. Sec. 3.10 [70]

A colossal number of people have read Terry Pratchett's *Discworld* novels, and it would likely be difficult to find many of them who do not think Pratchett has a distinctive writing style. They may find it difficult to describe what they feel its characteristics to be (past the requisite immediate mention of frequent word-play), but if explicit description were a prerequisite for any assumption of existence we would not have much of a world to interact with. One has to be wary of monolithic constructions like "style," but even were Pratchett's writing style to be entirely a product of the *belief* of individual readers, it would still be an interesting object of study (or series of objects of study)—after all, as Pratchett himself points out, just because something is a story does not mean that it is not important. We are, in any event, in little danger of being forced to describe Pratchett's writing as styleless: in contemporary stylistic analyses, style is frequently treated as involving systematic correlations between *any* textual features and *any* contextual factors relevant to the text.[1] Thus, it is almost impossible for anyone who has written more than a few lines to be "styleless," particularly as correlations do not require causation at all (though readers can be counted on to supply it) and authorship, even if it is only a matter of belief, can still easily be perceived as a conditioning factor until and unless contradictory evidence is encountered. Readers are humans, humans are good at perceiving patterns even in random noise (apophenia)—and an apophenogenic style is still a style.

Still, most of us would prefer epiphany to apopheny, even if we responsibly worry that the difference may turn out to be a matter mainly of ideology and marketing. If we are to venture a statement about what Pratchett's writing style is, how might we go about finding out, or at least convincingly cobbling together, what that might be? At some level the answer has to include some version of "examine Pratchett's texts and identify what is distinctive about them that can be attributed to authorship," although every part of that discussion is problematic. As Fish has pointed out in his critiques of New Critical approaches to literary analysis, anything one might want to say about a text in its meaningful sense (e.g., not "*Ulysses* is fairly heavy; I think we can break the window with it"[2]) is derived from interpretation at some level. None of the basic elements of lexicographic or grammatical analysis are universally accepted. A positivist stance toward text and style is simply one that is in denial; whatever comparisons we engage in are acts of interpretation, not of discovery in its unexamined sense. And we cannot expect "style" to be some unitary structural essence. David Lodge's image of the linguist homing in on the one essential linchpin of an author's style in *Changing Places* is memorable (especially to linguists, who are not accustomed to being represented in fiction that does not involve aliens, pyramids, or alien pyramids) but blessedly unrealistic.

Rather than attempting to provide an overall characterization of Pratchett's style, this paper will provide materials for characterizations, while demonstrating some very basic techniques of analysis drawn from the field of corpus linguistics. Much of it will entail word-counts, which can be more interesting than they sound. What I will arrive at will very much be open to the criticism of being a hunter-gatherer's collection of observations—it is completely *exploratory*, and no attempt will be made at exhaustiveness. As there are currently few analyses of Pratchett's style, such exploration may be useful nonetheless. One subsection will be focused on counting instances of discrete items—sequences with type-nouns (*the kind of / some sort of*), verbs indicating amplitude modulation (*sighed, yelled*) or type of utterance (*stated, demanded, asked*), combinations of verbs of vision with directional prepositions (*looked up, peered down*), and expressions using *bits* and *a bit*. These were all chosen as tests of hypotheses, in that use of "hypothesis" that banks on it sounding more scientific than "hunch": I had some impressions of Pratchett's style that I wanted to test, and they were of the sort amenable to useful destruction by data. A second subsection will examine some Pratchettian names—such as *Dangerous Beans*—in relation to the different ways in which they violate likely reader expectations. Both of these approaches position authorial style as a matter of shifts in potentials, allowing connection of specific observations about Pratchett's prose to wider discussions of the relation between humor and surprise.

However, since the discussion will involve some of the most loaded terms in the humanities and social sciences (*text, characteristic, author*), and since definitional differences among what deceptively appear to be the same words are one of the standard pitfalls in cross-disciplinary endeavors, I must first attempt to sketch out the space of discussion enough that readers can at least locate disagreement.

Text, Deviation, Foregrounding, Ostranenie, and Squance

The first issue is basic vocabulary. "Text" can refer to a physical artifact (or set of artifacts; in this case, volumes with pages that have black spots and non-black spots), it can refer to a basic grammatical construct of some sort (a string of words that is taken to also instantiate a set of grammatical categories, perhaps grouping into hierarchical formations that may include sentences as units), it can refer to a set of movements in an intersubjective discourse-community-constructed choice-space, and it can refer to whatever it is that the reader *experiences* interacting with (we have to assume this happens and admit that whatever it is may not be in every particular determined by community interaction).[3] The discussion to follow will primarily adopt the "temporal pattern in social choice-space" interpretation of text, in which the occurrence of any item is interpreted as signifying choices among a set of potential alternatives, with the choices each tied to different (potentially immense) sets of distinctions potentially relevant to the interaction in any way.[4] While the description is profoundly oversimplified, it should serve as an umbrella characterization of a wide range of contemporary programs of textual analysis, for example Systemic Functional Linguistics and Rhetorical Structure Theory to name but two.[5] Its foundations, as with most of modern linguistics, partly lie in Saussure's structuralist view that meaning is a function of distinction, although most contemporary versions do not adopt strict versions of Saussure's *langue/parole* distinction (nor Chomsky's derivative of it, *competence/*

("If there is a suitably high flux level, the inter-continuum pressure can probably overcome quite a high base reality quotient"—*Lords&Ladies* 36), a strong element of *Star Trek* physics to it (or of any of a number of other science-fiction presentations of technology), and although thaumotech in fantasy certainly existed before Pratchett (Poul Anderson's "Operation Afreet" in 1956, for example), it was in conflict, certainly, with stereotypes of fantasy literature.

Pratchett's footnotes are a clearer example of genre-bending. They are a scholarly graphotextual device and thus again a seemingly foreign import, although because the noted science-fiction and fantasy author Jack Vance was known for using them, they might be interpreted as primarily a Vance allusion and only secondarily a genre-skew (but to admit the existence of readers again, only for those with experience of Vance). In any event, the grammar of Pratchett's footnotes is different from Vance's.[13] Vance typically maintained strict verisimilitude to scholarly style; his footnotes are frequently noun phrases standing in apposition to a word they are defining in the text—a convention familiar to any user of dictionaries—or are full sentences. Pratchett adopts the visual form of the scholarly convention (in that they are quite recognizably footnotes, in the printed editions), but the footnotes are in some cases adverbial *which*-clauses—a colloquial feature actively prohibited by some formal style guides.[14]

Secondary deviation is frequently a matter of quantity, of a statistical difference (the word-counting in the next section will, in fact, be entirely an attempt to locate examples of secondary deviation). Cooper, in *Mysterious Music*, for example, has argued that one of the qualities that allows readers of free verse to *recognize* it as such is the greater-than-usual frequency with which syllables bearing primary stress are positioned immediately adjacent to each other in poetry using the form. The fact of Pratchett's frequent word-play, against the backdrop of the absence of such in most fantasy novels, thus may be counted as secondary deviation as well, although Pratchett may have been so successful at establishing his own subgenre that fewer readers now think of "fantasy" and "humor" as rarely intersecting categories. This does, of course, raise the thorny question of how much deviation is needed before there is *real* deviation, a question I will return to below.

Tertiary deviation occurs text-internally, so in application to Pratchett it would involve any of the devices Pratchett uses within his text to shift tone, to establish structure, to create or destroy parallelism. It is the primary locus of argument for close stylistic analysis (or any close reading, for that matter), and crucially depends on interlocking and hierarchical patterns of sequencing in the text. As this paper focuses primarily on elements at a fairly basic level (the longest sequence considered in the next section is four words) it is beyond the scope of most of the discussion here.

As an interpretive framework allowing texts to be viewed as existing in relation to networks of norms, the idea of deviation does useful work. Just what the norms are remain an issue, naturally, and we have to guard against slipping into any pretense that they somehow exist as some sort of Platonic true form, whose shadow we are attempting to delineate.[15] Corpus linguists establish them by recourse to collections of texts that act as reference sets but are always positioned *as* reference sets; they are simply what is possible for deviation to be measured in relation to, and the choice of what to include in them is never a neutral or theory-free matter. For trying to establish the extent to which an author's usage deviates from "overall" English, comparison against broad reference sets representing multiple registers is a logical choice (especially if the author is a humorist, and may be using anomalous register mixing as a technique; see Venour, Ritchie, and Mellish); if focusing on relations between the authors' usage and that of a set of similar authors, a much narrower set is warranted.

Deviation, however, might be seen as a set of potentials which *could* act upon a reader. It exists "in" the text that our model of text constructs, but it is necessarily divorced from even idealized readers. Terms like "distinctiveness," on the other hand, connote that something has acted on at least some *actual* readers. "It is distinctive" is much more difficult to disguise as objective than is "It deviates from the norm"; the damage historically wrought by the latter is directly tied to its sneakiness. Leech positions foregrounding as requiring psychological prominence; both produce measurable effects, but he defines foregrounding as aesthetically active—so neither requires conscious notice, but only the former affects aesthetic judgments (163). In principle, it would be possible for deviation to be "there" without having any behavioral or aesthetic effects at all (except on the analyst who finds it in the numbers; publication counts as an observable behavior, even in linguistics).

It is possible, of course, that all shifts in frequency do always affect readers at some level, and that all effects impinge on aesthetic impressions, thus rendering deviation, prominence, and foregrounding the same thing for an idealized reader. Absent the "always," the linkage between deviation and prominence, and between deviation and foregrounding, in actual readers can be a matter of empirical investigation. In linguistics, the role that input plays in shaping language is a perennial matter of contention, and the past several decades, with the explosive growth of technologies allowing statistical analysis of increasingly gigantic amounts of text, have seen the rise of usage-based theories of language. Thus, there is a robust and robustly-contested psycholinguistic literature attempting to measure such effects. Snyder's study serves as a possible boundary case; his study found that as few as five exposures to a particular type of ungrammatical sentence affect observers' judgment of grammaticality (but see Sprouse's arguments that Snyder's results were a side-effect of the experiment design).[16] Even if we adopt the "all deviation equals foregrounding" position, however, it remains the case that deviation is adduced from relations between reference sets and texts, and readers will never have identical reference sets, and (perceptual processes being what they are) will never encounter precisely the same text. If our view of foregrounding is one that involves alterations of reader behavior, they need to be actual readers (although one advantage of ideal readers constructed for thought experiments is that they are uncommonly cooperative).

It is also not the case that patterns of correlation that do affect the reader will be directly tied to an impression of distinctiveness (which need not be the same thing as an impression of literary quality), nor, conversely, that a pattern that a reader does feel to be distinctive be supported by a careful examination of the text. The possibility that all of the effects that, in other areas of human perception and reasoning, intervene between what is there and what people notice or react to—stereotyping, the illusion of frequency ("You notice what you look for"), and the like—would *not* apply to style is, I think, remote. Mark Liberman, for example, has noted pundits' ability to detect elevated use of the first-person singular pronoun despite the absence of any supporting evidence. Likewise implausible is the possibility that what might be considered emotional reactions *to* deviation or foregrounding would not affect perceptions of style, or more precisely, style-as-experienced. There is a very real sense in which attributions of difference require that something *feel* different from an experienced norm.[17]

In a perhaps-abusive exercise of an academic's deriving license, I will term "the felt difference between the felt expectations a reader has (derived in part from that reader's specific experience with previous texts), and what the text is perceived to be doing" *squance*.[18] To compound coinage with metaphor, we could adopt an image from Mukařovský (50) positioning norms as energy, as forces attracting speakers' usage, and view squance as a reaction to the torque produced by the reader's network of expectations (Hoey's "primings") interacting with the text. Torque will exist regardless; it can, however, be perceived as one or more of a multitude of things, e.g., a welcome diversion, a reconnection with object-as-event (ostranenie), a marker of regional or social difference, or, as with many older speakers encountering the changed usage of the young, an excuse for their inner Buckleys to stand athwart history yelling "Stop!" The perception that an author has a distinctive style requires that the reader link the text's squance to the author, rather than to a genre or some other conditioning factor. When readers of a text engage in tasks that are consciously, explicitly author-*focused*, their reactions are a function of squance, not directly of foregrounding or deviation.

Take, for example, the phenomenon of non–Terry-Pratchett writers consciously writing "in the style of Terry Pratchett," as in this description of the death of J. K. Rowling's Dumbledore from the 15 July 2005 online edition of *The Guardian*[19]:

> The hole was positioned immediately above a Dumbledore-shaped pile of robes currently resting on several cubic feet of stone and masonry, and, for some reason, a traffic cone.
> I LIKE WHAT YOU'VE DONE WITH THE PLACE.
> "Thank you," said a dozen portraits in unison.
> VERY KITSCH. YOU DON'T SEE MUCH KITSCH THESE DAYS.
> "Oh dear," said a muffled voice from somewhere within the robes.
> The Dumbledore-shaped pile got up, leaving behind another identical pile that looked distinctly less capable of upright posture. The ghost of Albus Dumbledore was wearing a traffic cone on his head.
> IS THAT A NEW LOOK? I HAVE SUCH A HARD TIME KEEPING UP WITH FASHION.

Such attempts presuppose that the writer thinks Terry Pratchett has a style that can be emulated and they are implicit verifications of the writer's attribution of distinctiveness to Pratchett's prose. They make sense in a way that writing a piece "in the style of books that are at 45-degree angles to someone's desk" would not. Their authors are drawing on their felt perceptions of Pratchett's writing, regardless of whether the writer succeeds (however we would measure that); at the same time, no one would be particularly surprised to discover that the piece's author had not come to the task with a meticulously articulated list of Pratchettic features to encode. Style emulation is more akin to attempting to mirror a movement. Trying to name the muscles involved during the process does not help in the slightest. While some of the features of the imitative text match those from Pratchett's writing in a way that is so obvious as to be probably uninteresting (having a Death figure speak in all caps might be regarded as a similarity of content rather than style, although that distinction is a vexed one), other sections suggest possibilities to investigate. "Dumbledore-shaped pile" uses a personal name as part of a compound modifier formed with the participle "shaped," and this certainly strikes me, at least, as distinctive. Does Pratchett use personal names like this, and if so, does he do so more than English-speakers do in general? (Spoiler: Yes.)

Similarly, given a set of sentences such as those below, at least some Pratchett-readers will be able to assign rankings based on how much each sentence sounds like an attempt at Pratchesimilitude. The issue here, again, is not whether the sentences *are* Pratchett-like, it is the degree to which they can be felt to be such:

1. A vista of tall cliffs, facing a sere wasteland, loomed before them, blocking any direct progress to the north.
2. "Not to be intrusive or anything, but is that your newspaper?" asked Harald.
3. It was the sort of side-alley that your average cormorant would never invite to *anything*.
4. Several of the crates were stacked against the far wall, skewed slightly ajar as if someone had moved them hastily into place.
5. She was far more concerned with where the chair wasn't.
6. Not being involved in the situation at all seemed like the absolute best state to be in, all things considered.
7. His hand slipped under the table and came up holding a meat cleaver honed to paper thinness.
8. It had been described as an odd shade of blue, particularly by people who keep their color terms down to what can be counted on one hand.

Traditional forms of stylistic analysis represent the results of style-description tasks, if only ones imposed by the analyst on herself in an attempt to articulate an impression; they exist only to the degree that they are explicit, and thus may seem different in kind to style-emulation and to the kind of style-categorization implicit in this list (to which I will return later). But all three originate in what those engaged in the task feel to be the author's style, whether the results converge or (perhaps more interestingly) do not.

If one's goal is to define authorial style as a stable set of correlations between author and text features relative to an abstract reader, as most stylistic analyses must, these squantic intuitions represent starting points, and some readers' intuitions will constitute better starting points than others.' A "sensitive and observant reader attuned to the use of the language," as Leech puts it (163), is presumably someone whose expectations approximate an intersubjective mean more closely than those of most randomly-chosen readers, and whose reactions to deviations from those expectations are perhaps more pronounced ("Only those who *feel* ideosomatic regulation can sense or feel the creative movement of 'blasphemy'; of deviation from the canon"; Robinson 125). Deviation data derived from text-mining, and statistical evaluation of those data, also represent starting points—"empirically-derived 'good bets' to follow up on in undertaking a subsequent stylistic analysis in terms of foregrounding" (Leech 164).

If, instead or in addition, one's goal is to use reader behavior as a way to

investigate "style-as-experienced," or the relations holding between actual readers and texts-as-experienced, or even relations holding between different *kinds*
of readers and texts-as-experienced, deviation data and squantic intuitions
remain relevant because of the disjunction between the two; it is a matter of
no little theoretic interest—and to no few fields—that a pundit can feel a
politician's speech to have a marked excess of first-person pronouns that it
does not in fact evince, or that adult readers are confident in judging Theodore
Geisel's prose to be quite simple. At a more general level, readers' native language varieties (e.g., British or American dialects) can certainly affect their
perceptions of authorial style (Francom and Ussishkin), a point that is particularly relevant to the discussion of writers read as widely as is Pratchett.

Counting Instances

In this section, I will examine the general frequency with which Pratchett
uses several sets of specific items, including single words and sequences of two
to three words. The term "sequence" is being used because some of the two-
word combinations (bigrams) and three-word combinations (trigrams) may
or may not act more as single units than as series of "slots" with items substi-
tutable within them in a manner fully predictable from knowledge of English
grammar and the denotations of the specific words.[20] The strategy adopted
here will be simply to dodge the issue, although at some points in the discussion
of results it will be worthwhile to return to the fact that it *is* an issue. Item frequencies from Pratchett will be compared to ones derived from two different
sources:

(a) A pair of large, balanced corpora of English—BYU-BNC (Davies) henceforth BNC for purposes of brevity, based on the British National Corpus, comprising roughly 100 million words of British English, and the Corpus of
Contemporary American English, henceforth COCA (Davies) comprising
roughly 450 million words of American English. Both allow classification of texts
by major register: spoken (usually via transcripts of live television interviews), fiction, magazines, news, academic writing, and in the case of the BNC, additional
"non-academic" and "miscellaneous" categories. Of these, only the spoken, fiction, news, and academic subcorpora were used. Pratchett's writing is fiction, of
course, so BNC-F and COCA-F are the closest comparators; spoken and academic are useful as extreme positions along a number of scales (formality, etc.)
and Pratchett's background as a journalist made comparing against the news category logical. Both corpora are accessible via web-based GUIs that allow the user
to search for orthographic words, lemmas (abstracting away from "cat" vs. "cats,"
for example), and lexical categories ("parts of speech"). Results can be viewed in
terms of total frequency and in terms of "words per million" (henceforth WPM),

a procedure that proportionalizes against the size of each subcorpus. If there are fewer words in the spoken–English sample than in the fiction sample, for example, then a lower total frequency in the former might still indicate a higher proportion than the same number in the latter; the WPM display compensates for this.[21]

(b) A set of single-author text collections (discussed in more detail below). These were chosen simply as samples of other authors' writing, and not structured in any way other than being incorporated as separate files within the composite whole for each author, so they are not formally corpora. However, they can be useful, particularly as a source of negative evidence ("Pratchett does X more than does typical British fiction, but definitely not more than Wodehouse"). These were downloaded as plain-text files from Project Gutenberg, and the Gutenberg-specific language at the beginning and end of each file was removed for processing. Tabulation of word counts and subsequent calculation of dispersion and correlation measures (also discussed below) were done using the R statistics / programming language (R Core Team), along with a graphical front-end interface and a set of extensions ("packages" in R).[22]

As with much traditional stylistic analysis, the choice of items to examine was partly driven by intuition and simple curiosity—I had the impression, for example, that Pratchett uses expressions such as *the sort of* and *a sort of* unusually frequently, and wanted to know if the impression was accurate to any degree. Similarly, I had noticed cases in which Pratchett had used an adjective to modify words like *bit* (e.g., "the important bit"), and, as I associated this type of usage with British comedy (particularly *Monty Python* with its "naughty bits"), I also examined instances of *bits* and *a bit*.

In addition, however, the choices were strongly shaped by limitations imposed by the method of access to the texts themselves. The *Discworld* texts may be purchased in electronic format, but the license agreement under which they are sold in the U.S. prohibits their conversion into a format amenable to very large-scale analysis; investigating the rate at which Pratchett introduces new vocabulary as a text proceeds, for example, rapidly becomes prohibitively labor-intensive if done by hand. The programs with which the texts may be read (Kindle, in this case) do, however, allow searching with an upper "hit" limit of 100.[23] Thus, it is possible to investigate orthographic sequences that (a) occur fewer than 100 times per text and (b) do not require part-of-speech tagging or syntactic analysis to locate. While the situation is far from ideal, the fact that there is comparatively little stylistic analysis of Pratchett's prose will, I hope, justify the profoundly approximate nature of the approach (quantitative linguists at this point may be wondering if the next step involves chipping flint). The texts and the reader program were sufficient to allow filling out "number of instances per text" charts (given time and patience), and these charts can then be used as the input for a limited range of analyses.

The additional author-based text collections were added because COCA and the BNC, while providing information about the frequency of items in different sub-corpora, do not provide measures of how "bunched up" or "dispersed" items are across the corpus.[24] One of the many ways linguistic elements depart from being normally distributed is that they are *bursty*; whatever factors lead an author to include an otherwise-unusual word in a text may be operant across a large section of that text, leading to multiple uses in that text but no others (and the first use of the word can constitute its own conditioning factor for subsequent use). Few people have any reason to make reference to the Despotate of Epirus, for example, but Byzantine histories do, and the ones that do have reason to mention it multiple times. Burstiness is the focus of a very large and growing body of research at the intersection of information theory and linguistics (see Altmann, Pierrehumbert, and Motter as an example), but if we are interested in the degree to which an author's use of an item may be a reliable indicator of authorship, or of the author's style, then logically items that are used consistently throughout the author's work should count more than those that appear frequently but in only one or two of the author's texts.[25] Imagining a corpus of all English text, we would want items that are author-bursty but not novel-bursty.

Comparisons of Pratchett to COCA and BNC subcorpora thus allow discussion of what the quantitative relationship is between Pratchett's total usage of an item and the total usage of the item across a very large set of texts in specific registers, but they do not allow any direct discussion of how much usage of the item is *characteristic* of Pratchett's texts in general, or how much the total frequency reported by BNC/COCA may represent a small number of texts' having a very large number of uses. To pick a trivial example, Pratchett uses the personal name "Polly" a sizeable number of times—but four instances are from *Eric* (a parrot), four are references to a kitchen-girl in *Soul Music*, and one hits the 100 limit fairly early on in *Monstrous Regiment,* of which Polly is the protagonist. Pratchett is hardly characterizable as an author who frequently goes around naming characters Polly; he named one major character that, and the character has dialog.

The measure used here to represent dispersion is Gries's DP score, which represents the difference between the proportional frequencies of an item per text and what would be *expected* if the item were evenly distributed across the texts based on the texts' relative "size" in the corpus. For example, if there are 100 instances of item X in the corpus, and one of the texts represents 20 percent of the total number of words in the corpus, one would expect 20 percent of the 100 to occur in that text. If 90 percent of the 100 appear in it instead, the items are clearly concentrated in that text. The DP score is lower the more evenly distributed the items are; in a set of measures of the "BNC Baby" subset of the BNC provided by Gries,[26] the most evenly-distributed word is "a" with a score of just over .1; very unevenly distributed items may have scores of .98. Since the goal in this discussion is to assign *more* weight to items that occur more consistently for that author, the dispersion-adjusted scores used in the charts below and the "by Author" tables in Appendix B were obtained by multiplying the frequency of the item, expressed in WPM, by (1-DP).

The selection of authors for comparison was shaped by pragmatic limitations similar to those affecting the choice of items to examine. Basic word-tabulations (for example, counting the instances of each (orthographically-defined) word in each text in a set of texts) can be done quite rapidly given "plain text" electronic versions of written works, but few recent humor, fantasy or science-fiction texts—the natural choices for initial comparison—are available in the public domain (and the "ebook-reader-count" method, while usable, is not an attractive choice for multiple corpora). Cory Doctorow, a contemporary author whose works interweave fantasy, science-fiction elements, and magic realism, has (thankfully!) made novels available to Project Gutenberg, and thus these were included. The other texts used were also drawn from Project Gutenberg, although the authors are obviously not contemporaries of Pratchett. Weird Fiction author H. P. Lovecraft (via Gutenberg Australia), British science-fiction author H. G. Wells, and American Golden-Age space-opera author E. E. Smith were included for comparison as speculative fiction samples, and texts by P. G. Wodehouse were added for comparison because of his status as a British humor writer. Because it is useful to have a sample that might serve as a boundary case, texts by Edward Bulwer-Lytton were used as well. Table 1, below, lists number of texts and total number of words per author while full lists of texts per author are in Appendix A. For the Pratchett texts, figures from the L-Space "Statistics" page and extrapolations from the ebook editions were used; the calculations used later in this section are based on a total word count approximating 3,510K.

Author	*N. of texts*	*Total words*
Bulwer-Lytton	23	3,424,494
Doctorow	7	525,655
Lovecraft	38	491,515
Wells	7	428,817
Wodehouse	38	2,145,828

Table 1: Number of texts in, and size of, author text collections.

Several of the Lovecraft texts and one of the E. E. Smith texts were co-written; for purposes of this paper, I am assuming that whatever stylistic differences their coauthors introduced are small enough to permit the texts' inclusion. Any detailed analysis of relations between stylistic features in particular texts of Pratchett's and particular texts of Lovecraft's or Smith's, however, would render the assumption highly problematic.

In addition to raw and proportionalized counts, Pearson correlation scores were computed between series of subcorpus counts to determine the extent to which author (or corpus in the case of BNC vs. COCA vs. Pratchett) appeared to affect frequency of occurrence. While the correlations provide no real information about differences between *items* in the series, they do provide a way of gauging how much one subcorpus is using the items similarly to another. For example, consider the following subset:

		BNCF	*COCAF*	*Doctorow*
looked	up	135.33	93.92	147.27
	down	67.76	43.74	81.5
	around	34.63	28.88	81.5
peered	up	1.32	1.11	2.63
	down	3.21	2.38	5.26
	around	1.07	1.08	2.63
glanced	up	16.91	11.33	0
	down	8.11	7.15	2.63
	around	5.03	7.74	0
stared	up	10.12	4.93	2.63
	down	15.02	7.02	2.63
	around	2.07	0.48	0

All three subcorpora use forms of *looked* more than forms of *glanced*, etc. Whatever is going on here, much of it has to do with population-wide differences in usage between forms like *looked up* and *peered down*—there are overall differences in how those combinations are used. Those differences are interesting in their own right (of course) but for current purposes, it is primarily useful to know how much each *column* "tracks" another *column* in terms of values in the one increasing when values in the other do, or decreasing in one when the values increase in the other; in other words, how much information one column provides about the other. If Doctorow, for example, always used each of these constructions exactly half as often as COCA-F does, those two columns would have a high correlation score—the only thing about Doctorow's usage that the COCA-F column *could not* provide would be the fact of the .5 frequency multiplier. Conversely, if the relationship between pairs of items in the columns were completely random, knowing the COCA-F distribution would tell us nothing about Doctorow's.

It is vital to point out some of the limitations of the analysis here:

- **Lack of part-of-speech tagging means extra ambiguity**. The verb forms that will be discussed are regular verbs with -ed suffixes, and are thus indeterminate out of context between past tense and past participle forms. From some angles, this is not necessarily a problem (a muttered word still involves muttering), but it does mean that the analysis does not take into account what the word is doing in the sentence. Also, the use of -ed forms ignores the use of *present* tense verbs, and authors are perfectly capable of adopting present tense as the primary tense of narration—so an author's having a low rate of usage of "muttered" might be ignoring a very high rate of "mutters." The novels used in the author collection are primarily past-tense narratives, but of course authors can shift to present tense for portions even so (it is one of the classic tertiary deviation moves, and my impression is that Doctorow uses it quite frequently). The investigation here is only intended to suggest avenues for further study.

- **Consistently low numbers are less informative**. Linguistic expressions do not conform to normal distributions in the statistical sense; they instead follow what information theorists term a Zipf curve, a category of what elsewhere are called power-law distributions or Pareto distributions. Essentially, a few items occur extremely frequently (e.g., "the"), and a very large number of items occur very infrequently (e.g., "vug"); single-occurrence items are familiar to philologists as hapax legomena. Because of this distribution, the larger the corpus, the more likely the total frequency of a given item is to jump from "zero" to "one" (and if the corpus is under a million words, that "one" can show up as something like "2.92"). Thus, the presence of low but non-zero scores can simply be a function of corpus size. COCA is over four times as large as BNC, and the BNC dwarfs any of the single-author collections used here. Thus, comparisons between items that occur only at very low frequency are much less likely to be telling us anything. Since the correlation scores used are calculated between columns that typically have a few low frequency values in them, I will be taking care to use the scores heuristically—e.g., using "these results suggest" rather than "these results indicate." Any shifts in frequency connected to the status of particular texts as co-written, as discussed above, can also be expected to manifest more strongly for items that do not occur as often (with a boundary case being items that only the co-author uses).

- **There is doubtless an error rate.** For a sequence like "looked up" to count *as* a sequence, there should be no sentence-final punctuation intervening ("I walked over and looked. Up on the hill, there were..."). Such cases are fairly rare for the sequences being investigated here, and I have attempted to eliminate any. However, I will avoid any arguments based on small differences in frequencies (e.g., 34.57 vs. 34.64 or even 36), since if there *is* an error, it could easily be the cause of the difference. This is particularly an issue with low frequency values, compounding the problem discussed above.

Type Noun Sequences

The nouns *kind*, *sort*, and *type* are the only three words that can occur in the frame "the ___ of thing," and the sequences *kind of* and *sort of* are interestingly indeterminate—"a sort of green bird," for example, may be a variety of bird that is green, or it may be a bird that is somewhat green, or a greenish shade the speaker does not want to commit to pinning down too much (there is frequently less structural ambiguity in spoken English, where the difference between "sort of" and "sorta" provides extra information). *Type of* is less common, and occurs proportionally more often in academic English; *type* was still being used at the end of the nineteenth century in some cases equivalently to *exemplar* or *eidolon*, while the general "subclass" uses of *kind* and *sort* are much older (see Denison; Brems and Davidse).

A growing body of literature has examined the ways these are used in modern English (see De Smedt, et al. for a detailed and careful review of the literature on different uses of type noun constructions). In their study of the constructions' use in two very different corpora (one based on samples from *The Times*, the other COLT, a corpus of teenage London spoken English), De Smedt et al. found striking dissimilarities in the use of different subtypes. In particular, adverbial qualifier uses of *sort of* and *kind of* (among the "sorta" types) were markedly (if perhaps not surprisingly) higher in the teenage spoken sample. What might be viewed as a more literal or componential use, positioning *kind, sort,* or *type* as a head noun followed by an *of*-phrase (i.e., what might be paraphrased as "a variety of" or "a class of") was more common in the written register. Similarly, Fetzer has analyzed the use of type noun constructions in political speech (interviews, for example), noting the differential use of certain types as hedging devices. Politicians may appear too colloquial if they use *sorta* as a discourse particle, for example, but *that sort of thing* as a reference to a discourse-established referent can allow a quite useful level of what Fetzer terms "fuzziness." De Smedt et al. posit six major categories of type-noun expressions, with subcategories of several of these. Achieving this level of delicacy was beyond the scope of the current paper, which limits itself to variations of two sequences: [Determiner + kind/sort/type + OF], and [kinds/sorts/types + OF]; in the first case, the determiners include *the, a(n), this, that,* and *some.*

Results are presented in Tables B1a and B1b in Appendix B. Versions using *types* were at low frequencies across the samples, as were expressions such as *these kind(s) of* and *those kind(s) of,* so these will not be discussed. Figure 1, below, highlights some of the interesting results. The pattern is consistent with the hypothesis that Pratchett generally uses type expressions with *sort* at a rate higher than usual (keeping in mind "usual" here is defined only by the reference corpora)—but with some interesting exceptions. He uses *the kind of* quite a bit more often than *the sort of,* although my initial impressions of his style would have predicted exactly the opposite. He also uses several expressions with *kind* more often than either the BNC or the COCA fiction rates, exceeding spoken rates in three cases as well—again, not something that my conscious impressions of his style included, although in general his usage correlates more strongly with BNC-F (.87, p < .0002) than COCA-F (.80, p < .002), as one might expect. One quite possible reason for the mismatch may lie in dialectal variation: a comparison of the *kind* and *sort* sides of the figures suggests a reversal of their frequencies between British and American English, with British preferring *sort.* From the perspective of an American English-speaker, *sort* is a marked choice: I was positioned to notice it more.

An additional point, not obvious from the charts in Figure 1, is that Pratchett's uses of *that sort of* and *this sort of* are usually positioned in front of the word *thing* (see Table 2, below). Across all examined registers of the BNC and COCA, *sort* is more likely to occur than *kind* in "[that/this] ____ of thing." This may indicate the status of "[that/this] sort of thing" as a multi-word unit (with limited flexibility in the front position) that, in U.S. English, is not as strongly affected by the general American preference for *kind. [A]nd that sort of thing* has specifically been discussed as a multi-word unit by McCarthy and Carter (17–26) and Tagg (211) so the possibility of *this/that sort of thing* functioning analogously does not seem unlikely (especially as it is shorter).

	Pratchett	BNC				COCA			
		S	F	N	A	S	F	N	A
that k/t	0.30	0.32	0.33	0.18	0.09	0.12	0.14	0.05	0.06
that s/t	0.87	0.45	0.60	0.32	0.28	0.40	0.56	0.34	0.22
this k/t	0.33	0.23	0.21	0.16	0.03	0.10	0.15	0.06	0.01
this s/t	0.82	0.32	0.50	0.34	0.07	0.22	0.46	0.22	0.07

Table 2: Proportions of *that kind of* and *this kind of* to *that kind of thing* and *this kind of thing.*

A detailed examination of how Pratchett uses *this sort of thing* and *that sort of thing* is beyond the scope of this paper, but the approach developed by Fetzer in her analysis of political discourse may be a useful starting point for further research.

When Pratchett's usage is adjusted for dispersion and examined relative to corresponding values from the additional author collections, he does not appear to be using these expressions to a much higher extent than at least some other authors: except in the case of *some sort of*, there is always at least one author who uses any given sequence at a higher rate, as shown in Figure 2, below (a number of sequences are again omitted because of their low overall frequency). Doctorow and Wodehouse, in particular, show much higher frequency of use than Pratchett, with Doctorow favoring *kind* and Wodehouse favoring *sort*. Doctorow is a Canadian author, and it is possible that Canadian use of *kind* vs. *sort* aligns more with AmE than BrE; Wodehouse, as a British author, might be expected to favor *sort* for similar national-variety issues.

In short, Pratchett's use of type-noun sequences can be argued, *provisionally*, to be higher than the general norm for British and American fiction, and as having some potentially interesting internal patterns for further exploration, but nothing well outside the envelope created by the six other, very disparate authors considered here. What he does *with* the type noun sequences, of course, could nevertheless be quite marked in a way that simple counts do not reveal. Type noun expressions, as discussed above, can be used both for creating/manipulating hyponymic relations and for hedging/"fuzzing." Some of Pratchett's hyponymic constructions certainly stand out:

> But if it's a lot heavier than you, then my suspicion is that you'll appear over there traveling at the sort of speed normally only experienced by sleepwalkers in clifftop villages in a very terminal way [*Times* 56].
>
> But people were people, even if they had four legs and had called themselves names like Dangerous Beans, which is the kind of name you gave yourself if you learned to read before you understood what all the words actually meant, and reading the warning notices and the labels on the old rusty cans gave you names you liked the sound of [*Maurice* 17].

The kind of archetypal "scientific" hyponymic expression one typically encounters introduces a subcategory based on a relevant feature that is presupposed to exist—"a fir tree is a kind of conifer with short needles," for example, presupposes that there are, in fact, conifers, and that having short needles is a characteristic of a subcategory that pre-existed the use of the expression, even if the hearer had not noticed it before. Pratchett sometimes establishes subcategories that *logically* could pre-exist the reference to them, but that outside of a philosophical argument or a comedy routine (assuming a clear difference

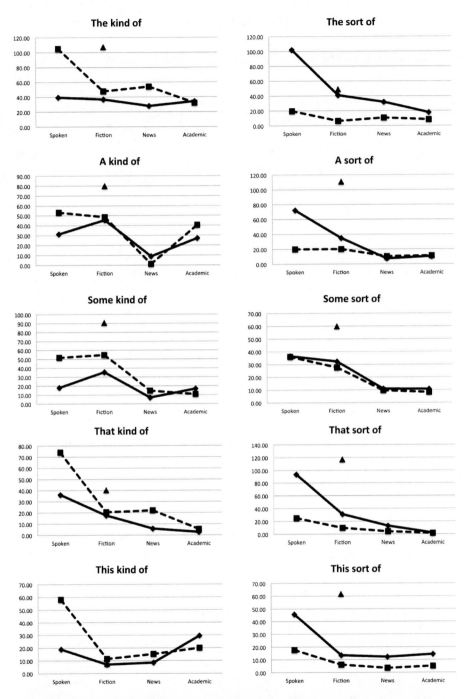

Figure 1: Total freq. (in WPM) for selected [DET] type expressions in BNC (solid line), COCA (dotted line) and Pratchett (triangle). Note that scales are not identical across sequence types.

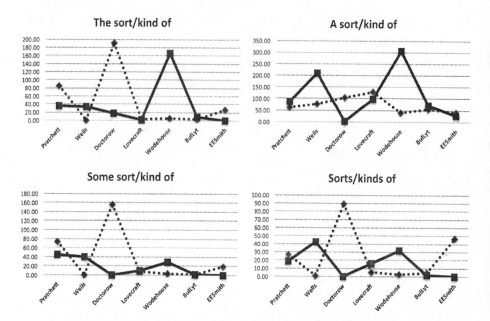

Figure 2: Frequencies for expressions with *kind* (dotted line) and *sort* (solid line) across author collections, adjusted for DP (WPM*(1-DP)).

for the moment) would be on the vanishing edge of possibility or relevance. We can talk about "the sort of marmot that rarely spontaneously combusts" (presumably this is 100 percent of marmots, but it is a standard feature of set theory that a subset can have exactly the same members as its superordinate set), but normally marmots would be put in subcategories on more socially-relevant critera.

Selected "Speech-Tag Verbs"

The term "speech-tag verb" here is an informal one; I am using it to refer to verbs whose selection is tied directly to choices in what Halliday and Matthiessen term speech function (108). They are among what are sometimes termed performative verbs in linguistic pragmatics, and their meaning is directly tied to what major interactional "moves" we view speakers as making. The set was chosen partly to test for contrast with the noise verbs in the next subsection; McGillis (in this book) has suggested that words referring to noise have particular significance in Pratchett, and these speech-tag verbs occupy some of the same functional space but with different affective implications. *Say*, of course, is an obvious member of the set, but its frequency precluded its investigation for the Pratchett corpus (because of the 100-item limit). The five verbs discussed here are *asked, declared, demanded, insisted,* and *stated,* although these are obviously not the only five verbs in the general category. Pratchett, like many writers, frequently tags dialog for the reader, using expressions such as "X, said Granny" or "X, Tiffany said"; he is not one of those authors for whom the reader has to carefully count lines to determine who has uttered what. The verbs used in such tags rarely occupy center stage, but can be particularly interesting *because* of that, influencing perceptions of tone without being obvious.

The tabulated frequency rates (see tables B2a and B2b in Appendix B) for Pratchett and the BNC and COCA subcorpora do not show Pratchett's use of these terms as standing out in any obvious way. As might be expected, rate of use is much higher in fiction (including Pratchett's), but Pratchett's scores correlated positively with all subcorpora except for the academic ones. English-speakers in general use *asked* more often than *insisted,* etc. Among the adjusted author rates, the author Pratchett *least* correlates with is Lovecraft (.77, p < .13), who uses fewer of these verbs overall. Most readers of Pratchett and Lovecraft, however, can probably articulate better candidates for stylistic differences between the two already.

Selected "Noise Verbs"

Like the speech-tag verbs, these can be used in dialog tags, e.g., "X, shouted Rincewind." Unlike the expression verbs, they directly indicate physical, acoustic properties of the utterance while simultaneously indicating affect—shouting and yelling are both loud, but if one is overcome with joy the first is the likeliest word choice; sighing and muttering may have equal amplitude but one would typically pair "mutinously" only with the second. As with the expression verbs, no attempt is made here to be exhaustive.

The tabulated frequency rates for these verbs (see tables B2a and B2b in Appendix B) suggest more interesting relations among subcorpora and authors than do those for the expression verbs. First, there appears to be more variation in general in their use. In terms of the unadjusted WPM rates, Pratchett correlates with the fiction subcorpora (BNC .97, p < .05; COCA .88, p < .05) but not the other subcorpora—this is not, perhaps, surprising. In comparison to BNC-F and COCA-F, Pratchett's usage rates appear to be markedly higher for all verbs except *yelled,* as shown in Figure 3 below; his use of *sighed* and of *shouted* are particularly high.

When compared to other authors' DP-adjusted rates, his use of these verbs still appears quite high; rates for the three most common verbs in the set are shown below in Figure 4. Wells edges ahead of Pratchett in shouting

Noise Verbs (BNC/COCA Fiction & Pratchett only)

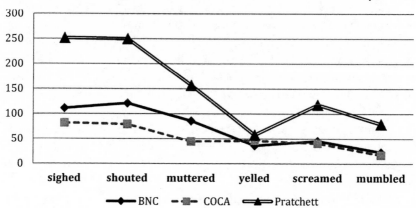

Figure 3: Noise verbs in BNC Fiction, COCA Fiction, and Pratchett (WPM).

and Bulwer-Lytton in muttering, but for those two authors those verbs constitute high proportions of their overall usage (*shouted* represents almost 77 percent of the noise verbs used by Wells, and *muttered* is almost 56 percent of Bulwer-Lytton's, but *sighed*, Pratchett's most frequent verb in this set, comprises only 30 percent of his total). Pratchett's adjusted scores correlate positively only with Wodehouse's (.90, $p < .05$), with Doctorow's being the next closest (.74, $p < .1$).

Sighed / Shouted / Muttered, DP-Adjusted, by Author

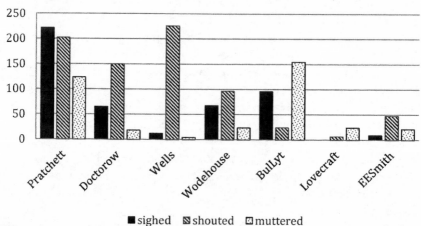

Figure 4: Selected noise-verb frequency per author, adjusted for DP (WPM*(1-DP)).

Vision Verbs with [Up / Down / Around]

This set of items comprises the four verbs *looked, peered, glanced,* and *stared* positioned before *up, down,* and *around,* and like the other items, they were chosen essentially as "probe expressions" to test whether they were more common in Pratchett (how authors present situated perception can be interesting). *Looked up* is, of course, ambiguous in English—"I looked up a word in the dictionary," "Things looked up after the fever passed," "Bjorn looked up the chimney," and "I looked up at the sky" all arguably involve different patterns, and "I looked a word up in the dictionary" is usually taken to involve the same pattern as the first of the previous even though *looked* and *up* are not contiguous. In many grammatical approaches, even when *up* refers transparently to a direction, cases in which *upwards* can substitute for it are considered to be adverbial, while in cases like "Bjorn looked up the chimney," it is taken to be a regular preposition. The approach used here is necessarily syntax-blind, since part-of-speech tagging and parsing was not a viable option for Pratchett. It cannot accommodate linking "looked up a word" to "looked a word up," nor can it treat "looked up a word" as an idiom separate from "looked up the chimney." However, on the specific topic of the adverbial vs. preposition distinction, Huddleston and Pullum (272–88) have argued strongly for considering the distinction void, claiming that both represent prepositional phrases, the difference being one of whether the preposition has a complement.

Results of the tabulation (tables B3a and B3b in Appendix B) show an interesting pattern of differences, although many of these expressions were too uncommon to serve as good bases for argumentation. Of the sequences that occur with moderate or higher frequencies, by far the most frequent are those with *looked,* all of which Pratchett uses quite regularly (his DP scores on these three are all under .2). He also uses *glanced up* and *stared down* with some frequency.

In terms of which sequences he uses more frequently than others, he appears to match almost every other subcorpus and author—correlations among all the subcorpora are extremely high. Among the adjusted author scores, the only ones not to correlate significantly were E. E. Smith and Lovecraft relative to each other and to Bulwer-Lytton and Wodehouse, who correlate with each other almost exactly (again, however, the low number of items suggests caution). In other words, it appears that most English-speakers in general use *looked up* more often than *peered down,* etc.—not very surprisingly—but Pratchett certainly uses looked+[up/down/around] *more.* Figure 5, below, illustrates the disparity.

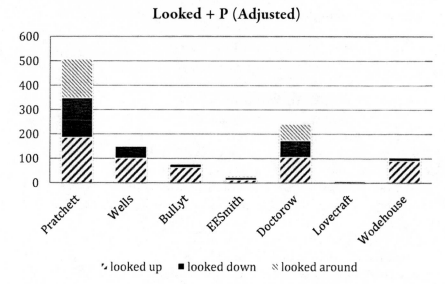

Figure 5: [Looked] + [up/down/around] by author, adjusted for DP (WPM*(1-DP)).

Vague Bits, Some Premodified

The set of terms examined here is heterogeneous; one of my impressions of Pratchett's style was that he uses the words *bit* and *bits* fairly often, particularly with modifying elements immediately before them (e.g., "burnt crunchy bits")—but I did not want to take the impression at face value. I was conscious of finding *bits* to be unaccountably funnier than *pieces* in general, and had to acknowledge that this (a) might be a completely idiosyncratic reaction, and (b) might well be causing me to notice differentially what instances are actually in the text.

Bit(s) can be used similarly to words like *fragment* or *piece*, but the (morphologically singular) form *bit* can also occur in the hedging or adverbial qualifying expression *a bit* ("the soup is a bit spicy"). This "noun/qualifier" split status is quite similar to that observed for *kind* and *sort* above, and may be motivated to some extent by a metaphor linking partitivity ("not the whole thing"-ness) to approximation and then to hedging. For purposes of this paper, only four expressions are considered: the plural *bits*, and the sequence *a bit* along with two comparators, *somewhat* and *vaguely*. Singular *bit* as an independent noun was left out because of its homography with the *bit* that is the past tense of *bite*, and while *rather* would be a natural comparator, its multiple functions rendered it similarly problematic for the limited form of analysis here.

Of course, not every example of "a" followed by "bit" is an instance of the qualifying expression *a bit*; in order to address this issue at least partially, values for *a bit* were determined by taking initial counts for the sequence "a bit" and subtracting counts for "a bit of" in the same text (thus the label "a bit (~of)" in the discussion to follow). This will leave in instances in which *a bit* refers to an indeterminate period of time ("We waited around a bit") and those in which it refers to a fragment but has no *of*-phrase ("I was looking for any aluminum foil that might have been left behind, and noticed a bit in the corner"). The "indeterminate period of time" use might be argued to be a form of hedge as well, and hence still relevant; the second type of case is fully a "false positive"; all of the figures for *a bit* discussed below should be interpreted as potentially including these.

Results of the tabulations are presented in Tables B4a and B4b in Appendix B; Figure 6, below, summarizes the per-corpora WPM counts for Pratchett in relation to the BNC and COCA subcorpora, while Figure 7 presents a summary of the DP-adjusted per-author results. Pratchett does, in fact, appear to use *bits* relatively frequently, both when compared to the BNC and COCA

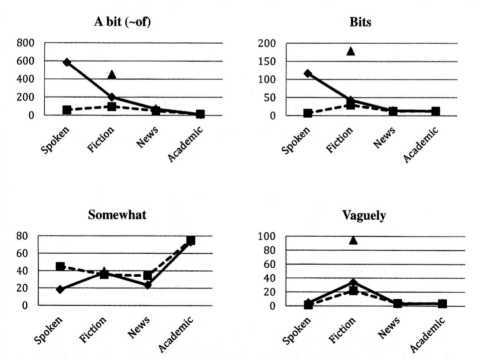

Figure 6: Total freq. (in WPM) for selected bit-expressions and qualifiers for BNC (solid line), COCA (dotted line), and Pratchett (triangle).

A Bit/Somewhat/Vaguely, DP-Adjusted WPM, by Author

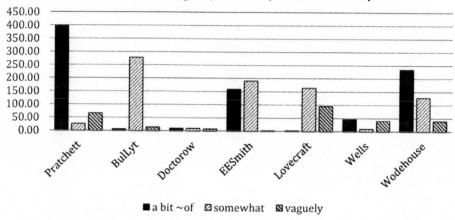

Bits/Pieces, DP-Adjusted WPM, by Author

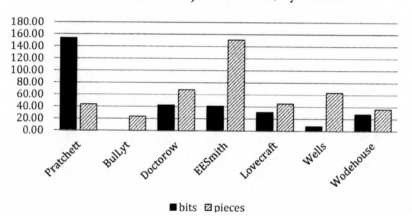

Figure 7: DP-adjusted scores per author for selected qualifying expressions (somewhat / vaguely / a bit) and portion terms (bits / pieces).

subcorpora scores for total WPM and when compared to the usage of other authors in DP-adjusted counts. He also appears to use *a bit (~of)* more frequently as well. Note that in the BNC and COCA, both of these items occur more often in the spoken register than in the others, and that in the spoken register, both occur more often in British than in American English. The situation thus appears analogous to the one with *sort*—there is a national-variety difference in usage that is likely to cause American readers to consider the item more marked than do British readers, who (if the BNC is representative) are positioned to consider *a bit (~of)* and *bits* simply as colloquial or informal.

My inference that *bits* is a comic option was quite likely based on heavy skewing in my reference set—until the cable-only channel explosion in the late 1980s and early 1990s, BBC programs in the U.S. were largely confined to PBS (Public Broadcast Service) stations, which showed BBC comedies very frequently but British dramas much less often (self-selection is likely a factor as well).

While part-of-speech tagging was not feasible in general for the Pratchett texts, it was possible to manually count the number of instances of *bits* with preceding adjectives for comparison with figures from the BNC and COCA; results are shown in Figure 8, below. Pratchett has a higher incidence of pre-modified *bits*, but this appears to be simply a function of his using *bits* more often in general; about 30 percent of his uses are premodified, compared to about 28 percent for spoken British English and (interestingly) 36 percent for American spoken English. Americans do not use the word nearly as often, but when they do, it is premodified at least as often as in British English. The lowest proportion is in British academic register (about 18 percent); perhaps the association with informality renders it more to be avoided.

As with *bits* in general, my association of premodified versions of the word with comedy is probably a result of a skewed reference set, although in this case it may be one shared by many other Americans. *Naughty* appears to be one of the top five adjectives distinctively associated with *bits* in COCA (as measured using mutual information scores, which are based on how much more often those two words occur together than random chance would predict)

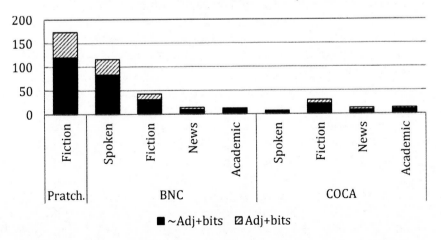

**Premodified and Non-Premodified Bits—
BNC, COCA, and Pratchett Only (WPM)**

Figure 8: Frequency (in WPM) of *bits* with and without premodifiers per corpus.

with the others being *browned, crunchy, stray,* and *leftover*; for the BNC, the top five are *boring, odd, pink, little,* and *various* (although eight of the ten instances of *pink bits* are all from the same source, dialog among a family whose children are confronting food with a pink garnish).

Counting Potentials

Discussion in the previous section focused on items that, in theory at least, the analyst could expect to find across a wide range of texts—*look up,* and *shouted,* and *the kind of* are familiar expressions, and were chosen partly because they are so familiar that one can imagine interestingly patterned use escaping conscious notice. They were also "observable," given a set of assumptions that a large group of ordinary literate language-users could be expected to agree on (there are specific Roman letters there, and there are spaces between some of them, etc.), and except for the sequencing internal to the item, the discussion did not have to make reference to any other facts about positioning within a specific text—what mattered was how many times it was there, not where it was. It is easy to imagine the question "how many times did X occur?" in these cases as providing information that *could* be useful. For uncommon words, basic frequency information may be useful as well because of its potential to let us identify author, or text topic (the latter through the phenomenon of burstiness discussed above). For example, the word *silts* is quite rare in everyday English, not occurring at all in many of the BNC and COCA subcorpora (it is most common in BNC Academic, where it occurs at .52 WPM); but it occurs more than forty times as often in Stephen Erikson's *Malazan* novels, a fact that may have something to do with Erikson's being an archaeologist. Pratchett's *knurd*, with its iconic letter-reversal altering *drunk* to a word for a state of pitched sobriety, likewise may tell us something about Pratchett the wordwright while acting as a marker of texts' association with Discworld.

Sentences and personal names are a different issue, and highlight the need for approaches that address the *potential* for a system to produce a given result—that go beyond past frequency of item occurrence, and allow constrained conjecture about the range of things that might occur, and in what proportions. We do not, by default, expect specific versions of either names or sentences to show up in identical form across a wide range of texts unless they are particularly famous. We expect this uniqueness despite it not holding as often as we might think—there is more use of formulaic sentences than one would expect ("Results are presented in Figure 1." occurs four times in COCA), and personal names are frequently far from unique (Guha and Garg, cited in Iria et.al. p. 480, found that 90,000 names covered a pool of 1,000,000 people). Given two equally rare examples, however, it is not the case that readers will view them as equally memorable. Take, for example, *Edgar Snow*, who appears in the BNC exactly once, the same number of times as *Clyde Kluckhohn*. It does not take any close reading to determine that frequency of occurrence may not accurately predict readers' ideas about which is more memorable in this case. Regardless of observed frequency, Edgar sounds the more *likely*. Likewise, neither "Cherry exports from the Traverse City area decreased last year despite increased consumption" nor "Bjarki deployed the surströmming to great effect against enraged marmots" appear to exist on the internet at the time this is being written, but they are unequally odd. Both are, however, much more likely than "City exports the from decreased year Traverse consumption cherry despite," because whatever patterns any given linguistic theory posits English uses, that sequence does not use enough of them. In addition to "how many times does X occur?" we need some way of addressing questions like "How likely is it that someone would *make* X?" and "How often would Recipe Y get you X?"

Many Discworld names strike readers as highly distinctive—*Mightily Oats, Dangerous Beans, Punctuality Riddle, Hrun*—but if I can venture generalizing from personal experience, they do not sound equally distinctive and they do not sound distinctive in the same ways; they may thus serve as interesting examples to work with. For this discussion, I will use *Mightily Oats* and *Dangerous Beans,* and as comparators *John Smith, Jeremiah Silts,* and the usefully and awkwardly ambiguous *Sleep Orange,* along with the *Edgar Snow* and *Clyde Kluckhohn* we met earlier. As an initial step, one of the simplest approaches to the "How likely is it...?" question is to ignore the possibility of recipes: pretend that there *is* total chance and that a speaker makes multi-unit expressions by randomly picking words out of a bag (this is rather uninventively termed a "bag of words model"; see Goldsmith for a general introduction).

If we adopt a probability scale ranging from 0 ("never") to 1 ("always"), and start with a bag containing tokens with letters on them, the chance of getting the sequence AB can be figured by simply multiplying the chance of getting A by the chance of getting B (assuming there is no chance we will run out of tokens any time soon). For example, if *all* the tokens have either an A or a B and they are in equal proportions, this would make the chance for drawing AB equal to .5 times .5, or .25. We can thus derive one value of likelihood for two-part names by assigning probabilities to their parts—using the BNC Fiction values for those words, for example—and cross-multiplying. The WPM measures, used in the previous section, are not directly pertinent here; the actual proportional probabilities for the words must be used, and the results are usually percentages small enough that converting them back into WPM yields figures that are still hard to read. An alternate measure for the results, one that remains readable for very low probabilities, is *surprisal* (Jaeger), also known as Shannon information; it is the inverse log probability in base 2, and *increases* as a combination becomes less probable. For example *the* is the most common word in English; in COCA, it has a surprisal value of about 4.16, while any word that occurs only once in COCA's 450 million words would have a surprisal value of 28.75. Using the BNC Fiction counts for our set of names and plugging in a value of 1/100,000,000 for words that do not occur at all in BNC-Fiction (e.g., *silts*), produces the following[27]:

Combination	Surprisal (using BNC-F frequencies)
Jeremiah Silts	49.36
Clyde Kluckhohn	38.46
Mightily Oats	36.83
Edgar Snow	30.14
Dangerous Beans	29.73
John Smith	27.78
Sleep Orange	26.96

Table 3: Bag-of-words *predicted* surprisal values for name set.

These values only partially match up with intuition (mine, at any rate). For the non-fictional names, base frequency suggests that *John Smith* will seem less surprising than *Edgar Snow*, who in turn is less surprising than *Clyde Kluckhohn*; so far, so good. Names that we probably already think could be "normal" may seem differentially distinctive based on componential rarity. But Clyde is more surprising than Mightily, and *Dangerous Beans* and *Sleep Orange* both end up being less surprising simply by virtue of their parts being frequent—this does not seem right.

Of course, language is not random—Kilgarriff has argued that it never is—and part of either the reason or the explanation is grammar. The field of linguistics has proven robustly immune from consensus about exactly *which* categories to use and how to talk about their arrangements (the situation is one that invites comparisons with the social dynamics of Pratchett's wizards, minus any actual power whatsoever), but the fact remains that words appear to go in categories, and the categories do not combine by chance; adjective-ish words are far more likely to go before noun-ish ones than after them. Both the BNC and COCA code words for part-of-speech category, and the "Phrases in English" site allows frequency counts for the BNC by part-of-speech code. It is thus possible to calculate the same kind of surprisal values as used for orthographic words above, but this time for category pairs; a sample is given below in Table 4 (the scores are much lower because there are far fewer category-labels than words).

Combination	Surprisal (Using BNC in general via PIE)
Adv + plural common noun (AV0 NN1)	11.60
Adverb + singular common noun (AV0 NN1)	10.87
Verb finite base + adjective (VVB AJ0)	10.44
Verb finite base + singular common noun (VVB NN1)	10.16
Verb finite base + adverb (VVB AV0)	10.00
Adverb + verb finite base (AV0 VVB)	9.30
Proper noun + proper noun (NP0 NP0)	6.44
Adjective + plural common noun (AJ0 NN2)	5.84
Adjective + singular common noun (AJ0 NN1)	4.56

Table 4: Surprisal values for selected part-of-speech bigrams occurring in the BNC (via *Phrases in English*; codes in parentheses are PIE POS tags).

Note that each of the names in our set can be interpreted as one or more of these category combinations. To the degree that we can successfully think of them as proper names, they are all "NP0 NP0" combinations and hence have a categorical surprisal value of 6.44—and if words really did act like variables to which we could seamlessly attach new meanings by spot-patching the social contract, that would be the end of it. But some of those names lend themselves easily to other interpretations, and English-speakers cannot simply block those interpretations by noting the initial capital letters on a sequence. Capitalization is a cue, but it is one among many.

If we start with the assumption that readers' prototypes for personal names involve words that are specialized for *being* personal names (as the experience of most native English-speakers would suggest), then the probability of a two-word sequence being a personal name should be inversely proportional to the degree to which either of the component parts has non-personal-name uses. *Mightily Oats,* for example, does not sound like a pair of personal names; it sounds like an adverb followed by a plural common noun, although enough family names are derived from plural common nouns to render that perhaps less incongruous. Neither *dangerous* nor *beans* occurs in BNC Fiction as a proper noun, although COCA has a couple of examples of a *Mr. Beans.* *Sleep Orange* is particularly ambiguous (it was designed to be), since *sleep* can be used as either a noun or a verb and *orange* can be a noun or adjective, but only the second word occurs more than a few times as a proper noun, and it only rarely (*sleep* is not found as a proper noun in the BNC at all; in COCA, it exists because of text pertaining to the movie *Dark City,* one of whose more disturbing characters is a Mr. Sleep). *Edgar* and *Jeremiah*, on the other hand, rarely appear as anything but proper nouns, *Smith* occurs in non-proper-noun service comparatively rarely (proper-noun use outnumbers common-noun use in the BNC at about an 11:1 ratio, and the verb use does not appear at all), and *John* is likewise far more often a proper noun than a common one (the ratio in BNC Fiction is approximately 460:1). Words such as *Kluckhohn* are quite easily assigned to the proper noun category because of the frequency of non–English-origin names in English (the other option is that it is being used as a foreign borrowing). If we calculate surprisal values for personal-name use by taking percentages representing the proportion of total uses of each term in BNC Fiction that are proper names (again using a dummy value of 1/100,000,000 instead of zero) and cross-multiplying, we get the following:

Sleep Orange	32.83
Dangerous Beans	30.06
Mightily Oats	22.97
Jeremiah Silts	9.97
Edgar Snow	4.36
John Smith	.08
Clyde Kluckhohn	.001

Table 5: Approximate surprisal values for combinations as proper noun + proper noun sequences.

At this point, we are in a position to assign composite scores that attempt to measure the likelihood of drawing tokens that, rather than having sequences of two words or two category labels, have each of the words attached to specific category labels. One of the useful points about logarithms is that adding them together is equivalent to multiplying what they stand for (which is why slide rules and logarithm tables were standard tools before calculators), so figuring out the surprisal value for drawing *dangerous* as a proper noun and *beans* as a proper noun in that order—again, within a dramatically simplified model of language—is a matter of adding together (a) the value for the word combination, (b) the value for the proper-noun + proper-noun combination, and (c) the value representing how unlikely (a) is to match up with (b). For *Dangerous Beans,* this is 29.73 + 6.44 + 30.06, or 66.23. For *dangerous beans* interpreted as an "adjective + plural common noun" sequence, on the other hand, it is 29.73 + 5.84 + 0 (the last being the rounded form of the dummy value .001), or 35.57. *Mightily Oats* as a proper name ends up with a 66.24, very close to *Dangerous Beans,* although what I regard to be its likely interpretation—as an adverb followed by a plural common noun, is at 48.43. The total ranking for these combinations as proper names is presented below in Table 6:

Sleep Orange	69.23
Mightily Oats	66.24
Dangerous Beans	66.23
Jeremiah Silts	55.80
Clyde Kluckhohn	44.90
Edgar Snow	40.94
John Smith	34.30

Table 6: Composite surprisal scores for names.

This kind of ranking is obviously highly artificial and has numerous flaws. We do not draw tokens out of a bag at random when we produce language; when given a two-word sequence in which the first is almost always a proper name, we are probably far more likely to expect the second to be a proper noun (since we commonly operate with two-word personal names in everyday life); and barring favism, for most of us the world is a place in which beans are among life's less dangerous components, placing references to dangerous beans in roughly the same category as those to nominalist porpoises or elegiac accountants. We know far more about our language and what we do with it than this approach represents, which is simply a construal of some frequency information. We know, for example, that many parents actively avoid giving their children names that sound like sentences or noun phrases, making those names that do seem the more surprising. And readers of fantasy and science-fiction know, when reading a novel in these forms, to expect names that are not ordinarily expected—that is part of what "learning the genre" entails. Names like *Hrun* are, in fact, not very surprising at all as a class once the reader places Pratchett's texts in a relation to Robert E. Howard's or August Derleth's; *Margaret Thatcher* in the Discworld very much would be, despite the fact that both Margarets and Thatchers would be initially unremarkable.[28]

But despite its flaws, this is a construal that lets us explicitly describe proposals about *where* some of the unlikeliness of expressions resides, and it does seem to capture some of what is going on, albeit in a way that appears cumbersome when applied to small sets of examples (after all, why not just say "that's a rare word, and it's not usually a name?"). It is, significantly, a kind of construal that can be implemented automatically and applied to vast amounts of text; many of the natural-language processing algorithms that underlie contemporary search engines and data mining techniques involve much more elegant and elaborated versions of similar strategies. It can connect narrow discussions of Pratchett's naming strategies to much wider discussions of how language works, and to what degree an automated construal fails.

Counting Humor (an Inconclusion)

In the sections above, readers have been barraged with a set of technical terms (some insidiously disguised as normal words like "text"), item inventories that treat language examples in somewhat the same way *Going Postal*'s Stanley Howler treats pins and stamps, and some exposition on how to take pieces of common sense ("you don't expect rare words, but you don't expect some of them less in fantasy") and somehow subject them to logarithms. Pratchett readers are likely suspecting that whatever I have put in the bun and tried to sell them, it warrants caution at least proportional to the sales pitch (and arcane terminology and the trappings of math(s)[29] most certainly serve as a sales pitch, even if that is not all they do and even if scholars try not to admit it even to themselves). The discussion has largely avoided trying to position linguistic description in detailed relation to theories of humor. This is in part because humor is yet another enormous area of study in its own right, and other scholars—for Pratchett, specifically, Butler, Scholz, and particularly Haberkorn (in this book)—have dealt with it in much more detail than I can begin to. Also, of course, humor is notoriously resistant to algorithmic approaches.

But Pratchett's humor is relevant to the subject at hand, and regardless of the complexity of questions about *why* we think things are funny, or about what the different varieties of attempts at funniness are, I am probably safe in saying that humor frequently involves incongruity, and that it frequently uses a "setup + punch" structural pattern. The reader (or hearer, or viewer) has to be able to build up a certain confidence in what is going on before it is overturned. Humor can, and frequently does, involve a moment of confusion leading to surprise, but the transition from confusion to surprise does not happen if the confusion is constant. Jokes in languages that we do not understand are never funny, although we might laugh anyway if native speakers do. The incongruity in humor has to be "spread out" to some extent for it to work, and this creates an interesting area of intersection between work on humor and work on information flow, with Pratchett's texts, I think, being a particularly interesting area for further study. All I will be able to do here is sketch out connections between domains that are entire fields of study; the difference between "interdisciplinarity" and "dabbling" will be rather thin. But the potential connections *are* interesting.

Attempts to apply quantitative text-analysis procedures to humor have frequently focused on puns, because they are viewed as *comparatively* easy; i.e., not obviously impossible. The archetypal pun is centered around a single word that can be perceived as having two meanings, or around a pair of words that either sound or look very similar. If meaning is considered as a function of the word's context, and context is interpreted as constituted by or realized as "which other words are around that one," then in principle, part of detecting or generating a pun involves sudden shifts in word co-occurrence. As a dismal, but illustrative example, consider "He didn't wreak havoc in that epic, but he did reek epically." *Wreak* is the standard classroom example of a word that collocates with one particular other word—*havoc*. The *epically* in the second clause is a cue for the context shift even in the absence of spelling, and given sufficient exposure to large amounts of tagged text, a machine-learning algorithm can acquire "expectations" that are sensitive to such shifts in co-occurrence, and similarity between non-identical forms (*wreak/reek*) can be evaluated using Levenshtein distances between the spellings, pronunciations, or both (see Mihalcea and Strapparava; Kao et al.; Mihalcea et al.).

In Prachett, of course, even what seem like simple puns frequently do not fit the archetype; Prachett sometimes waits until the next sentence to confound the reader's interpretation, and the item acting as the "hinge" of the play does not have to be orthographically a single word:

> As they said, you always knew where you stood with Quezovercoatl. It was generally with a lot of people on top of a great stepped pyramid with someone in an elegant feathered headdress chipping an exquisite obsidian knife for your very own personal use [*Eric* 40].

The sequence "[KNOW] where [PRONOUN] [STAND] with X" is formulaic; in Sinclair's terms, it would be a lexical item. Pratchett lets the reader glide through it before suddenly dissolving it with the next sentence, using a sort of syllepsis (or crypto-antanaclasis; either term dresses types of puns in loftier clothing, and makes a better sales pitch). In principle, these types of structures are computationally not too different from the simple puns research like Mihalcea et al.'s or Kao et al.'s has already started working with.

At a more general level, separate from discussions of humor (although Kao et al. is an exception) there is a rapidly growing body of research exploring how a range of linguistic phenomena might be explained by language-users' attempting to manage information flow rate in a "noisy" channel so that it stays within optimal boundaries (see Jaeger, who terms this the "uniform information density" hypothesis, for an overview to 2010) and by the communicative role of ambiguity (see Piantidosi et al.). These are highly relevant to humor because of its reliance on the "confidence/disruption" pattern: humor has to be more like walking along effortlessly and then being tripped up than like carefully picking one's way across broken glass, staring at one's feet every minute.

If those *comprehending* language attempt to keep the incoming information flow rate within an envelope created by processing and channel constraints, readers would, logically, react to higher information density by slowing down—a point which corresponds well to most of our experiences of attempting to read material such as dense philosophical texts or poems by Gerard Manley Hopkins. Douthwaite has noted that "[n]ormality in reading is proceeding at a breakneck speed, making predictions as to what will come next, then sampling the text to verify these forecasts, in a cyclical fashion" (103); high information density means that predictions made at full speed would fail more often (keeping in mind that if the text is doing something the reader already expects, its information density is lower for that reader). For most verbal humor, ambiguity has to be present—for puns, for example, the reader has to *know* the other word—but drawing the reader's attention to specific ambiguities immediately, or placing the reader in a constant state of alert, is counterproductive. If a humorist is to keep her audience at a useful level of incaution, information has to be "spread out" sufficiently; comedy is a confidence game, although comics, unlike public relations flacks or politicians, operate by revealing the scam. Density-*lowering* devices may therefore be of particular interest for humor analysts.

It might be interesting to note, for example, that among the sequences examined in section two, above, the type-noun constructions and the visual-verb constructions are "information-sparse" in certain respects. Given the way human vision works, we know that if someone looks (or glances or peers), the act will involve at least one direction; there is an implied "x-wards," and a preposition can supply direction without having to supply any targeted detail (compare "look up" and "look towards the sky"). Type-noun constructions in which *kind/sort/type* act as heads modified by *of*-phrases manage to warn the reader that some kind of "thing" is about to be mentioned in advance of mentioning it, thus parceling out part of the meaning of the expression early. In addition, *any* multi-word unit, to the extent that it constitutes an "item" that is distributed across a longer span than (on average) many single-word units, can be seen as comparatively less dense than a short (especially monomorphemic) alternate choice. In other words, you know where you stand with them (until you don't). Verbs like *yelled* or *stated*, on the other hand, move more specific information about the utterance into the same word that bears the primary tense; they could be seen as denser. However, they are doing so by incorporating the information into a schema that is already predictable in other ways. We *know* narrative can have tags like this, and the tags usually do not introduce new participants (in Pratchett, the unsettling advent of small-caps frequently lacks the tag). We expect them in a way we do not usually expect other subject + verb pairs, and they prevent us from having to engage in the unnatural speaker-matching task their absence would necessitate.[30] Pratchett's word-play may certainly slow down readers for a moment, but these devices do not.

And this, of course, brings us back to *Ulysses*, and to the Russian Formalists. If we think of "surprise" in terms of the frequency of unexpected items or item-combinations within a given stretch of the text, and consider the kind of "encumbrance" the Formalists celebrated as being a function of a high surprise-frequency in this sense, then most humor will fail to meet their criterion for literariness. It cannot be dense enough and remain humor—except to audiences who are already familiar enough with the material that it is not dense to them (this may be why many post–Structuralist texts that valorize playfulness so seldom appear to achieve it; they wear it like the more dutiful sort of hipster wears a fedora, and performance art rarely manages to rollick). If, however, we consider the amount of surprise *per time unit per reader per act of reading*, we might get a different picture entirely. The surprises are more spread out in humor, but the reader moves towards them faster; to misuse yet another term from physics (and science fiction), they are blue-shifted. This may not, of course, produce the same effect that slow, encumbered reading does; the humor reader (typically) does not feel her grasp of the language, and her understanding of the context, challenged at every instant. But it still does *something*. And if we are talking about Pratchett's novels, it does that something to a great many people. Audiences *voluntarily* read Pratchett. If we view texts through the lens of social praxis, Pratchett has been enormously effective.

Roman Jakobson, with good reason by his definitions, described poetry as "organized violence committed on ordinary language" (Erlich *Russian* 219*n*33); literariness is positioned as revolution, storming the Bastille of automatization (and hence of ideology) to free its prisoners. While the discourse of literary theory appears to have largely abandoned Jakobson's intrinsically binarist approach, and certainly the Formalists' early sharp distinction between literary and non-literary language, some of the framing of the approach endures. "Writerly" texts with high encumbrance are valorized. A reader forced to become acutely aware of constant squance can make it an object of consideration rather than a window that s/he does not know s/he is looking through—while also emphasizing the author's power even if the author denies authority. *Rupture* and *interrogate* are uncommonly common terms in literary theoretic parlance; it's all about the leather, and the theorist is firmly cast in the role that gets the cop hat. Adora Belle would probably add a comment about horseradish.

Pratchett, however, does not seem to be the type to commit organized violence on his language; he is honestly playful with it. If we accept a position advocated by usage-based theories of language—that the process of reading a text alters readers' expectations about language in general—the juxtapositional surprises he distributes across his text may act as a form of noise injection, preventing the reader's model of English, or of genre, from assigning too high a probability to only what has gone before. By decreasing confidence *a bit*, it increases flexibility (see also Haberkorn, in this book). To borrow terms from Sinclair, Pratchett's word-play emphasizes the *Thespian* model of language (in which production and comprehension are seen as actively interpretational and performative) over the *Academician* one, in which language is interpreted via a conduit metaphor and seen as "transmission" of optimally-stable meanings (see also Reddy). Pratchett's dissolution of formulaic sequences lays bare the devices of linguistic convention, but in measured doses.

Does reading Pratchett produce ostranenie? Here, we are firmly in the realm of the subjective. Ask his readership (but define the term first, and expect them to attempt to find the snake behind it,[31] armed with third thoughts and/or a pan and some garlic butter). As for the eight-question Pratchesimil-itude survey that section one carelessly informed the reader that I would get back to, it may be interesting to note that number seven is actually from Pratch-ett, that the cormorant sentence in number three is indeed a transparent ploy to make my discussion of type-noun sequences slightly more relevant, that number two deploys a level of tentativeness arguably somewhat similar to that achieved by hedging, and that pointing out where things aren't is both Pratch-ettic and Structuralist.[32]

Grammars and style guides, as we typically think about them, are a bit like Discworld's gods. As soon as they do something useful, they start garnering belief and can easily end up pretending they created what prompted them ("tiny bundles containing nothing more than a pinch of pure ego and some hunger" [*Turtle* 130] is an excellent description of the archetypal grammar pedant). Pratchett's prose adopts roughly the same stance towards grammars as the witches do toward gods: Regardless of the gods' (constructed) existence, "[there's] no call to go around believing in them; that only encourages them" (*Lords&Ladies* 59). Despite the splendor of the language below them, gram-marians are seldom satisfied. It is embarrassing to know that one's job is to document a creative phrase that only exists because every improbability curve must have its far end; especially when one can peer into other grammars that work seamlessly because their Creators have more mechanical aptitude than imagination (to steal a phrase from *Turtle* 131 and do something untoward with it). Pratchett readers, accustomed to seeing gaps treated joyfully as loop-holes, can Rob Anybody.

NOTES

1. See, for example, Leech (54), "A style X is the sum of linguistic features associated with texts or textual samples defined by some set of contextual parameters, Y."

2. This would, however, be displacing signs from their places, and quite arguably inciting insurrections among things.

3. See Leech (179–207) for a much more nuanced discussion of different models of text and the basis of stylistic analysis, and Fischer-Starcke (34–62) for a comparatively recent overview of a range of linguistic stylistic studies (and the volume as a whole for a good example of modern corpus stylistic analysis). The approach taken here will, in addition to being highly exploratory, differ from these approaches via an internalization move, heavily emphasizing reader variability and what might be called *style-as-experienced* as opposed to *style-as-external-pattern*. Any problems inherent in this—and any misuse of terminology—are entirely my fault.

4. Note that *choice* here is not used with its typical connotations of intention. The sense is that the language presents only certain forms as "within the pale"—I can, for example, use a present-tense verb, or a past-tense verb (usually with an -ed suffix), but English doesn't provide any basis for expecting a proleptic perfect with a -kzarr suffix. Someone can certainly use one (providing whatever "proleptic perfect" means can be devised or at least convincingly prophesied), but it will not *mean* anything from a discourse-community standpoint unless the speaker can manage social interaction so as to "bootstrap" the item into the language.

5. See Halliday and Matthiessen's *Introduction to Functional Grammar* for an overview of SFL, and Mann and Thompson's "Rhetorical structure theory" for an outline of RST.

6. By author fiat, if nothing else.

7. For Russian Formalism in general, see Erlich's overview in "Russian Formalism" and his detailed discussion in *Russian Formalism: History—Doctrine*. For Shklovsky, see the translated collection of essays in *Theory of Prose,* and, for a recent discussion of his positions in relation to Brecht and Tolstoy, see Robinson, who advances an analysis drawing on theories of embodied cognition. For Jakobson's stylistics, see the collected essays in *Language and Literature* and "Closing Statement: Linguistics and Poetics." For a discussion of Mukařovský's typology of deviation, see Leech 61–64.

8. See Erlich's *Russian Formalism* and particularly Robinson for detailed discussions of the development of this concept; as a term, *ostranenie* has been used in a number of different senses, some of which appear synonymous with terms like *estrangement, verfremdung* and *foregrounding* and others not. As with any critical movement, Formalism was not static. Since I will be concerned partly with the degree to which textual features might be perceived as distinctive, I would like to have a term for an upper boundary, something that the reader is fairly sure *happened* even if she does not completely know what it is. I therefore want to use ostranenie (with the warning lack of italics) specifically in the sense Bogdanov discusses it: "In the most common cases of *ostranenie,* the object still remains recognizable but it undergoes a transition on the plane of representation and signification that involves a revelatory participation of the other (reader) who experiences this shift [sdvig] as an instance of being-as-event (in Bakhtin's terms) or as vision (in Shklovsky's terms)" (51–2).

9. See Douthwaite for an in-depth discussion of foregrounding, from a cogni-

tivist/functionalist perspective, within a model of reading and textual interpretation.

10.   "There is no requirement that foregrounding should be consciously noted by the reader" (Leech 61).

11.   E.g., the Karrank%, a species in David Brin's *Startide Rising* whose name, we are conclusively informed by the glossary, "[i]s impossible for humans to pronounce correctly" (606).

12.   Even without readers' other likely experiences with eye dialect, these could be viewed a substitution-based English language-games (like Pig Latin), with the "distance" of each word from what is expected in standard English prose being a function of the number of substitutions necessary to get from one to another, a measure known as Levenshtein distance.

13.   I noted this informally in an entry on *Hogfather* in terms of Pratchett commenting on his own text (199).

14.   Labels vary by linguistic theory, but these are *which*-clauses that are usually set off with a comma in standard written English and that introduce a comment about the previous material; they are relative clause structures conscripted as the grammatical equivalent of parentheses.

15.   Not adumbrate; that creates a recursion problem.

16.   For recent discussions of how long-lasting effects can be, and different factors establishing them, see Ivanova et. al; and Zervakis and Mazuka. As examples of usage-driven models of grammar, see Croft; Tomasello; and Hoey (it may be useful to note that Hoey uses the term *priming* with a different specific sense than it has in psychology). Arguments *against* the centrality of usage have been most strongly articulated by Chomsky, most of whose work in linguistics has addressed the issue; see Berwick, Chomsky, and Piattelli-Palmarini for a recent statement of the position.

17.   There is also a very real possibility that the reader may be suspecting circularity at this point: "it's distinctive because it feels distinctive." I am viewing "distinctive" as a label for a category that presupposes the experience of Robinson's somatic response but is not identical to it. One might, for example, interpret a somatic response as meaning that an item is *wrong*, rather than that it is *distinctive*; centuries of linguistic chauvinism exemplify exactly this.

18.   The term is based on an American dialect expression *squantswise*, "off from the perpendicular," famous among U.S. teachers of undergraduate linguistics courses because of its use in the documentary *American Tongues*.

19.   As distinct from writers who have found after lengthy exposure to Pratchett's prose that it has worn grooves in their heads, even if whatever is flowing through them is not nearly as entertaining.

20.   The position that words, as usually conceived, are not always the basic unit relevant to textual meaning—that sequences of n words are actually the primary "ground level" of linguistic production and comprehension, with single words being simply cases with n being equal to 1—has been strongly argued by John Sinclair. The usage-based theories mentioned above draw in part on this position, and there is an active field of research on the following: the extent to which particular sequences might act as multi-word units (see Arnon and Snyder); of what the consequences of this may be for models of how the lexicon works (or whether it exists—see Elman); how much the frequency of particular sequences affects learning and production (see Ellis).

21. Proportional frequencies, which are expressed with numbers between 0 and 1, are the values actually used to calculate probabilities of co-occurrence, etc., but these typically involve either a large number of zeroes after the decimal place or scientific notion; for presentation purposes, alternate presentations such as WPM are preferable.

22. RStudio was used as the interface; additional packages used were tau (Buchta, Hornik, Feinerer and Meyer), openNLP (Feinerer and Hornik), stringr (Wickham), and Hmisc (Harrell et al.).

23. As of the time of writing, the iBook reader allows searches that produce more than 100 hits, but does not appear to recognize spaces at the ends of search expressions—e.g., "looked up" will also match "looked upon."

24. An additional reason for including the author-based text collections is that BNC and COCA, as they are compiled from very wide-ranging samples (the point, after all, is to be representative), can be expected to demonstrate regression to the mean. The larger the pool of measurements, the more average the average. Single-author collections can provide a few "envelope" points.

25. See Gries for a discussion of this topic, including the DP metric that is discussed below.

26. http://www.linguistics.ucsb.edu/faculty/stgries/research/dispersion/links.html.

27. The choice of .000000001 to represent the probability of all items that do not appear in the BNC is obviously rather arbitrary. It treats *any* possible sequence as equivalent to a hapax legomenon in the BNC, and thus overestimates frequency wildly for those that violate basic conventions of English, e.g., *vrksl%nnnnk*. It should suffice for the present argument, however.

28. "Initially" because Pratchett does not allow one to rest comfortably in one's assumptions about occupation titles; witness the seamstresses.

29. As a speaker of American English, I find one of them hard enough as it is.

30. In spoken language, even if one does not know exactly who is speaking, the speakers rarely have exactly the same voice. Matching lines up to speakers is not something pre-literate societies usually have to do.

31. "The thing about words is that meanings can twist just like a snake, and if you want to find snakes, look for them behind words that have changed their meaning" (*Lords&Ladies* 122).

32. There are thirteen instances of "<personal-name>-shaped NOUN" sequences in Pratchett (far more than in the BNC or COCA), and at least seven of them involve <personal-name>-shaped holes, gaps, or shadows.

Appendix A

Edward Bulwer-Lytton

Alice, or the Mysteries—Book 01
The Caxtons—A Family Picture
The Coming Race

Devereaux—Complete
The Disowned
Earnest Maltravers—Complete

Godolphin, Complete
Harold: The Last of the Saxon Kings—
  Complete
The Haunted and the Haunters
Kenelm Chillingly—Complete
The Lady of Lyons
The Last Days of Pompeii
The Last of the Barons
Leila, or, the Siege of Granada, Book I

Lucile
Lucretia—Complete
The Pilgrims of the Rhine
The Parisians
Rienzi: The Last of the Roman Tribunes
A Strange Story
What Will He Do with It?
Zanoni
Zicci: A Tale—Complete

Cory Doctorow

Down and Out in the Magic Kingdom
Eastern Standard Tribe
Home Again
Little Brother

Makers
A Place so Foreign
Someone Comes to Town, Someone
  Leaves Town

H. P. Lovecraft

"The Affair of Charles Dexter Ward"
"The Alchemist"
At the Mountains of Madness
"Azathoth"
"Beyond the Wall of Sleep"
"The Call of Cthulhu"
"The Color Out of Space"
"Cool Air"
"The Crawling Chaos"
"The Dream Quest of Unknown Kadath"
"Dreams in the Witch House"
"The Dunwich Horror"
"Ex Oblivione"
"Facts Concerning the Late Arthur
  Jermyn"
"The Festival"
"The Haunter of the Dark"
"He"
"Herbert West: Reanimator"
"The Horror of Red Hook"

"The Hound"
"Imprisoned with the Pharaohs"
"The Lurking Fear"
"Medusa's Coil"
"Memory"
"The Music of Erich Zann"
"Pickman's Model"
"The Picture in the House"
"The Rats in the Walls"
"The Shadow Out of Time"
"The Shadow Over Innsmouth"
"The Shunned House"
"The Strange High House in the Mist"
"The Temple"
"The Thing on the Doorstep"
"Through the Gates of the Silver Key"
"The Tomb"
"What the Moon Brings"
"The Whisperer in Darkness"

E. E. Smith

The Galaxy Primes
Masters of Space
The Skylark of Space
Skylark Three

Spacehounds of IPC
Subspace Survivors
Triplanetary
The Vortex Blaster

H. G. Wells

The First Men in the Moon
The Food of the Gods
The Island of Dr. Moreau
The Sleeper Awakes

The Time Machine
War of the Worlds
The World Set Free

P. G. Wodehouse

The Clicking of Cuthbert
The Coming of Bill
A Damsel in Distress
Death at the Excelsior
The Gem Collector
The Gold Bat
The Head of Kay's
The Indiscretion of Archie
The Intrusion of Jimmy
Jill the Reckless
The Little Nuggett
The Little Warrior
Love Among the Chickens
A Man of Means
The Man Upstairs & Other Stories
The Man with Two Left Feet
Mike
Mike & PSmith

My Man Jeeves
Not George Washington
Piccadilly Jim
The Politeness of Princes
The Pothunters
A Prefect's Uncle
The Prince & Betty
PSmith in the City
PSmith, Journalist
Right Ho, Jeeves
Something New
Swoop!
Tales of St. Austin's
Three Men and a Maid
Uneasy Money
The White Feather
William Tell
A Wodehouse Miscellany

Appendix B

B1a: Type-Noun Sequence Frequency (WPM) for the BNC, COCA, and Pratchett

	BNC				COCA				Pratch.
	Spoken	Fiction	News	Acad.	Spoken	Fiction	News	Acad.	Fiction
the kind of	39.60	36.76	28.00	34.19	105.09	47.70	53.99	32.16	107.44
the sort of	102.10	40.94	31.91	17.88	19.77	6.37	10.75	8.38	49.02
the type of	12.10	3.71	8.09	34.69	12.16	4.57	12.44	30.26	4.10
a kind of	31.30	45.35	9.00	27.13	53.17	48.44	1.22	40.42	79.97
a sort of	72.20	35.06	7.55	10.69	20.07	20.26	10.57	11.49	110.96
a type of	2.00	0.76	1.36	6.69	2.17	1.42	3.02	8.42	4.40
some kind of	18.20	35.35	7.00	16.88	51.66	54.67	14.73	10.70	90.70
some sort of	36.50	32.24	10.91	10.75	36.00	27.53	9.59	8.19	59.89
some type of	0.20	0.06	0.09	0.44	6.39	0.96	2.47	4.79	0.00
kinds of	24.70	10.41	8.18	76.69	117.62	27.62	42.37	65.60	34.35
sorts of	75.50	15.18	11.91	22.75	26.07	13.69	10.90	12.42	25.83
types of	24.10	3.00	13.18	127.56	23.22	4.06	24.53	136.64	15.56
that kind of	36.13	17.60	5.83	2.74	74.10	20.49	22.13	5.33	40.21
that sort of	93.74	31.05	12.90	1.89	25.12	9.63	4.02	1.50	117.00
that type of	8.63	0.38	1.24	0.91	8.02	0.72	2.86	1.59	0.30
this kind of	18.97	7.10	8.60	29.61	58.14	11.50	15.29	20.03	7.86
this sort of	45.77	13.51	12.23	14.35	17.69	6.14	3.48	5.07	61.67
this type of	6.02	0.57	5.83	32.42	9.14	1.16	5.27	27.36	0.00

B1b: Type-Noun Sequence Frequency Per Author (DP-Adjusted WPM)

	Pratchett			Wells			Doctorow			Lovecraft		
	WPM	DP	ADJ	WPM	DP	ADJ	WPM	DP	ADJ	WPM	DP	ADJ
the kind of	107.44	0.21	84.88	2.98	0.89	0.33	223.47	0.15	189.95	12.32	0.76	2.96
the sort of	49.02	0.30	34.31	56.70	0.41	33.45	23.66	0.28	17.04	9.85	0.91	0.89
the type of	4.10	0.71	1.19	0.00	1.00	0.00	0.00	1.00	0.00	4.93	0.90	0.49
a kind of	79.97	0.22	62.38	158.16	0.51	77.50	123.57	0.15	105.03	204.47	0.37	128.82
a sort of	110.96	0.22	86.55	316.31	0.34	208.76	5.25	0.60	2.10	140.52	0.31	96.96
a type of	4.40	0.67	1.45	0.00	1.00	0.00	0.00	1.00	0.00	7.39	0.83	1.26
some kind of	90.70	0.19	73.47	2.98	0.84	0.48	189.29	0.18	155.22	24.63	0.67	8.13
some sort of	59.89	0.27	43.72	53.71	0.27	39.21	2.62	0.98	0.05	22.17	0.60	8.87
some type of	0.00	1.00	0.00	0.00	1.00	0.00	0.00	1.00	0.00	0.00	1.00	0.00
kinds of	34.35	0.24	26.11	8.95	0.89	0.98	107.79	0.17	89.47	14.78	0.66	5.03
sorts of	25.83	0.29	18.34	74.60	0.43	42.52	2.62	0.96	0.10	41.88	0.63	15.50
types of	15.56	0.43	8.87	11.94	0.49	6.09	0.00	1.00	0.00	14.78	0.75	3.70
that kind of	40.21	0.28	28.95	2.98	0.84	0.48	49.95	0.21	39.46	2.46	0.94	0.15
that sort of	117.00	0.18	95.94	29.84	0.50	14.92	23.66	0.17	19.64	0.00	1.00	0.00
that type of	0.30	0.97	0.01	0.00	1.00	0.00	0.00	1.00	0.00	0.00	1.00	0.00
this kind of	7.86	0.50	3.93	0.00	1.00	0.00	42.06	0.49	21.45	4.93	0.92	0.39
this sort of	61.67	0.18	50.57	17.90	0.51	8.77	0.00	1.00	0.00	2.46	0.99	0.02
this type of	0.00	1.00	0.00	0.00	1.00	0.00	0.00	1.00	0.00	0.00	1.00	0.00

	Wodehouse			Bulwer-Lytton			EESmith		
	WPM	DP	ADJ	WPM	DP	ADJ	WPM	DP	ADJ
the kind of	10.80	0.60	4.32	6.93	0.57	2.98	33.85	0.23	26.06
the sort of	203.79	0.19	165.07	18.95	0.55	8.53	0.00	1.00	0.00
the type of	10.79	0.62	4.10	6.93	0.42	4.02	8.46	0.67	2.79
a kind of	69.51	0.42	40.32	73.96	0.24	56.21	63.47	0.38	39.35
a sort of	360.35	0.15	306.30	91.06	0.23	70.12	33.85	0.21	26.74
a type of	6.07	0.77	1.40	9.70	0.51	4.75	4.23	0.85	0.63
some kind of	10.12	0.70	3.04	2.77	0.70	0.83	42.31	0.57	18.19
some sort of	43.86	0.35	28.51	2.77	0.72	0.78	0.00	1.00	0.00
some type of	0.00	1.00	0.00	0.46	0.96	0.02	0.00	1.00	0.00
kinds of	8.77	0.72	2.46	9.24	0.50	4.62	63.47	0.27	46.33
sorts of	53.98	0.41	31.85	5.55	0.66	1.89	0.00	1.00	0.00
types of	2.70	0.93	0.19	6.00	0.50	3.00	8.46	0.70	2.54
that kind of	10.80	0.58	4.54	18.03	0.46	9.74	97.32	0.37	61.31
that sort of	211.22	0.31	145.74	26.35	0.53	12.38	8.46	0.67	2.79
that type of	0.67	0.98	0.01	1.39	0.88	0.17	0.00	1.00	0.00
this kind of	9.45	0.69	2.93	3.24	0.67	1.07	38.08	0.43	21.71
this sort of	124.84	0.28	89.88	3.70	0.67	1.22	0.00	1.00	0.00
this type of	0.00	1.00	0.00	0.00	1.00	0.00	0.00	1.00	0.00

B2a: "Noise" and "Speech-Tag" Verb Frequency (WPM) for the BNC, COCA, and Pratchett

	BNC				COCA				Pratch.
	Fiction	Spoken	News	Acad.	Spoken	Fiction	News	Acad.	Fiction
asked	225.82	914.24	274.69	131.36	286.77	790.02	286.03	208.53	217.37
declared	6.72	29.35	64.97	36.59	22.51	22.32	39.08	37.56	14.81
demanded	3.21	84.42	39.94	23.02	9.86	40.00	21.27	19.59	90.09
insisted	4.82	61.28	62.58	10.07	14.23	46.30	30.08	21.05	24.18
stated	12.45	16.03	26.37	95.10	16.13	10.67	20.14	101.97	3.63
sighed	0.20	111.19	1.43	0.33	0.25	82.03	2.13	0.57	251.53
shouted	9.13	121.25	17.10	2.48	3.21	79.22	10.13	2.84	250.02
muttered	0.20	85.74	2.01	0.26	0.16	44.52	1.52	0.27	156.91
yelled	0.20	36.08	2.29	0.13	4.38	46.29	7.65	1.15	57.74
screamed	1.91	45.82	6.97	0.46	3.90	40.84	5.42	0.87	118.21
mumbled	0.00	22.75	1.15	0.13	0.19	17.22	0.70	0.23	79.51

B2b: "Noise" and "Speech-Tag" Verb
Frequency Per Author (DP-Adjusted WPM)

	Pratchett			Bulwer-Lytton			Doctorow			EESmith		
	WPM	DP	Adj	WPM	DP	Adj	WPM	DP	Adj	WPM	DP	Adj
asked	217.37	0.31	149.99	428.50	0.17	355.66	625.72	0.17	519.35	1493.62	0.18	1224.77
declared	14.81	0.34	9.77	85.05	0.23	65.49	13.15	0.27	9.60	275.02	0.32	187.01
demanded	90.09	0.15	76.58	43.45	0.31	29.98	26.29	0.36	16.83	380.81	0.25	285.61
insisted	24.18	0.32	16.44	47.61	0.23	36.66	34.18	0.16	28.71	97.32	0.15	82.72
stated	3.63	0.66	1.23	35.59	0.30	24.91	2.63	0.68	0.84	88.86	0.22	69.31
sighed	251.53	0.12	221.35	116.95	0.18	95.90	78.87	0.18	64.67	16.92	0.47	8.97
shouted	250.02	0.19	202.52	42.53	0.43	24.24	178.78	0.16	150.18	63.47	0.25	47.60
muttered	156.91	0.21	123.96	198.30	0.22	154.67	26.29	0.30	18.40	42.31	0.49	21.58
yelled	57.74	0.35	37.53	3.69	0.77	0.85	26.29	0.43	14.99	135.40	0.15	115.09
screamed	118.21	0.21	93.39	2.31	0.82	0.42	68.36	0.31	47.17	88.86	0.33	59.54
mumbled	79.51	0.24	60.43	2.77	0.76	0.66	34.18	0.39	20.85	0.00	1.00	0.00

	Lovecraft			Wells			Wodehouse		
	WPM	DP	Adj	WPM	DP	Adj	WPM	DP	Adj
asked	150.27	0.40	90.16	558.02	0.15	474.32	830.69	0.13	722.70
declared	51.73	0.60	20.69	32.82	0.49	16.74	24.29	0.43	13.85
demanded	12.32	0.70	3.70	23.88	0.53	11.22	113.37	0.35	73.69
insisted	54.20	0.47	28.73	56.70	0.30	39.69	35.76	0.39	21.81
stated	25.56	0.61	9.97	14.92	0.38	9.25	43.18	0.38	26.77
sighed	0.00	1.00	0.00	17.90	0.33	11.99	95.15	0.29	67.56
shouted	24.63	0.73	6.65	289.46	0.22	225.78	136.31	0.29	96.78
muttered	49.27	0.51	24.14	11.94	0.64	4.30	41.84	0.43	23.85
yelled	4.92	0.96	0.20	38.80	0.31	26.77	24.96	0.5	12.48
screamed	71.44	0.57	30.72	32.82	0.35	21.33	15.52	0.51	7.60
mumbled	24.63	0.74	6.40	11.94	0.64	4.30	15.52	0.67	5.12

B3a: Visual-Verb + P Frequency (WPM) for the BNC, COCA, and Pratchett

		BNC				COCA				Pratch.
		Spoken	Fiction	News	Acad.	Spoken	Fiction	News	Acad.	Fiction
looked	up	5.12	135.33	2.87	0.78	6.11	93.92	4.33	1.45	219.49
	down	1.91	67.76	0.96	0.52	2.39	43.74	2.16	1.13	187.74
	around	1.00	34.63	0.76	0.26	1.89	28.88	1.70	0.59	190.16
peered	up	0.00	1.32	0.00	0.00	0.00	1.11	0.04	0.00	4.53
	down	0.00	3.21	0.00	0.00	0.03	2.38	0.12	0.01	5.14
	around	0.00	1.07	0.00	0.00	0.03	1.08	0.02	0.02	16.33
glanced	up	0.00	16.91	0.00	0.00	0.03	11.33	0.23	0.10	35.26
	down	0.10	8.11	0.00	0.00	0.05	7.15	0.10	0.04	16.02
	around	0.00	5.03	0.00	0.00	0.20	7.74	0.12	0.03	8.16
stared	up	0.10	10.12	0.10	0.00	0.04	4.93	0.10	0.02	17.23
	down	0.00	15.02	0.00	0.00	0.14	7.02	0.36	0.09	18.14
	around	0.00	2.07	0.00	0.00	0.00	0.48	0.00	0.00	8.16

B3b: Visual-Verb + P Frequency Per Author (DP-Adjusted WPM)

		Pratchett			Doctorow			Lovecraft			Wodehouse		
		WPM	DP	ADJ	WPM	DP	ADJ	WPM	DP	ADJ	WPM	DP	ADJ
looked	up	219.49	0.15	186.57	147.27	0.28	106.03	7.39	0.75	1.85	114.72	0.21	90.63
	down	187.74	0.14	161.46	81.50	0.17	67.65	17.24	0.71	5.00	26.32	0.48	13.69
	around	190.16	0.16	159.73	81.50	0.17	67.65	7.39	0.88	0.89	2.02	0.95	0.10
peered	up	4.53	0.73	1.22	2.63	0.92	0.21	0.00	1.00	0.00	0.67	0.98	0.01
	down	5.14	0.65	1.80	5.26	0.47	2.79	0.00	1.00	0.00	0.67	0.97	0.02
	around	16.33	0.43	9.31	2.63	0.79	0.55	0.00	1.00	0.00	0.00	1.00	0.00
glanced	up	35.26	0.27	25.74	0.00	1.00	0.00	0.00	1.00	0.00	4.05	0.82	0.73
	down	16.02	0.35	10.41	2.63	0.77	0.60	0.00	1.00	0.00	4.72	0.82	0.85
	around	8.16	0.48	4.24	2.63	1.00	0.00	0.00	1.00	0.00	0.67	0.99	0.01
stared	up	17.23	0.42	9.99	2.63	0.79	0.55	0.00	1.00	0.00	2.70	0.86	0.38
	down	18.14	0.37	11.43	2.63	0.91	0.24	0.00	1.00	0.00	1.35	0.92	0.11
	around	8.16	0.56	3.59	0.00	1.00	0.00	0.00	1.00	0.00	0.00	1.00	0.00

		Bulwer-Lytton			E. E. Smith			Wells		
		WPM	DP	ADJ	WPM	DP	ADJ	WPM	DP	ADJ
looked	up	73.50	0.15	62.48	16.92	0.29	12.01	122.35	0.17	101.55
	down	19.88	0.30	13.92	21.15	0.49	10.79	65.50	0.26	48.47
	around	7.86	0.47	4.17	16.92	0.65	5.92	5.97	0.73	1.61
peered	up	0.00	1.00	0.00	0.00	1.00	0.00	17.90	0.49	9.13
	down	0.00	1.00	0.00	0.00	1.00	0.00	2.98	0.84	0.48
	around	0.00	1.00	0.00	0.00	1.00	0.00	0.00	1.00	0.00
glanced	up	0.46	0.90	0.05	12.69	0.63	4.70	20.89	0.51	10.24
	down	0.92	0.88	0.11	0.00	1.00	0.00	2.98	0.84	0.48
	around	0.92	0.90	0.09	25.39	0.38	15.74	0.00	1.00	0.00
stared	up	0.00	1.00	0.00	0.00	1.00	0.00	8.95	0.49	4.56
	down	0.46	0.95	0.02	4.23	0.82	0.76	5.97	0.67	1.97
	around	0.46	0.92	0.04	4.23	0.77	0.97	2.98	0.89	0.33

B4a: Bits and Pieces Frequency (WPM) for the BNC, COCA, and Pratchett

	BNC				COCA				Pratch.
	Spoken	Fiction	News	Acad.	Spoken	Fiction	News	Acad.	Fiction
a bit ~of	584.52	200.7	70.7	11.94	59.17	97.92	51.54	15.93	453.8
somewhat	18.17	37.71	23.41	73.12	44.85	35.56	34.37	74.84	39.6
vaguely	4.52	33.82	3.06	3.91	1.4	21.95	3.85	3.58	94.63
bits	116.32	43.06	14.24	12.72	7.17	29.63	12.75	13.22	178.67
pieces	55.8	62.42	41.27	28.7	42.55	69.44	69.9	46.04	55.63
adj+bits	32.82	12.19	4.49	2.35	2.62	7.71	4.15	3.12	53.33

B4b: Bits and Pieces Frequency, Per Author (DP-Adjusted WPM)

	Pratchett			Bulwer-Lytton			Doctorow			EESmith		
	WPM	DP	Adj	WPM	DP	Adj	WPM	DP	Adj	WPM	DP	Adj
a bit ~of	453.80	0.12	399.34	10.63	0.41	6.27	23.66	0.57	10.17	198.87	0.20	159.10
somewhat	39.60	0.34	26.14	330.87	0.16	277.93	13.15	0.27	9.60	221.56	0.14	190.54
vaguely	94.63	0.30	66.24	25.42	0.45	13.98	13.15	0.39	8.02	8.46	0.75	2.12
bits	178.67	0.14	153.66	1.48	0.80	0.30	49.95	0.15	42.46	59.24	0.31	40.88
pieces	55.63	0.22	43.39	36.51	0.35	23.73	99.90	0.32	67.93	173.48	0.13	150.93

	Lovecraft			Wells			Wodehouse		
	WPM	DP	Adj	WPM	DP	Adj	WPM	DP	Adj
a bit ~of	24.63	0.87	3.20	77.59	0.40	46.55	373.85	0.37	235.53
somewhat	221.71	0.26	164.07	17.90	0.45	9.85	170.72	0.25	128.04
vaguely	145.35	0.34	95.93	56.70	0.28	40.82	51.96	0.23	40.01
bits	49.27	0.37	31.04	14.92	0.47	7.91	51.96	0.46	28.06
pieces	76.37	0.41	45.06	80.57	0.21	63.65	53.98	0.33	36.17

WORKS CITED

Altmann, Eduardo G., Janet B. Pierrehumbert, and Adilson E. Motter. "Beyond Word Frequency: Bursts, Lulls, and Scaling in the Temporal Distributions of Words." *PLoS ONE* 4.1 (2009): e7678. 15 July 2013.

Alverez, Louis, and Andrew Kolker. *American Tongues*. Center for New American Media, 1988.

American Psychological Association. *Publication Manual of the American Psychological Association*. 6th ed. Washington, DC: American Psychological Association, 2009.

Anderson, Poul. "Operation Afreet." *The Magazine of Fantasy and Science Fiction*. Sept. 1956.

Arnon, Inbal, and Neal Snyder. "More Than Words: Frequency Effects for Multi-Word Phrases." *Journal of Memory and Language* 62 (2010): 67–82.

Barnwell, Colin. "Dumbledore's Death in the Style of Terry Pratchett." *Guardian* 15 July 2009. Web. 22 May 2013.

Berwick, R. C., N. Chomsky, and M. Piattelli-Palmarini. "Poverty of the Stimulus

Stands: Why Recent Challenges Fail." *Rich Languages from Poor Inputs.* Eds. M. Piattelli-Palmarini and R. C. Berwick. Oxford: Oxford University Press, 2012. 19–42.

Bogdanov, Alexei. "Ostranenie, Kenosis, and Dialogue: the Metaphysics of Formalism According to Shklovsky." *The Slavic and East European Journal* 49.1 (2005): 48–62.

Brems, Lieselotte, and Kristin Davidse. "The Reanalysis and Grammaticalization of Nominal Constructions with Kind/Sort of: Chronology and Paths of Change." *English Studies* 91.2 (2010): 180–202.

Brin, David. *Startide Rising.* 1983. New York: Spectra, 2010.

Burchta, Christian, Kurt Hornick, Ingo Feinerer and David Meyer. "tau: Text Analysis Utilities." *R Package* version 0.0–15. *CRAN Repository.* 2012.

Chiaro, Delia. *The Language of Jokes.* New York: Routledge, 1992.

Cooper, Gordon Burns. *Mysterious Music.* Stanford: Stanford University Press, 1998.

Davies, Mark. *BYU-BNC (Based on the British National Corpus from Oxford University Press).* 2004–. Web. 2012–13.

_____. *The Corpus of Contemporary American English: 450 Million Words, 1990–Present.* 2008–. Web. 2012–13.

De Smedt, Liesbeth, Lieselotte Brems, and Kristin Davidse. "NP-Internal Functions and Extended Uses of the 'Type' Nouns *Kind, Sort,* and *Type*: Towards a Comprehensive, Corpus-Based Description." *Language and Computers* 62.1 (2007): 225–255.

Douthwaite, John. *Towards a Linguistic Theory of Foregrounding.* Alessandria: Edizione dell'Orso, 2000.

Dżereń-Głowacka, Sylwia. "Imagery in Terry Pratchett's Discworld." *Imagery in Language.* Ed. Barbara Lewandowska-Tomaszczyk and Alina Kwiatkowska. Frankfurt am Main, Germany: Peter Lang, 2004. 723–32.

Ellis, Nick C. "Frequency Effects in Language Processing." *Studies in Second Language Acquisition* 24 (2002): 143–188.

Elman, J. L. "On the Meaning of Words and Dinosaur Bones: Lexical Knowledge Without a Lexicon." *Cognitive Science* 33 (2009): 547–582.

Erlich, Victor. "Russian Formalism." *Journal of the History of Ideas* 34.4 (1973): 627–638.

_____. *Russian Formalism: History—Doctrine.* 2d rev. ed. The Hague: Mouton, 1965.

Feinerer, Ingo, and Kurt Hornik. "openNLP: openNLP Interface." *R package* version 0.0–8. *CRAN Repository* 2010. Code.

Fetzer, Anita. "Hedges in context: form and function of *sort of* and *kind of.*" *New Approaches to Hedging.* Ed. Gunther Kattenböck, Wiltrud Mihatsch, and Stefan Schneider. Bingley, UK: Emerald. 49–71.

Fish, Stanley. *Is There a Text in the Class? The Authority of Interpretive Communities.* Cambridge: Harvard University Press, 1980.

_____. "What Is Stylistics and Why Are They Saying Such Terrible Things About It?" *Approaches to Poetics: Selected Papers from the English Institute.* Ed. S. Chatman. New York: Columbia University Press, 1973. 109–52.

Fischer-Starcke, Bettina. *Corpus Linguistics in Literary Analysis: Jane Austen and her Contemporaries.* New York: Continuum, 2010.

Francom, Jend, and Adam Ussishkin. "Converging Methodologies: Assessing Corpus Representativeness Through Psycholinguistic Measures." *American Association of Corpus Linguistics.* Georgia State University. October 2011. Presentation.

Goldsmith, John. "Probability for Linguists." 2008. Web. 15 July 2011.

Gries, Stefan Th. "Dispersions and Adjusted Frequencies in Corpora: Further Explorations." *Corpus Linguistic Applications: Current Studies, New Directions.* Ed. Stefan Th. Gries, Stefanie Wulff, and Mark Davies. Amsterdam: Rodopi, 2010. 197–212.

Halliday, M. A. K., and Christian Matthiessen. *Introduction to Systemic Functional Grammar.* 3d ed. New York: Routledge, 2004.

Harrell, Frank E., Jr., et al. "Hmisc: Harrell Miscellaneous." *R package* version 3.10– 1.1. *CRAN Repository.* 2013.

Hoey, Michael. *Lexical Priming: A New Theory of Words and Language.* New York: Routledge, 2005.

_____. "Lexical Priming and Literary Creativity." *Text, Discourse, and Corpora: Theory and Analysis.* Ed. Michel Hoey, Michaela Mahlberg, Michael Stubbs, and Wolfgang Teubert. New York: Continuum, 2007.

Huddleston, Rodney, and Geoffrey K. Pullum. *The Cambridge Grammar of the English Language.* Cambridge: Cambridge University Press, 2002.

Iria, José, Lei Xia, and Ziqi Zhang. "WIT: Web People Search Disambiguation Using Random Walks." *Proceedings of the 4th International Workshop on Semantic Evaluations (SemEval-2007).* Prague: Association for Computational Linguistics, 2007. 480–83. PDF.

Ivanova, Iva, et al. "The Comprehension of Anomalous Sentences: Evidence from Structural Priming." *Cognition* 122.2 (2012): 193–209.

Jaeger, T. Florian. "Redundancy and Reduction: Speakers Manage Syntactic Information Density." *Cognitive Psychology* 61.1 (2010): 23–62.

Jakobson, Roman. "Closing Statement: Linguistics and Poetics." *Style in Language.* Ed. T. A. Sebeok. Cambridge: MIT Press, 1960. 149–63.

_____. *Language in Literature.* Cambridge: Harvard University Press, 1987.

Kao, Justine T., Roger Levy, and Noah D. Goodman. "The Funny Thing About Incongruity: A Computational Model of Humor in Puns." *Proceedings of the 35th Conference of the Cognitive Science Society.* 2013.

Kilgarriff, Adam. "Language Is Never, Ever, Ever Random." *Corpus Linguistics and Linguistic Theory* 1.2 (2005): 263–275.

Leech, Geoffrey. *Language in Literature: Style and Foregrounding.* New York: Routledge, 2008.

Liberman, Mark. "Presidential Pronouns, One More Time." *Language Log.* 22 May 2011. 25 July 2013.

McCarthy, M., and R. Carter. "*This that and the other*: Multi-Word Clusters in Spoken English as Visible Patterns of Interaction." Ed. M. McCarthy. *Exploration in Corpus Linguistics.* Cambridge: Cambridge University Press, 2006. 7–26.

Mihalcea, Rada, Carlo Strapparava, and Stephen Pulman. "Computational Models for Incongruity Detection in Humour." *Proceedings of the Conference on Computational Linguistics and Intelligent Text Processing.* Iasi, Romania. 2010.

Mukařovský, Jan. *Structure, Sign, and Function.* New Haven: Yale University Press, 1977.

Mann, William C., and Sandra A. Thompson. "Rhetorical Structure Theory: Toward a Functional Theory of Text Organization." *Text* 8.3 (1988): 243–281.

Neumann, Robert. "Statistics." *L-Space.* 2012–13.

Piantadosi, Steven T., Harry Tily, and Edward Gibson. "The Communicative Function of Ambiguity in Language." *Cognition* 122.3 (2012): 280–291.

Pratchett, Terry. ~~Faust~~ *Eric*. 1990. New York: HarperCollins, 2007.

_____. *Interesting Times*. 1994. New York: HarperCollins, 2007.

_____. *Lords and Ladies*. 1992. New York: HarperCollins, 2007.

Reddy, Michael J. "The Conduit Metaphor: A Case of Frame Conflict in our Language About Language." *Metaphor and Thought* 2 (1979): 164–201.

Robinson, Douglas. *Estrangement and the Somatics of Literature: Tolstoy, Shklovsky, Brecht*. Baltimore: Johns Hopkins University Press, 2008.

Rossbacher, Peter. "Šklovskij's Concept of *ostranenie* and Aristotle's *admiratio*." *MLN* 92.5 (1977): 1038–1043.

Scholz, T. "The Making of a Hilarious Undead: Bisociation in the Novels of Terry Pratchett." *Fastitocalon: Studies in Fantasticism Ancient to Modern* 1.2 (2010): 141–152.

Shannon, C. E. "A Mathematical Theory of Communication." *The Bell System Technical Journal* 27 (1948): 379–423.

Shklovsky, Viktor. *Theory of Prose*. Trans. Benjamin Sher. Elmwood Park, IL: Dalkey Archive, 1990.

Sinclair, John. *Trust the Text*. New York: Routledge, 2004.

Snyder, William. "An Experimental Investigation of Syntactic Satiation Effects." *Linguistic Inquiry* 31.3 (2000): 575–582.

Sprouse, John. "Revisiting Satiation: Evidence for an Equalization Response Strategy." *Linguistic Inquiry* 40.2 (2009): 329–341.

Spruiell, William. "*Hogfather*." *Beacham's Encyclopedia of Popular Fiction*. Vol. 13. Ed. Kirk H. Beetz. New York: Gale, 2001. 197–201.

Tagg, Caroline. "A Corpus Linguistics Study of SMS Text Messaging." Diss. University of Birmingham, 2009. 27 July 2013.

Tomasello, Michael. *Constructing a Language*. Cambridge: Harvard University Press, 2003.

Venour, Chris, Graeme Ritchie and Chris Mellish. "Dimensions of Incongruity in Register Humour." *The Pragmatics of Humour Across Discourse Domains*. Ed. Marta Dynel. Amsterdam: John Benjamins, 2011. 125–146.

Wickham R. "stringr: make it easier to work with strings." *R package* version 0.6.2. *CRAN Repository*. 2012.

Zervakis, Jennifer, and Reiko Mazuka. "Effect of Repeated Evaluation and Repeated Exposure on Acceptability Ratings of Sentences." *Journal of Psycholinguistic Research*. N. pag. 23 Nov. 2012.

Debugging the Mind
The Rhetoric of Humor and the Poetics of Fantasy
GIDEON HABERKORN

The human brain is a device for making the world meaningful. It is the hardware on which our mind, the software, endlessly weaves patterns of meaning by creating connections and relationships. Fantasy can foreground the tools we use to make meaning. Humor can help us notice and correct mistakes our mind makes in its meaning-making. The space opened up by the interplay between humor and fantasy is one in which readers can probe their mental patterns for mistakes and try out new ones. This interplay is present in Terry Pratchett's Discworld novels, which are both funny, and fantasy: Thus, the rhetoric of humor and the poetics of fantasy are central aspects of the Discworld novels.

The course this essay will take begins with a few notes about minds making meaning, leads to a discussion of the humor of the Discworld novels, progresses to their position in the fantasy tradition, and ends with a look at the interplay between the two aspects. Let me emphasize that this essay does not, and cannot, aim to achieve a definite and final statement, since books can be, and have been, written on all theoretical areas touched upon—cognition, humor, fantasy—and since the Discworld series itself has long become extensive enough to warrant several books and articles of analysis. This article is the product of much research, but more importantly, it will, hopefully, provoke much research. With that in mind, let us begin.

Cognition, and the Making of Meaning

The mind makes meaning—it takes the straw of sensual perception and spins it into the gold of a meaningful pattern, by creating connections and relationships (cf. Baumeister 16). Things *mean* by being part of a pattern, and it is this pattern of connections and relations that Geertz refers to when he describes man as "an animal suspended in webs of significance he himself has spun" (5; see also Baumeister 16–17).[1] Since the crucial relationships, such as causal connections, cannot be observed, they have to be inferred. That is why the webs within which man is suspended are effectively self-made rather than found—and this is a problem.

The problem lies in the fact that, as a rule, we are very good at weaving webs: Paul Valéry maintained that "[t]here is no discourse so obscure, no tale so odd or remark so incoherent that it cannot be given a meaning" (qtd. W. Martin 86)—and Culler suggests that

> [i]f a computer were programmed to produce random sequences of English sentences we could make sense of the texts it produced by imagining a variety of functions and contexts. If all else failed, we could read a sequence of words with no apparent order as signifying absurdity or chaos and then, by giving it an allegorical relation to the world, take it as a statement about the incoherence and absurdity of our own languages [161].

Yet if everything is connected, connections become meaningless. If the urge to make patterns is irrepressible, inevitable, we need other processes which help ensure as much internal coherence as possible, make sure the pattern is still adequate to the reality it structures—and if necessary, weed out the mistakes. That is part of what philosophy, critical thinking, and the empirical sciences do. As a rule, though, we do not much like criticizing our ideas. We like to regard them as natural, permanent and without alternative: Baumeister notes that symbolic systems tend to overestimate the stability of the phenomena of which they make sense, i.e., "[t]he idea is unchanging, but the reality changes" (Baumeister 66)—and Midgley notes that "we assume that the ideas we are using are the only ideas that have ever been possible," and go on to do so, "[u]ntil they explode" (6). In this context, the question of whether the work of a widely read author offers a chance to practice making meaning and troubleshooting that meaning is an important one.

A Rhetoric of Humor, or Why Did the Goat Cross the Bridge?

Terry Pratchett often writes things that are funny. Fantasy writer Michael Moorcock calls the Discworld novels "broad comedy" and "excellent farce"—

"one of the few specifically comic series in epic fantasy (if that's what it is)" (119). Fantasy scholar Brian Attebery calls them "endlessly inventive, self-reflexive"—parody which has taken on "a life beyond that of its ostensible target" ("Foreword" 310). John Clute, editor of the *Encyclopedia of Fantasy*, has written repeatedly and very eloquently about the way in which Pratchett's Discworld is home, for the most part, to comedy but not to comic novels—it is "a Garden of Repose" precisely because its creator does not "shiver it to growth, which is another Death" (*Evidence* 168). For the intents and purposes of this essay, all such distinctions can be put aside. It is sufficient that Pratchett uses language in a way readers tend to find funny.

There have been many theories of what exactly, as Martin puts it, "are the mental processes involved in 'getting a joke' or perceiving something as funny" (*Psychology* 31). Serious overviews of humor theory reach back as far as Plato and Aristotle,[2] and the most prominent explanations are based on *superiority*, *relief* or *incongruity*—humor is a context in which we can feel superior to the butt of the joke, can release suppressed feelings and thoughts, or can stumble across cracks in our mental landscape. Although "most researchers agree that humor can often be used to express aggression" (Martin 55), the superiority theory, favored by Plato and Hobbes, has a problem: As Morreall notes, there are many instances in which we feel superior, but are not likely to be amused (9). Superiority and aggression are apparently neither necessary nor sufficient for perceiving something as funny. While the relief theory offers a neat explanation for the "predominance of aggressive and sexual themes in most (if not all) jokes" (Martin 43), it has its roots, via supporters like Spencer and Freud, in "an outdated hydraulic theory of the mind" (Morreall 23). Philosophers like Kant, Kierkegaard and Schopenhauer have supported variations of the incongruity theory—an approach vulnerable to the criticism that "only young children are irrational enough to enjoy incongruity by itself," while "rational adults should, or even can, face it only one way, by trying to eliminate it" (Morreall 15). This criticism contains the seeds of a promising alternative—one which preserves aspects of theories focused on superiority and incongruity, but is grounded in cognitive linguistics.

Before we get to this theory, I will just quickly note that I am aware that there are other theories of humor; indeed, there are other theoretical discussions of humor in Pratchett's writing. Most notably, a discussion of Pratchett's work in the context of Pirandello, Bergson, Freud, Lacan and Bakhtin has been undertaken by Andrew M. Butler. In some cases, these authorities in their field have produced humor theories long discredited; in some, they deal with humor as a mood or mode or social phenomenon, rather than addressing the question of *how* something is funny. In some cases, one might be forgiven for suspecting that, instead of explaining humor, the aim is simply to prop up an existing theoretical framework. In any case, it is neither useful nor necessary to retrace Butler's steps here. All that is necessary is a rhetorical theory of humor, an argument for humor as a kind of mental spellchecker, and evidence for the claim that it is an important aspect to Pratchett's Discworld novels.

If a psychological theory of humor needs to explain "the mental processes involved in 'getting a joke' or perceiving something as funny," a rhetorical theory of humor needs to explain how to provoke such processes. Rhetoric is the art and science of speaking well—*ars et scientia bene dicendi*—"well" in the sense of "effectively," and most often, the effects rhetorical theorists are interested in are things like *persuasion* and *defense*. However, language can be used to achieve quite a few other effects. A rhetoric of humor deals with the question of how the tools of language can be used to make something funny. The desired effect is what John Morreall calls *a playful cognitive shift*—a rapid move from a *set-up*, which embodies a "background pattern of thoughts and attitudes," to a *punch*, which "causes our thoughts and attitudes to change quickly" (50). Such patterns can be thought of as *schemas, frames* or *scripts*. It is possible to think of set-ups as activating one script and punches as activating another, incongruous with the first (R. Martin 86–87). One of the most prominent current theories in the humor research community is the *Semantic-Script Theory of Humor* (SSTH), or rather its revised incarnation, the *General Theory of Verbal Humor* (GTVH), which offers a complex set of tools and concepts for the analysis of jokes and, by extension, longer humorous narratives (Attardo 108, 121). To apply it in all its complexity is not necessary to support my thesis, and would indeed be beyond the scope of this argument, but briefly: A joke expresses in *language* (L) a *narrative* (NS) which puts a *target* (T) in a *situation* (SI) evoking at least two distinct and *opposed scripts* (SO)—and it contains a *logical mechanism* (LM) with which this opposition can be playfully explained and resolved (Attardo 108). We will have to leave it to future research to attempt a more detailed survey of Pratchett's most common Ts and LMs. For now, it is sufficient to note that humor can be seen as a playful process of noting that there is more than one way of looking at something, and then resolving the opposition. In humor, it is fun to change your script, if not your mind. At that point, those who follow the shift and discover the mistake get a chance to feel superior, if only to their own erring, pre-shift selves. The shift or reinterpretation usually moves from "higher" to "lower"—"towards what is less desirable, such as failure, mistakes, ignorance, and vice" (Morreall 51). A rhetoric of humor deals with ways in which we can create that moment of discovery and shift—and make it enjoyable.

This is vital: There is research that indicates we are happy if we can fit our experience into a pattern, and unhappy if we cannot (Csikszentmihalyi 36, 39), and Baumeister even describes human beings as addicted to meaning (358). We also hate to find inconsistencies in our views or actions, which may lead to *cognitive dissonance*, resulting in tension and the urge to find the easiest way to resolve it (Cooper 6–9). Since we like to see ourselves as intelligent, we do not like the thought of making mistakes—and thus cognitive dissonance means we have a hard time admitting being wrong (96). Humor not only provides a context in which we can probe our meaningful patterns for flaws, it provides a context in which finding and correcting such flaws can be enjoyable.

A Pun, on Any Other Name...

Armed with this basic theoretical framework, onwards to Discworld. One aspect of Pratchett's humor fairly frequently remarked upon is wordplay, specifically funny names and puns. To begin with, there is Lord Havelock Vetinari, ruler of the city state of Ankh-Morpork. His last name sounds vaguely suitable for a Renaissance Italian nobleman, which fits the context, but it also is a near homophone of *veterinary physician*, or *veterinarian*. His first name is a real name, but also alludes to his habit of collecting information by various secret means—it is, after all, a near homophone of *have a look*. Another such name is Magrat Garlick. While Magrat sounds near enough to Margaret to be a simple corruption, the witch herself notes unhappily that it "sounded like something that lived in a hole in a river bank and was always getting flooded out" (*Abroad* 31). Sure enough, we find Magrat, muck rat, muskrat—*ondatra zibethicus*, a semi-aquatic rodent living in wetlands.

Places on the Disc often get similarly humorous names, such as Djelibeybi and Hersheba, suitably Middle-Eastern sounding desert locations, both of which are near enough in sound to the sweets *Jelly Baby* and *Hershey bar*. Rhetorically, what is interesting about these and other funny names in Pratchett's writing is that the two scripts are activated by the same one or two words, based on identical or similar sound. These sounds can make sense in two contexts: They usually sound more or less fitting and reasonable as names, but they appear in a context related to the alternative meaning. As in the cases of Havelock and Magrat, the better examples allude to an alternative meaning which also fits the context—like Qu, one of the history monks featured in *Thief of Time* and *Night Watch*, who provides various gadgets and devices: His name sounds suitably oriental, while also sounding enough like the Q who performs a similar job for James Bond. At the heart of these names is the pun.

One way in which Pratchett adds complexity to his puns is the inclusion of additional languages: Here, readers will only understand the pun if they know the necessary language(s), and often some more or less obscure facts. For example, the Director of Music at the Ankh-Morpork Opera House in *Maskerade* is called Mr. Salzella. This sounds suitable enough, but you need to know Italian, have some knowledge of the history of table paraphernalia, and remember some music history—or the plot of *Amadeus*—to understand why his name sounds so much like s*alt cellar*—after all, the Italian for the *salt cellar*, the precursor of the salt shaker, is *Saliera*.

The Discworld country of Überwald contains mountains and dark coniferous forests, peopled by werewolves and vampires, which makes sense to any reader who knows both German and Latin: *Überwald* translates as *over* or *across (the) wood*, which, via Latin, gets you to *Transylvania*. A particularly nice group of names occurs in *The Truth*, where the dwarfs who own and operate Ankh-Morpork's first printing press using movable type are called Boddony, Caslong and Gunilla Goodmountain. The first two are the names of typefaces, while Goodmountain sounds like a fairly standard Discworld dwarf name, until you translate it into German and get *Gutberg*, which is near enough to Johannes Gutenberg, who invented printing with movable type. One of the most complex examples concerns the heads of two feuding noble families: Lord Albert Selachii and Lord Charles Venturi. The *venturi effect* is a principle utilized in jet engines, while *Selachii* refers to the biological classification of sharks. Two warring families associated with *jets* and *sharks* should lead you, via the gang names from *West Side Story*, to the Shakespeare play the musical is based on: *Romeo and Juliet*, with its two households, both alike in dignity. After such mental gymnastics, we do not need to discuss at length why the nation of Klatch is famous for its coffee.[3]

For each of these cases, two different patterns are activated in the mind of the reader. More complex humor creates the *assumption/mistake/correction* sequence not in the minds of the audience but rather in other minds, which the audience can witness in the act—more complex because readers have to infer what is going on in the minds of fictional characters for the humor to work. Pratchett offers such puns as well:

> Sergeant Colon went back to his desk, surreptitiously opened his drawer and pulled out the book he was reading. It was called *Animal Husbandry*. He'd been a bit worried about the title—you heard stories about strange folk in the country—but it turned out to be nothing more than a book about how cattle and pigs and sheep should breed [*Feet* 29].

The pun at the core of this joke is based on the true meaning of animal husbandry—the breeding and raising of livestock—and Sergeant Colon's misinterpretation, which connects it to bestiality. It is complicated by the fact that the mistaken interpretation is only vaguely hinted at—"strange folk in the country"—so that the reader needs to fill in the blanks.

Another way to complicate puns is to slip them into dialogue, as illustrated in this snippet from a conversation between Death and one of his customers:

> "I wish to make a complaint. I pay my taxes, after all."
> I AM DEATH, NOT TAXES. I TURN UP ONLY ONCE.
> The shade of Mr Hopkinson began to fade. "It's simply that I've always tried to plan ahead in a sensible way..."
> I FIND THE BEST APPROACH IS TO TAKE LIFE AS IT COMES [*Feet* 27].

While the connection of death and taxes is a straightforward allusion, the taking of life as it comes is a pun, which has one meaning as a piece of advice for mortals, and quite another when applied to Death.

Pratchett's use of puns and wordplay links him to two British traditions, which are embedded in a general fondness for puns notable in a lot of British humor. The first specific tradition is that of the *Carry On* films, made mostly from the late 1950s to the 1970s, which Porter describes as a "frantic mix of farce, parody and double entendres" (61). The films' frequent use of "puns both in dialogue and character and location names" can be compared to Pratchett's style, although Pratchett is usually less bawdy (61). The second tradition is that of the cryptic crossword, where "such a range of food is said to be satisfactory" leads readers to connect *food* to *fare* and *fare* to *fair*, which is another word for *satisfactory*, or "headgear on communist evokes intense dislike" prompts them to connect *hat* (headgear) to *red* (communist) to get *hatred*, which is an *intense dislike* (Manley 38, 50). Against that background, the move from *Salzella* to *Salieri* seems almost straightforward.

Low, Linked and Like: Understatement, Footnote and Simile

It is practically common knowledge that English humor is especially fond of irony and understatement. To understand what that means, it is useful to look at Jerome K. Jerome's *Three Men in a Boat*, and almost anything by P. G. Wodehouse. Both work with what Muecke calls *impersonal irony*: They create a "rational, casual, matter-of-fact, modest, unemotional" narrator, who affects a tone of "dryness or gravity of manner" (52). But there is more to their humor than that. When Wodehouse writes, "In life it is not aunts that matter but the courage which one brings to them" (11) or, "She wrinkles her nose at me as if

I were a drain that had got out of order" (157), then there are at least two steps involved: First, there is an exaggeration—aunts are included among the serious trials life has in store, and people are linked to blocked drains with all that can entail. Second, the exaggerated image is put in understated language—instead of aunts described in harsh words as catastrophes, the drama is only hinted at in the notion that one needs courage to deal with them. Instead of reading distressing descriptions of raw sewage bubbling up from god knows where, readers are simply given a "drain that had got out of order." Things are taken one step further in two of the better-known episodes from Jerome's novel: After a detailed description of the destruction caused by the narrator's uncle Podger trying to hang a picture, the man finally leans over too far and falls off his chair and onto the piano, "a really fine musical effect being produced by the suddenness with which his head and body struck all the notes at the same time" (20). And then his wife comments, "that she would not allow the children to stand around and hear such language" (21). A man's incompetent attempts to hang a picture are extended to near epic proportions, then described with impersonal irony. The inevitable crash is turned into a musical interlude, and the final explosion of cursing is left out completely, only commented on by an earwitness. Similarly, when the eponymous three men want to open a tin of pine-apples, they fail miserably—and dramatically—until finally, one of them holds the tin, another holds a sharp stone, and the third brings down the boat's mast on the whole affair.

> It was George's straw hat that saved his life that day. He keeps that hat now (what is left of it), and, of a winter's evening, when the pipes are lit and the boys are telling stretchers about the dangers they have passed through, George brings it down and shows it round, and the stirring tale is told anew, with fresh exaggerations every time.
> Harris got off with merely a flesh wound [100–101].

Again, the event climactic to an exaggerated series is left out completely, and only hinted at mysteriously with the mention of stirring tales, hats and flesh wounds.

All of these devices can be found in Pratchett's Discworld novels. Here is an example from *The Truth*:

> "What happened to Mr Dibbler?"
> The dwarf put his head on one side. "The skinny man with the sausages?" he said.
> "That's right. Was he hurt?"
> "I don't think so," said the dwarf carefully. "He sold young Thunderaxe a sausage in a bun, I do know that."
> William thought about this. Ankh-Morpork had many traps for the unwary newcomer. "Well, then, is Mr Thunderaxe all right?" he said.

"Probably. He shouted under the door just now that he was feeling a lot better but would stay where he was for the time being," said the dwarf [23–24].

First, CMOT Dibbler's famous sausages in a bun are described as traps for unwary newcomers, and shown to be a reason to worry about a man's health. However, what these fiendish foods might do to the unwary is then mercifully only described in terms of its vague results. Similarly, *Lords and Ladies* features a delay involving a troll, who ill-advisedly refers to Unseen University's librarian, who happens to be a orang-utan, as a *monkey*, when he obviously is an *ape*. "Several minutes later, the travellers leaned on the parapet, looking down reflectively at the river far below" (194). In both cases, humor is created through a pattern of *expectation* (first script), *discovered mistake* (opposition) and *reinterpretation* (second script). A sausage and the rather common confusion of apes and monkeys should be trivial things, but they turn out to be dramatic. Yet these dramatic events are described without the expected emotion, and when we expect dramatic results, we get not even an understated description—we get a metonymic description of an event through its effects (and those, again, rather understated).

Feet of Clay contains a further example of this, which also illustrates Pratchett's use of a device not usually associated with narrative fiction—the footnote. A golem, who finds himself with money, but no need for it, gives it to a beggar. Ordinarily, readers have every right to expect that to be the end of it, the beggar being only on the fringes of the narrative and of no consequence to its further course. He is surely a trivial character. Yet, as soon as he is made "richer by a whole thirty dollars," he is annotated: "He subsequently got dead-drunk and was shanghaied aboard a merchantman bound for strange and foreign parts, where he met lots of young ladies who didn't wear many clothes. He eventually died from stepping on a tiger. A good deed goes around the world" (12). The note ends in a statement that refers to a saying, but also to the literal fact that the man has gone around the world as a result of a good deed—it's a play on words. The description of the "young ladies" who do not "wear many clothes" is clearly an understatement, and the description of the man's death is again metonymic, substituting the cause for the effect—the act of stepping on the tiger was not what killed him, it was what presumably followed. Finally, Pratchett uses the footnote, which in non-fiction is often used to expand on tangential topics, to give a trivial character a whole adventure worthy of its own novel.[4]

In a final example we can see two more cases of glossing, one case of a footnote containing a comment or aside, a further pun, and more funny names:

"Right you are, Captain Carrot!" said the dwarf baker. "C'mon, lads! Let's hang 'em up by the *bura'zak-ka*!"

"Ooo," murmured the weak of heart, damply.

"Now, now, Mr Ironcrust," said Carrot patiently. "We don't practise that punishment in Ankh-Morpork."

"They bashed Bjorn Tightbritches senseless! *And* they kicked Olaf Stronginthearm in the *bad'dhakz!* We'll cut their–"

"Mr Ironcrust!" [*Feet* 47].

Now, even without the footnotes, there is humor here. Pratchett's dwarf names often contain metals or connections to mining, but a baker called Ironcrust has additional meaning. (We will skip discussing Tightbritches and Carrot.) If you read through it too quickly, you almost miss the metonymic "damply"— Pratchett has a tendency to have people wet themselves in moments of fear or panic, although he never mentions it directly. The passage gets three footnotes. *Bura'zak-ka*, which readers might assume to be a part of the human anatomy, possibly a tender one, turns out to mean "town hall." This completely changes the meaning of the surrounding sentence, because "by" does no longer refer to the part the rope will be attached to, but rather specifies the location. Captain Carrot's note on Ankh-Morpork legal custom is annotated "Because Ankh-Morpork doesn't have a town hall," changing what sounded like the moral high ground into simple pragmatism. Finally, *bad'dhakz*, which readers might again have associated with tender elements of the anatomy, turns out to mean "yeast bowl"—thus, again, forcing us to reassess our reading of the context, specifically the meaning of "in."

Another aspect which links Pratchett's writing with that of Wodehouse is the use of figurative language, specifically the use of metaphor and simile. Wodehouse writes of people moving "slowly off with bowed heads, like a couple of pallbearers who have forgotten their coffin and had to go back for it" (163), and describes somebody as "looking like a bereaved tapeworm" (169). Pratchett describes geography as "physics slowed down and with a few trees stuck on it" (*Feet* 12), Nobby Nobbs as having "a certain resemblance to a chimpanzee who never got invited to tea parties" (*Guards* 54), and summer as "a moving creature" which "likes to go south for the winter" (*Feet* 12). Getting an education, to add a final example, is described in *Hogfather* as "a bit like a communicable sexual disease," in that "[i]t made you unsuitable for a lot of jobs and then you had the urge to pass it on" (40). If one thing is described by a comparison with something else, we expect a certain degree of similarity. The first moment of readjustment is caused, therefore, by the outlandish point of reference. A second is quite often caused by the realization that the comparison makes sense nevertheless. One of the most brilliant examples comes from *Moving Pictures*:

Over Holy Wood, the stars were out. They were huge balls of hydrogen heated to millions of degrees, so hot they could not even burn. Many of them would swell enormously before they died, and then shrink to tiny, resentful dwarfs remembered only by sentimental astronomers. In the meantime, they glowed because of metamorphoses beyond the reach of alchemists, and turned mere boring elements into pure light [121].

If stars are mentioned in the context of the Discworld's version of Hollywood, we expect the equation of people with celestial objects along the usual lines—above us, bright and beautiful, etc. Instead, Pratchett provides a fairly literal description of physical properties of real stars—and in the process, actually offers a far less glamorous but probably far more realistic image of celebrities.

Just Asking

Apart from the impersonal irony described above, at least one more of Muecke's types of irony can be found in Pratchett's writing: self-disparaging irony, in which a character puts on the mask of an "ignorant, credulous, earnest, or over-enthusiastic person" (56). The two most famous practitioners of this type of irony are possibly Socrates and Columbo. In the Discworld novels, this ironic stance is often taken in conversations with people who feel very sure that they are in possession of the one true interpretation of the world—only to find themselves faced with innocent questions they have no good answers for. An example from *Hogfather* takes place in Unseen University's Great Hall, where Archchancellor Ridcully and the Senior Wrangler discuss the mistletoe hanging from the ceiling. Ridcully opens with, "we never invited any *women* to the Hogswatchnight Feast, did we?"—Hogswatch being the Discworld equivalent of Christmas. It turns out that, of course, women would spoil everything, and have therefore never been invited. Ridcully then wonders, what purpose the mistletoe could possibly serve—which leads to a discussion of symbolism:

> "Well, er ... it's ... well, it's ... it's symbolic, Archchancellor."
> "Ah?"
> The Senior Wrangler felt that something more was expected. [...]
> "Of ... the leaves, d'y'see ... they're symbolic of ... of green, d'y'see, whereas the berries, in fact, yes, the berries symbolize ... symbolize white. Yes. White and green. Very ... symbolic."
> [....]
> "What of?"
> The Senior Wrangler coughed.
> "I'm not sure there *has* to *be* an *of*," he said.

"Ah? So," said the Archchancellor, thoughtfully, "It could be said that the white and green symbolize a small parasitic plant?"
"Yes, indeed," said the Senior Wrangler.
"So mistletoe, in fact, symbolizes mistletoe?" [182–183].

By patiently and perceptively asking harmless questions from the point of view of one who merely wants to understand, Ridcully gets the Senior Wrangler to admit that the mistletoe hanging in the Great Hall is in fact a thing of no practical use, which may be symbolic, but not of anything in particular. It is, in fact, a rather pointless tradition. The whole scene takes place in a novel about the point of Hogswatch stories and traditions, and therefore makes an important point in a humorous way. The same device is used on a different topic in *The Last Hero*, when Lord Vetinari asks,

"What exactly has Cohen the Barbarian done that is *heroic*?" he said. [....]
"Well ... you know ... heroic deeds ... [....] Fighting monsters, defeating tyrants, stealing rare treasures, rescuing maidens ... that sort of thing," said Mr Betteridge vaguely. "You know ... heroic things."
"And who, precisely, defines the monstrousness of the monsters and the tyranny of the tyrants?" said Lord Vetinari, his voice suddenly like a scalpel—not vicious like a sword, but probing its edge into vulnerable places.
Mr Betteridge shifted uneasily. "Well ... the hero, I suppose."
"Ah. And the theft of these rare items ... I think the word that interests me here is the term 'theft,' an activity frowned on by most of the world's major religions, is it not? The feeling stealing over me is that *all* these terms are defined by the hero. You could say: I am a hero, so when I kill you that makes you, *de facto*, the kind of person suitable to be killed by a hero. You could say that a hero, in short, is someone who indulges every whim that, within the rule of law, would have him behind bars or swiftly dancing what I believe is known as the hemp fandango. The words we might use are: murder, pillage, theft and rape. Have I understood the situation?" [20].

Again, careful questioning leads to the rather important point that the difference between a hero and a villain may have much more to do with perspective than we care to admit. In both cases, the questioning of the ironic persona forces a discovery of flaws in a certain thought pattern. The characters in question *may* see the flaws and learn. The readers who are made to laugh—via the *assumption/mistake/correction* sequence—by definition see the flaws and may well correct them in their own mental landscape.

Pratchett's rhetoric of humor first of all creates a playful atmosphere—the puns and the plays on words have a central role in this. The use of understatement, humorous footnotes and comparisons—as well as several types of irony—creates a safe environment in which to practice questioning our mental patterns and assumptions. If the mind is usually busy cheerfully spinning the straw of sensual perception into the gold of a meaningful pattern, Pratchett's humor gets it to happily check the end result for knots and flaws. Since such questioning can become a habit, it is not crucial whether these examples of humor deal with important mental constructions or not. A mind that has learned how much fun can be had questioning its own assumptions will not be stopped that easily. Whether you want to pigeonhole them as broad comedy, farce, parody, or even comic novels—humor is a central aspect of the Discworld books, and their use of humor helps make them a training ground for joyfully debugging the mind.

Fantasy, a Modern Tradition

I have mentioned John Clute's essay about Discworld, comedy and the comic novel. His argument may not have been central to my discussion of humor, but it is keenly relevant to my discussion of fantasy, because he argues that Pratchett keeps his novels in the realm of comedy rather than comic novels by preventing change. Discworld characters are resigned to an untransformable world, writes Clute—and "in this sense" he argues "they are not native creatures of fantasy" ("Coming of Age" 26). Clute's point here is that it is the "true secret of Discworld ... that it has remained free ... of the dangerous pieties of transformative healing"—and thus free of fantasy (30). However, the next step in my argument will be that, based on my understanding of fantasy, the Discworld novels are not free of fantasy at all, but are in fact steeped in it. Fantasy is a central element of their makeup.

Modern fantasy as a distinct literary field is a surprisingly young phenomenon, younger than for instance *detective fiction*, and it crystallized in the middle of the late 20th century. What does it mean that modern fantasy crystallized at that point? The rules of genre, just like natural laws, are predictions or expectations based on experience: If you drop a stone, it will fall to the ground. If you read a mystery, it will feature a crime, a victim, a detective, an investigation, a culprit, and a resolution. Human beings tend to understand categories, such as genres, "through a very concrete logic of typicality," taking "a robin or a sparrow to be more central" to the category *birds* "than an ostrich" (Frow 54); this is known as the prototype effect. As a result it seems that, "[r]ather than having clear boundaries, essential components, and shared and uniform properties, classes defined by prototypes have a common core and then fade into fuzziness at the edges" (Frow 54).[5] In this view, we would expect literary genres to aggregate around a core text, or a collection of such texts.

Thus, any definition of fantasy as a genre ought to presuppose something of a tradition. The beginning of such a tradition, its wellspring, should supply the prototypical core texts around which to cluster the genre. Any future text is part of the tradition if it relates in one of three ways to relevant aspects of the core texts: It can *repeat* what has gone before, it can *amplify* what has gone before, or it can *repudiate* what has gone before. Amplification, which expands on its precedents, can be seen as an evolutionary method of change, while repudiation, which opposes or contradicts its precedents, can be seen as a revolutionary one (cf. Carroll 63, 67–69).

When I say that modern fantasy as a distinct literary field crystallized in the late middle of the twentieth century, I am referring to a moment when two separate traditions came together. The two unwitting founding fathers were J. R. R. Tolkien and Robert E. Howard (cf. Schweitzer, "Conan" 977, and "Heroic" 379), and Pesch thus pinpoints the birth of modern fantasy to the unauthorized publication of Tolkien's *The Lord of the Rings* in the United States by Ace in 1965, and the publication of the paperback edition of Howard's *Conan* stories in 1966 (36–37).[6]

On Howard's side, fantasy is a child of *pulp fiction* with its cursory characterization and formulaic plots (cf. Pesch 36; Attebery, "Magazine Era" 34). It "emphasizes physical conflict between heroes and supernatural creatures like gods and goddesses, demons, witches, or wizards" and is hence most commonly labelled *sword and sorcery* (Gramlich 779). In *science fiction*, the pulp plots "were often thinly disguised westerns, mysteries or lost-world romances" (Attebery, "Magazine Era" 34), and in *fantasy*, it is not difficult to see the barbarian hero in the tradition of either the lone western hero or the hardboiled detective: The heroes of sword and sorcery are "bigger than life, violent and wield swords or axes," and are usually far less moral and altruistic than the term hero implies (Gramlich 779–780; cf. also Clute, "Howard" 481). They may face "monsters or survivors of elder races," but they seldom encounter elves, dwarfs, or fairies (Gramlich 779). "The setting is generally a recognizable version of Earth where magic works, either in the distant past or future" (780). This tradition shares with classical science fiction a *sense of wonder*. Nicholls and Robu argue for this concept as a feature that distinguishes *science fiction* from all other forms of fiction, "including most fantasy," and describe it as "a sudden opening of a closed door in the reader's mind"—a moment in which readers "can glimpse for themselves ... a scheme of things where mankind is seen in a new perspective" (1084). Sawyer agrees that this sense of wonder, "the thrill of being forced into new ways of seeing things," is "[o]ne of the core effects of science fiction," but he is far less adamant when it comes to its exclusivity (707). In science fiction, wonder can be triggered through "vastness of scale," or a level of alien complexity which "causes readers to reflect upon their own positions as inhabitants of a universe stranger than they imagined"—but also, in more naïve readers, through "technological effects" and "big dumb objects" (707).[7] In general, wonder is a profound shift of perspective which makes new insights available to the reader. It can be provoked by any "description of the indescribable," any "charting of places no one has ever been," any "encounter with aliens" (708). It has the power to make readers conscious of their world, to transform acceptance into amazement, and to make the mundane appear spectacular (cf. Senior 117–118). As such, a sense of wonder is definitely an aspect of modern fantasy.

The second tradition which spawned modern fantasy is the one which culminated, in the first half of the twentieth century, in Tolkien's *Lord of the Rings*, and which Schweitzer refers to as the "literary stream" ("Heroic" 379). This stream "grew out of and has been greatly influenced by fairy tales, the body of narratives derived from the oral folktales of magic" (Eilers 319). It can be argued that the main reason fantasy does not simply form a continuous tradition with most if not all fiction that went before is simply the profound shift in the horizon of expectation effected, at least in Europe and Anglo-America, by the rise of the novel (see Eilers 335; Clute, "Taproot" 921).[8] Clute emphasizes the changes the realist novel brought to readerly expectations, while Eilers insists that fantasy "originated when writers began applying the techniques of literary realism in stories in which the extranatural played a fundamental role" (335). Thus, the literary stream brings to fantasy a fusion of conventional realism with the subject matter of non-realistic fiction. Its writers "manifested a modern emphasis on the individual by developing original plots, particular characters, and particular settings," and employed "a largely descriptive, referential prose instead of the refined, condensed style that had been traditionally employed" (335). In essence, the tradition of literary fantasy carries at its heart the depiction of extranatural events in a way which creates an "illusion of reality" (318). Clute suggests that texts on which modern fantasy clearly draws but which were written before this shift be labelled taproot texts ("Taproot" 921).[9] Through its taproot texts, the literary tradition of fantasy links back to a largely oral tradition of storytelling.

The modern fantasy tradition is largely a body of narratives featuring *existents* (i.e., characters and settings) and *events* (i.e., actions and happenings) which are to a large extent not consistent with what we see as reality. These are inherited from traditions which worked with a different understanding of reality. The narratives will usually feature physical conflict, and heroes more or less deserving of the label. They will link both to the formulas of pulp and the rich traditions of myth and legend, and will in some way provoke wonder—i.e., a profound shift of perspective. Yet they will present these events and existents using techniques of realism established by the tradition of the modern novel. Modern fantasy in this sense could not begin to congeal as a genre before the conventions of literary realism had fully developed. The modern fantasy novel is, if you will, a counterfactual realistic novel.

Some Boundary Issues

I will digress for a moment and mention two theoretical concepts from which the modern fantasy tradition needs to be distinguished. The first is the *fantastic*, the second is *magical realism*.

The concept of the fantastic is inextricably linked to Todorov's work on the subject, which is still widely regarded as the central text (see Durst 12–13, Horstkotte 14, 17). In essence, the Todorovian *fantastic* is not so much a genre as a state of indecision between two genres: it is the dividing line between the *uncanny* and the *marvelous*—a critical and a magical reading (see *Fantastic* 27). "In a world which is indeed our world, the one we know," i.e., the world of the enlightened western industrial nations, "there occurs an event which cannot be explained by the laws of this same familiar world" (25). Either this event is not real within the fictional world, "and laws of the world then remain what they are," or the event is indeed real within the fictional world, "but then this reality is controlled by laws unknown to us" (25). The fantastic evaporates as soon as the reader decides to read certain events and existents as either real or imaginary within the world of a work, thereby reading the work as either uncanny or marvelous. The fantastic exists only in the moment of uncertainty, of hesitation (25, 31–33, 41). It should be obvious why the Todorovian fantastic is of little use in working with modern fantasy fiction. Even in so-called "urban fantasy"—narratives set in a world resembling ours very closely, but containing elements of magic—it is made perfectly clear to the reader that the counterfactual or non-mimetic events or characters depicted are in fact intended to be as real as their mimetic, factual context. This is even more so when the whole setting is counterfactual: Discworld really is a disc resting on the backs of four giant elephants—Berilia, Tubul, Great T'Phon, and Jerakeen—who in turn stand on the back of an even more gigantic turtle, Great A'Tuin. Not everybody may believe it—the Omnians hold the absurd belief that the world is in fact round—but readers are left in no doubt that it is fact.

While the lexical similarity between *fantasy* and *the fantastic* has caused many a scholar to attempt to connect, relate, and compare the two, there is no conceptual similarity to warrant this. As Italo Calvino pointed out at the time of its publication, the subject of Todorov's study is not what it may sound like, since the French term *fantastique* refers mainly to horror stories "which involve a somewhat nineteenth-century relationship with the reader" (71).[10] In Italian, he notes, "the words *fantasia* and *fantastico*" imply "the acceptance of a different logic based on objects and connections other than those of every-day life or the dominant literary conventions" (72)—and of course Tolkien makes a similar point regarding *fantasy* and *fantastic* when he links them to the notions of both imagination and unreality, and thus to "images of things that are not only 'not actually present,' but which are indeed not to be found in our primary world at all, or are generally believed not to be found there" (69). Unfortunately, then, a perfectly useful concept, which can be applied with great benefit to discussions of horror and the Gothic, has come to be associated with a genre to which it adds nothing and to which it was never intended to add anything—bear in mind that a Todorovian literature of the fantastic would have to exclude works like *The Lord of the Rings*—simply through an intercultural translation problem.

In fact, the notion that this is a world where different things are real than in the reality we all agree to live in is emphasized as well as turned on its head for comic effect in *The Colour of Magic* and *The Light Fantastic*, when Two-flower—a boring accountant looking for romance (*Colour* 27–28)—meets Rincewind the failed wizard. If you like to see fantasy literature as escapist, you could regard Twoflower as a caricature of a fantasy reader. In this, as in so many other things, he is balanced by Rincewind, a sort of inverted romantic: He lives in a world that works by magic and longs for a rational world of science. He feels there must be a "better way of doing things.... Something with a bit of sense in it" (*Colour* 53). When he tells Twoflower: "I just think the world ought to be more sort of organized[,]" the tourist replies: "That's just fantasy" (*Colour* 80). Even while our notions of reality and fantasy are turned on their heads, it is made very clear to the reader that there is no room for the ambiguity of the fantastic.

This also separates the modern fantasy tradition from *magical realism*. There is a tendency, it is true, to use that label for those select works of modern fantasy which a critic might want to distance from what he or she perceives to be literature of lesser quality.[11] Such a rather unqualified usage seems to equate magic realism with respectable literature of a vaguely fantastic nature. Indeed, its "increasingly ubiquitous use for any text that has a fabulous or mythic dimension" has opened it up to the accusation "that it has become a catch-all for any narrative device that does not adhere to Western realist conventions" (Ashcroft, Griffith, Tiffin 133). Briefly, magic realism, or magical realism, has come to mean "all narrative fiction that includes magical happenings in a realist matter-of-fact narrative" (Bowers 2), making the supernatural ordinary and everyday, "admitted, accepted, and integrated into the rationality and materiality of literary realism" (Zamora and Faris qtd. Bowers 2). It "combines realism and the fantastic in such a way that magical elements grow organically out of the reality portrayed" (Faris qtd. Horstkotte 41). Like modern fantasy, magic realism uses the tools of realism to depict magic as mundane. It does so, however, simply because it depicts a different social reality (cf. Bowers 1, 25).[12] Magic realism suggests that the world is different from the way it is commonly believed to be. Modern fantasy makes no such claim. It presents a world patently unlike the world we agree to live in, and it acknowledges this. There is a tension between the accepted social world and the outrageous claims of fantasy. Just as realism explicitly excludes unacceptable magical thinking, so fantasy explicitly excludes the usual mundane explanations for its magic. Magic realism does not create such tension, simply because it does not accept consensus reality (cf. Easterbrook 491–492). Returning to Rincewind's yearning for a rational world of science, it is perfectly clear that the wizard has no chance of realizing this dream—just as none of us can ever ride a dragon or unfurl a set of giant wings and soar into the warm air of a summer evening.

Magic realism is inherently political. Because it works from a different consensus reality, magical realism is useful to writers writing against totalitarian governments as "a means to attack the definitions and assumptions which support such systems (e.g., colonialism) by attacking the stability of the definitions upon which these systems rely" (Bowers 4). It becomes possible to subvert modern western consensus reality by presenting a different reality in the same terms, i.e., using the tools of realism (cf. Bowers 22; Horstkotte 39–40).[13] It offers a different vision, a different point of view. Essentially, magic realism is an alternative realism, based on an alternative concept of reality.

Fantasy is also political—but quite differently so. Attebery suggests that such politics manifests in three strategies, namely the deliberate violation of the norms of Western consensus reality, the deliberate anachronism of locating the work in a time other than the here and now, and "the borrowing of motifs and story structures from folk tradition" ("Politics" 10). If I understand his text correctly, he equates the impossible of fantasy with the consensus reality of non–Western cultures, a notion that seems to entail the view that there is such a thing as a singular non–Western reality. I would rather argue that modern fantasy accepts the social reality it exists in, while at the same time contrasting it with a world that violates accepted rules of reality. Because no single part of it is to be taken metaphorically, the whole work can be likened to a metaphor. The truth of a metaphor emerges from the tension between two irreconcilable concepts, and the truth—and with it the politics—of fantasy emerges from a similar tension.

Thus, unlike the fantastic, modern fantasy is openly and decidedly counterfactual—its narratives deal with things that cannot be; yet these narratives present these things that cannot be, using various tools usually employed to ensure things seem very real. Unlike magical realism, modern fantasy does not make statements about the nature of reality because it is concerned with real politics—it makes statements about the nature of reality because it is concerned with the politics of the real.

I have elsewhere presented an argument about how Pratchett fits into the twin traditions of fantasy, and how he builds on and reinvents the figure of the traditional fantasy hero (Haberkorn, "Cultural Palimpsests"). Coming at it from a different direction, Verena Reinhardt and I have also discussed the Discworld in the context of magical education in various fantasy worlds, again locating Pratchett's work within that tradition (Reinhardt and Haberkorn). I will here take yet another approach, and locate Pratchett within the politics of fantasy, which allows writers to foreground the tools we use to make sense of the world, and allows readers to practice using them. Fantasy has this potential largely because of its counterfactual or non-mimetic realism.

The Poetics of Non-Mimetic Realism

Poetics is the theory of literary form. It explores not so much *what* a text is about as *how* it is about what it is about. It deals with literariness, with style, form, genre, as well as structural elements like grammar and syntax; tropes and figures; assonance and echo. A poetics of fantasy needs to concern itself with the question: What makes a text a fantasy text? What does a fantasy text do? And how does it do that?

Let us begin with the realistic representation of counterfactual events and existents. In this context, it is worth remembering Avram Davidson's point that, "although the wombat is real and the dragon is not, nobody knows what a wombat looks like and everyone knows what a dragon looks like" (207). And the Discworld equivalent occurs when, in *Hogfather*, the Auditors pay the Guild of Assassins to assassinate the Hogfather, Discworld's equivalent of Santa Claus. When Lord Downey, head of the Guild, observes that "[t]here are many who would say this ... person does not exist" the Auditor replies: "He must exist. How else could you so readily recognize his picture?" (26). Since fantasy texts cannot create verisimilitude through accuracy, they must compensate through adequacy—i.e., the deficit in historical plausibility is compensated through narrative plausibility.

I need not argue here that novels set upon the back of a giant turtle and peopled with dwarfs and trolls and whatnot are non-mimetic, counterfactual.

Even if we frequently recognize familiar thoughts and mindsets, even if the dialogue often appears familiar, the Discworld novels are very clearly not set in our consensus reality. But how are such narratives made plausible?

Right from its early days, the novel achieved realism through its "its sober, secular, hard-headed, investigative spirit" (Eagleton 7). A novel appears realistic if it conforms to the way we, the readers, tend to see the world: Loofbourow suggests that a realistic novel is "a kind of fiction that results when the artist and his audience share the same assumptions" (257; cf. also Culler 164). As discussed in Morris, Barthes claims that "the very gratuitousness of apparently insignificant detail in a realist story" serves as what he terms the *reality effect*—it makes fiction seem real (101). Making sense of reality entails sorting through endless detail, determining what matters and what does not. The more reality-like a work is in its challenge to our meaning-making faculties, the more filtering a reader has to do, the more realistic it will seem.[14] Culler, finally, lists several further ways in which a novel creates realism, among them what he calls "the natural attitude to the artificial" (164)—that is, the text explicitly draws attention to literary conventions and claims not to follow them—but of course "the forms that such claims take are also literary conventions" (173; cf. Martin, *Theories* 69). I think it is easily apparent, but perhaps difficult to prove with isolated snippets, that Pratchett writes in a naturalistic, realistic manner about the unnatural things he describes. I will nevertheless try it with a short excerpt from *Reaper Man*:

> Death stood at the window of his dark study, looking out onto his garden. Nothing moved in that still domain. Dark lilies bloomed by the trout pool, where little plaster skeleton gnomes fished. There were distant mountains.
>
> It was his own world. It appeared on no map.
>
> But now, somehow, it lacked something.
>
> Death selected a scythe from the rack in the huge hall. He strode past the huge clock without hands and went outside. He stalked through the black orchard, where Albert was busy about the beehives, and on until he climbed a small mound on the edge of the garden. Beyond, to the mountains, was unformed land—it would bear weight, it had an existence of sorts, but there had never been any reason to define it further.
>
> Until now, anyway [*Reaper* 285].

I would contend that this passage is soberly described. It actually has, despite being set in such a fantastical location, a certain almost mundane feel to it—as indeed it should from the perspective of the characters involved. It contains gratuitous detail: The skeleton gnomes are there for a joke, but the lilies and the trout pool, even the bees, are there not because they are relevant. They are irrelevant. Albert could be doing anything, and Pratchett could be mentioning any other details to suggest that there is in fact an infinite grab-bag of details waiting to be grabbed because this is a real place, which he is not inventing but merely describing. The passage also implies assumptions we all share, among them that you cannot look through walls but have to use windows; that you cannot appear elsewhere but have to walk the distance; that if death is in fact personified as Death, he has to be some place; that if you work from home you are likely to have a study; and so on and so forth.

What the passage does not really do is draw attention to literary conventions and then claim not to follow them. Yet if we turn to *The Wee Free Men*, we find the protagonist Tiffany Aching investigating the case of a witch. When the Baron's son disappears, people decide that it was the fault of the lonely old woman living all by herself in her cottage, because she must obviously be a witch. So they burn her cottage and her books, kill her cat, and she is reduced to begging from door to door. She dies that winter. When Tiffany goes to inspect the ruins of her house, she wonders how an old woman with no teeth and a tiny oven could possibly have cooked and eaten a strong young boy (*Free* 45–47).

> And all the stories had, somewhere, the witch. The *wicked old witch*.
> And Tiffany had thought: Where's the *evidence*?
> The stories never said *why* she was wicked. It was enough to be an old woman, enough to be all alone, enough to look strange because you had no teeth. It was enough to be *called* a witch [*Free* 37].

In passages like this, Pratchett clearly draws attention to the way things are supposed to happen in stories and makes the implicit argument that they do not happen like this here, because this is after all not a story. This is real.

This is a statement about the politics of the real. The old woman becomes a witch because people's minds have created a pattern in which she is clearly labelled as one. She becomes a witch because enough people call her one. Figments of people's imagination have a very real, very negative effect on this woman's life.

Attebery maintains that fantasy's political claims are "that reality is a social contract, easily voided; that the individual character is a conditional thing, subject to unnerving transformations into trees and axolotls and cockroaches and disembodied discourses" ("Politics" 23). Finally, fantasy can "let the Other become a self," at which point "the past threatens to break into the present, colonies become capitals, and the natural world takes its revenge on civilization" (23). I would go further and claim that modern fantasy—a specialized version of the literary game in which players agree to treat things as real which they in fact believe to be empirically impossible—creates fictional worlds which depart from the consensus reality of the social world, but which are nevertheless depicted using the tools and conventions of realism, and that it thereby potentially foregrounds the narrative techniques and the fictionality of narratives. That means that it can be a commentary on the narrative construction of the human world, and readers can use it to practice dealing with their narrative worlds and their narrative selves. Modern fantasy fiction can not only thematize the fictionality of consensus reality, but the tools and techniques used to manufacture such realities. Such are the politics of fantasy. As Attebery poetically claims, "the untruth shall make you free" ("Politics" 25).

Fantasy as Theoretical Fiction

Tiffany Aching is clearly in a story about stories—such fiction is commonly called *metafiction*; Currie calls it *theoretical fiction*. Pratchett's characters frequently find themselves at least in scenes and moments which are clearly about stories, and about the fact that the human mind cannot help making them up. There is a moment in *Hogfather*, for example, when Archchancellor Ridcully declares that "man is naturally a mythopoeic creature," and when the Senior Wrangler asks what that means, the Dean responds, without looking up, that it "[m]eans we make things up as we go along" (245–246). This is clearly a comment on the human tendency to construct meaning-making patterns.

Tiffany questions the pattern of a traditional fairy tale story. In the excerpt quoted earlier, Lord Vetinari deconstructs the hero. In *Hogfather*, Susan Sto-Helit, Death's grand-daughter, takes the approach a step further when she tells the story of Jack and the Beanstalk:

> and then Jack chopped down the beanstalk, adding murder and ecological vandalism to the theft, enticement and trespass charges already mentioned, but he got away with it and lived happily ever after without so much as a guilty twinge about what he had done. Which proves that you can be excused just about anything if you're a hero, because no one asks inconvenient questions [40].

And she does not only subvert stories by retelling them. In her job as a governess, she physically intervenes: When the little girl Twyla tells her she is afraid of the monster in the cellar, Susan gets a poker and follows her downstairs (*Hogfather* 15–16). Susan is fighting stories the previous governess has put into the heads of Twyla and her brother—but not in the way other adults think: "Little gel gets it into her head there's a monster in the cellar, you go in with the poker and make a few bashing noises while the child listens, and then everything's all right" (17). In fact, after Susan enters the cellar, "[t]here was a short period of silence and then a terrifying scream" (17–18). When Susan finally comes back upstairs, "[t]he poker was bent at right angles. There was nervous applause" (18). Later, when the other adults have gone, "Susan went back into the cellar and emerged towing something large and hairy with eight legs" (18). The final confrontation of that novel reveals that Susan has not just taught the children that monsters can be defeated: she has taught them what makes a monster. When an insane murderer called Teatime threatens to kill Death, the children have no problem identifying Death as normal and Teatime as "creepy"—so when Susan throws her poker, it passes right through Death and impales the man (429–431).

In *Witches Abroad*, Granny Weatherwax fights her sister Lily, who manipulates people through stories, and treats others "like they was characters, like they was things" (270). Throughout the book, Granny subverts traditional fairy tales, and the fact that story structure is alien to her is illustrated, amusingly, by the fact that she cannot tell a joke—although she keeps trying (176, 205, 227).

On Discworld, stories are real. When the human mind processes the world, gives it a pattern, that pattern is real. The law of cliché is a law of nature, as we can observe if we open *Soul Music* and witness a crashing vehicle: "Satchelmouth shut his eyes and held on tight until the last scream and crackle and splinter had died away. When he opened them, it was just in time to see a burning wheel bounce down the canyon" (278). Compare this with a similar event in *Night Watch*: "Vimes counted under his breath, and had only reached two when a cartwheel rolled out of the smoke and away down the road. This always happens" (293). Of course, once such patterns have become observable laws, characters are bound to recognize and understand them, and they begin using them for their own ends. When the City Watch want to kill a dragon by shooting an arrow at its vulnerable spot, they consider their chances highly unlikely—but they know that "[w]hen you really need them the most ... million-to-one chances always crop up. Well known fact" (*Guards* 262). The problem then becomes whether it really is a million-to-one chance. The situation, it turns out, has to be finely tuned: "No-one ever said 'It's a 999,943-to-one chance but it just might work'" (266). And so, the City Watch begin to adjust the odds, that is, make success ever more unlikely, until they are truly faced with a million-to-one chance—which cannot fail (267, 271–272). All of these examples are ways of saying that the patterns human minds spin can become a kind of reality. Believing things can make them true. Not, I hasten to add, in a factual sense; belief cannot move physical mountains. In that sense, Discworld is counterfactual. But if all of us believe that the mountain is the home of our gods, then to all intents and purposes, within our community, it will be. If all of us believe that an old woman is a witch, then to all intents and purposes, within our community, she will be.

Pratchett goes beyond that, however. If we recognize and understand these patterns, if we understand that they are merely creations of our minds, then we can use them, we can reinterpret them, we can change them. This is where Pratchett's Discworld novels clearly become theoretical fiction, i.e., self-reflexive fiction, fiction about fiction (Currie 52). Waugh defines the more usual term for this kind of fiction, *metafiction*, as works that "create a fiction and ... make a statement about the creation of that fiction" (6). Not all works of modern fantasy realize this potential, of course, in fact the majority probably do not, at least not fully. Not all of Pratchett's Discworld novels realize this potential either. Nevertheless, they often "contemplate the logic and the ideology of narrative in the act of construing the world" (68).[15] Such works can be read as commentaries on narrative worldmaking, and thus can be used by readers to better understand the way in which their worlds and their selves are narrative constructions.

Debugging the Mind

Terry Pratchett's Discworld novels are funny, and they are fantasy. Using the poetics of the modern fantasy tradition, Pratchett creates a space in which he can foreground our mind's act of spinning sensory perception into meaningful pattern. Employing the rhetoric of humor, he encourages his readers to practice questioning such mental patterns. By combining the two, the Discworld novels are at least potentially a space in which readers can probe their mental patterns for mistakes and try out new ones.

Discworld is not just about recognizing stories and conventions, using them, playing with them. It is about resisting them. In *Feet of Clay*, Pratchett introduces golems to Discworld. Traditionally, a golem is "a man made out of clay (replicating God's creation of Adam) brought to life through words of power ... written on paper and inserted into the golem's mouth" (Ashley 421). In *Feet of Clay*, however, the words are stuck inside the creature's forehead: Golems are people who are enslaved by words in their heads. It is widely believed they cannot exist without those words, but then one golem survives their removal—as it puts it: "Words in the heart can not be taken" (374–5). When someone comments that this is the first golem which has got no words written by a priest in its head, Captain Carrot observes: "He'll make up his own words" (*Clay* 381). When Vetinari probes our unquestioning acceptance of the means a hero uses, when Susan helps the children overcome the nightmarish stories of their previous governess, even when Ridcully gently questions the traditions of Hogswatchnight, Pratchett uses the Discworld to explore the role of the words in our heads, and how they control us. And how we can make up our own.

Notes

1. Even though Geertz notes that he believes this "with Max Weber," he gives no further reference (5). While his "webs of significance" are frequently quoted, they are usually either attributed solely to him, or Weber is mentioned only in passing. This article is, alas, no different.

2. Both Morreall and Martin provide examples of such detailed summaries, which are beyond the scope of this article. There is also a fairly recent article by Perks on "The Ancient Roots of Humor Theory" that is well worth reading.

3. The German term *Kaffeeklatsch* has entered the English language as coffee klatch. It refers to a meeting for coffee and conversation or gossip.

4. A second footnote on the same page expands on the term "real science," which is glossed as, "the sort you can use to give something three extra legs and then blow it up" (12)—combining wild exaggeration (real science causes mutation/monstrosity and explosions/destruction), impossible precision (three extra legs), and a fairly conversational tone, underscored by the vagueness of "something."

5. Attebery is repeatedly referenced as describing genres as fuzzy sets—categories clustered around one or more central texts and fading out towards the edges—and some scholars erroneously treat this as a concept somehow particular to the fantasy genre, even though Attebery himself clearly refers to genres in general (*Strategies* 12). Some scholars even seem to think that Attebery invented the concept.

6. The emphasis is thus on publication in the United States, and in book form. The first volume of the *Lord of the Rings* had been published in Great Britain in 1954, its precursor, *The Hobbit*, in 1937. Conan the Cimmerian had first appeared in the short story "The Phoenix and the Sword" published in *Weird Tales* in 1932 (cf. Tiner 221).

7. It is perhaps in this context that the term *gosh-wow! effect* is most appropriate (cf. Sawyer 707).

8. Texts which can arguably be termed fantasy do not appear with any frequency before the middle of the nineteenth century, and noteworthy works include William Morris' *The Wood Beyond the World* (1894), E. R. Eddison's *The Worm Ouroboros* (1922), Lord Dunsany's *The King of Elfland's Daughter* (1924), and T. H. White's *The Once and Future King* (1958), among others (see Schweitzer, "Heroic" 379–380, and Eilers 318).

9. Tolkien himself drew on a large number of such texts, including *Beowulf*, the *Völsung Saga*, the *Elder Edda* and other Old English and Old Norse poetry, but also fairy tale collections such as those by Asbjörnsen, Campbell, and the Grimms, as well as the ballad tradition (see Shippey 344–347). Indeed, Tolkien did not read—and was thus not influenced by—much contemporary or even recent literature, although he knew the work of William Morris, and probably Rudyard Kipling (351), and he had a "relationship of intimate dislike" with the work of Shakespeare, Spenser, George MacDonald, Hans Christian Andersen, and Wagner (344).

10. Cf. also Attebery, *Strategies* 20.

11. Attebery, by contrast, sees magic realism as a rather patronising label, allowing

critics of such literature to "dismiss it while pretending to admire it" ("Politics" 17).

12. Attebery does not accept the division between fantasy and magic realism, on the grounds that fantasy entails a deliberate deviation from an accepted social world, apparently because he does not accept the notion that different cultures might have different concepts of reality. He caricatures it as the claim that "people from those Other places obviously don't know the difference between the real and the fantastic, so it all gets jumbled together in their work" ("Politics" 17). Such an argument seems to be based on the notion that the real and the fantastic are somehow interculturally accepted absolute concepts instead of cultural constructs which may well not exist in some cultures (17).

13. Thus, most proponents of magic realism write from a cultural perspective situated outside Western Europe, such as Russia (e.g., Mikhail Bulgakov, *The Master and Margerita*), India (e.g., Salman Rushdie, *Midnight's Children*), or South America (e.g., Gabriel García Márquez, *One Hundred Years of Solitude*). They usually write against a predominant, oppressive political power, e.g., Bulgakov, in some cases after the fact, e.g., Günther Grass, *The Tin Drum*.

14. Similarly, Iser argues that the gaps of fiction are the reason "why the reader often feels involved in events which, at the time of reading, seem real to him, even though in fact they are very far from his own reality" (283).

15. Cf. also Cupp and Arsinger, who explore the postmodern politics of science fiction and fantasy.

WORKS CITED

Ashcroft, Bill, Gareth Griffith, and Helen Tiffin. "Magic Realism." *Post-Colonial Studies: The Key Concepts.* 1998. London: Routledge, 2000. 132–133.

Ashley, Mike. "Golem." *The Encyclopedia of Fantasy.* Ed. John Clute and John Grant. London: Orbit, 1997. 421–422.

Attardo, Salvatore. "A Primer for the Linguistics of Humor." *The Primer of Humor Research.* Ed. Victor Raskin. Berlin: Mouton de Gruyter, 2008. 101–155.

Attebery, Brian. "Foreword." *Journal of the Fantastic in the Arts* 22.3 (2011): 310–312.

_____. "The Magazine Era: 1926–1960." *The Cambridge Companion to Science Fiction.* Ed. Edward James and Farah Mendlesohn. Cambridge: Cambridge University Press, 2003. 32–47.

_____. "The Politics (If Any) of Fantasy." *Journal of the Fantastic in the Arts* 13 (1991): 7–28.

_____. *Strategies of Fantasy.* Bloomington: Indiana University Press, 1992.

Baumeister, Roy F. *Meanings of Life.* New York: Guilford, 1991.

Bowers, Maggie Ann. *Magic(al) Realism.* London: Routledge, 2004.

Butler, Andrew. "Theories of Humor." *Terry Pratchett: Guilty of Literature.* Ed. Andrew M. Butler, Edward James, and Farah Mendlesohn. Baltimore: Old Earth, 2004. 67–88.

Calvino, Italo. "Definitions of Territories: Fantasy." *The Uses of Literature.* San Diego: Harcourt Brace, 1986. 71–73.

Carroll, Noël. "Art, Practice, und Narrative." *Beyond Aesthetics: Philosophical Essays.* Cambridge: Cambridge University Press, 2001. 63–75.

Clute, John. "Coming of Age." *Terry Pratchett: Guilty of Literature.* Ed. Andrew M. Butler, Edward James, and Farah Mendlesohn. Baltimore: Old Earth, 2004. 15–30.

_____. "Howard, Robert E(rvin)." *The Encyclopedia of Fantasy.* Ed. John Clute and John Grant. London: Orbit, 1999. 481–483.

_____. *Look at the Evidence: Essays and Reviews.* New York: Jarconia, 1995.

_____. "Taproot Texts." *The Encyclopedia of Fantasy.* Ed. John Clute and John Grant. London: Orbit, 1999. 921–922.

Cooper, Joel. *Cognitive Dissonance: Fifty Years of a Classic Theory.* Thousand Oaks, CA: Sage, 2007.

Csikszentmihalyi, Mihaly. *Flow: The Psychology of Happiness.* London: Rider, 1992.

Culler, Jonathan. *Structuralist Poetics: Structuralism, Linguistics and the Study of Literature.* 1975. New York: Routledge, 2002.

Cupp, Jeff, and Charles Arsinger. "Do Science Fiction and Fantasy Writers Have Postmodern Dreams?" *Literature, Interpretation, Theory* 4 (1993): 175–184.

Currie, Mark. *Postmodern Narrative Theory.* Basingstoke: Palgrave, 1998.

Davidson, Avram. "The Spoor of the Unicorn." *Adventures in Unhistory: Conjectures on the Foundations of Several Ancient Legends.* New York: Tor, 1993. 207–223.

Durst, Uwe. *Theorie der phantastischen Literatur.* Tübingen: Franke, 2001.

Eagleton, Terry. *The English Novel: An Introduction.* Malden, MA: Blackwell, 2005.

Easterbrook, Neil. "Magical Realism." *The Greenwood Encyclopedia of Science Fiction and Fantasy: Themes, Works, and Wonders.* Ed. Gary Westfahl. Westport, CT: Greenwood Press, 2005. 490–492.

Eilers, Michelle L. "On the Origins of Modern Fantasy." *Extrapolation* 41 (2000): 317–337.

Frow, John. *Genre.* London: Routledge, 2006.

Geertz, Clifford. "Thick Description: Toward an Interpretive Theory of Culture." *The Interpretation of Cultures: Selected Essays.* 1973. London: Fontana, 1993. 3–30.

Gramlich, Charles. "Sword and Sorcery." *The Greenwood Encyclopedia of Science Fiction and Fantasy: Themes, Works, and Wonders.* Ed. Gary Westfahl. Westport, CT: Greenwood Press, 2005. 779–781.

Haberkorn, Gideon. "Cultural Palimpsests: Terry Pratchett's New Fantasy Heroes." *Journal of the Fantastic in the Arts* 18.3 (2008): 319–339.

Haberkorn, Gideon, and Verena Reinhardt. "Magic, Adolescence, and Education on Terry Pratchett's Discworld." *Supernatural Youth: The Rise of the Teen Hero in Literature and Popular Culture.* Ed. Jes Battis. Lanham, MD: Lexington, 2011. 43–64.

Horstkotte, Martin. *The Postmodern Fantastic in Contemporary British Fiction.* Trier: Wissenschaftlicher Verlag Trier, 2004.

Iser, Wolfgang. "The Reading Process: A Phenomenological Approach." *New Literary History* 2 (1972): 278–299.

Jerome, Jerome K. *Three Men in a Boat & Three Men on the Bummel.* Oxford: Oxford University Press, 2008.

Loofbourow, John W. "Realism in the Anglo-American Novel. The Pastoral Myth." *The Theory of the Novel.* Ed. John Halperin. Oxford: Oxford University Press, 1974. 257–270.

Manley, Don. *Chambers Crossword Manual*. 1986. Edinburgh: Chambers, 2001.

Martin, Rod A. *The Psychology of Humor: An Integrative Approach*. Burlington: Elsevier, 2007.

Martin, Wallace. *Recent Theories of Narrative*. Ithaca: Cornell University Press, 1986.

Midgley, Mary. "Philosophical Plumbing." *Utopia, Dolphins and Computers: Problems of Philosophical Plumbing*. London: Routledge, 1996. 1–14.

Moorcock, Michael. *Wizardry and Wild Romance*. Austin: Monkeybrain, 2004.

Morreall, John. *Comic Relief: A Comprehensive Philosophy of Humor*. Malden, MA: Wiley-Blackwell, 2009.

Morris, Pam. *Realism*. London: Routledge, 2003.

Muecke, D.C. *Irony*. London: Methuen, 1970.

Nicholls, Peter, and Carnel Robu. "Sense of Wonder." *The Encyclopedia of Science Fiction*. Ed. John Clute and Peter Nicholls. London: Orbit, 1999. 1083–1085.

Perks, Lisa Glebatis. "The Ancient Roots of Humor Theory." *Humor* 25:2 (2012): 119–132.

Pesch, Helmut W. *Fantasy: Theorie und Geschichte*. Diss. U Köln, 1982. Passau: Erster Deutscher Fantasy Club, 2001.

Porter, Alan J. "Carry-On Films." *An Unofficial Companion to the Novels of Terry Pratchett*. Ed. Andrew M. Butler. Oxford: Greenwood, 2007. 60–61.

Pratchett, Terry. *The Colour of Magic*. London: Corgi, 1985.

_____. *Feet of Clay*. London: Corgi, 1996.

_____. *Guards! Guards!* London: Corgi, 1990.

_____. *Hogfather*. London: Corgi, 1997.

_____. *The Last Hero: A Discworld Fable*. London: Gollancz, 2001.

_____. *The Light Fantastic*. London: Corgi, 1986.

_____. *Lords and Ladies*. London: Corgi, 1993.

_____. *Maskerade*. London: Corgi, 1995.

_____. *Moving Pictures*. London: Corgi, 1992.

_____. *Night Watch*. London: Gollancz, 2002.

_____. *Reaper Man*. London: Corgi, 1992.

_____. *Soul Music*. London: Gollancz, 1994.

_____. *Thief of Time*. London: Corgi, 2001.

_____. *The Truth*. London: Corgi, 2000.

_____. *The Wee Free Men*. London: Doubleday, 2003.

_____. *Witches Abroad*. London: Corgi, 1992.

Sawyer, Andy. "Sense of Wonder." *The Greenwood Encyclopedia of Science Fiction and Fantasy: Themes, Works, and Wonders*. Ed. Gary Westfahl. Westport, CT: Greenwood, 2005. 706–708.

Schweitzer, Darell. "Conan the Conqueror by Robert E. Howard (1959)." *The Greenwood Encyclopedia of Science Fiction and Fantasy: Themes, Works, and Wonders*. Ed. Gary Westfahl. Westport, CT: Greenwood, 2005. 975–977.

_____. "Heroic Fantasy." *The Greenwood Encyclopedia of Science Fiction and Fantasy: Themes, Works, and Wonders*. Ed. Gary Westfahl. Westport, CT: Greenwood, 2005. 379–381.

Senior, William A. "Oliphaunts in the Perilous Realm: The Function of Internal Wonder in Fantasy." *Functions of the Fantastic*. Ed. Joe Sanders. Westport, CT: Greenwood, 1995. 115–124.

Shippey, Tom. *The Road to Middle Earth: How J. R. R. Tolkien Created a New Mythology*. New York: Houghton Mifflin, 2003.

Tiner, Ron. "Conan." *The Encyclopedia of Fantasy*. Ed. John Clute and John Grant. London: Orbit, 1999. 221.

Todorov, Tzvetan. *The Fantastic: A Structural Approach to a Literary Genre*. 1970. Ithaca: Cornell University Press, 1975.

Tolkien, J. R. R. "On Fairy-Stories." *The Tolkien Reader*. New York: Ballantine, 1966. 33–99.

Waugh, Patricia. *Metafiction: The Theory and Practice of Self-Conscious Fiction*. London: Routledge, 1984.

Wodehouse, P. G. *Wodehouse Nuggets*. Ed. Richard Usborne. 1983. London: Vintage, 1992.

Primary Bibliography
of Terry Pratchett's Works
Published in English

This list indicates first editions of UK imprints; the ⊗ symbol indicates the work does not include any Discworld or Discworld-related material.

The Amazing Maurice and His Educated Rodents. Illus. David Wyatt. London: Doubleday, 2001.

The Amazing Maurice and His Educated Rodents. Stage Adaptation. Adapt. Stephen Briggs. Oxford: Oxford University Press, 2003.

Ankh-Morpork City Watch Warrant Card. Wincanton, UK: Cunning Artificer, 2005.

A Blink of the Screen: Collected Shorter Fiction. Foreword A. S. Byatt. London: Doubleday, 2012.

The Bromeliad: Containing Truckers, Diggers *and* Wings. London: Doubleday, 1998. ⊗

Carpe Jugulum. Illus. Josh Kirby. London: Doubleday, 1998.

Carpe Jugulum, the Play. Adapt. Stephen Briggs. Illus. Stephen Player. London: Samuel French, 1999.

The Carpet People. Illus. by the author. London: Colin Smythe, 1971. ⊗

The Colour of Magic. London: Colin Smythe, 1983.

The Dark Side of the Sun. London: Colin Smythe, 1976. ⊗

Diggers. London: Doubleday, 1990. ⊗

Dodger. London: Doubleday, 2012. ⊗

Dodger's Guide to London. Doubleday, 2013. ⊗

Equal Rites. Illus. Josh Kirby. London: Gollancz, 1987.

~~*Faust*~~ *Eric.* Illus. Josh Kirby. London: Gollancz, 1990.

Feet of Clay. Illus. Josh Kirby. London: Gollancz, 1996.

The Fifth Elephant. Illus. Josh Kirby. London: Doubleday, 1999.

The Fifth Elephant, the Play. 1999. Adapt. Stephen Briggs. Illus. Josh Kirby. London: Methuen, 2002.

From the Discworld. Music by Dave Greenslade. London: Virgin, 1996.

Going Postal. Illus. Paul Kidby. London: Doubleday, 2004.

Going Postal. Stage Adaptation. Adapt. Stephen Briggs. Illus. Paul Kidby. London: Methuen, 2005.

Guards! Guards! Illus. Josh Kirby. London: Gollancz, 1989.

Guards! Guards! A Discworld Big Comic. Illus. Graham Higgins. Adapt. Stephen Briggs. London: Gollancz, 2000.

Guards! Guards!, the Play. 1993. Adapt. Stephen Briggs. 1993. Illus. Stephen Player. London: Corgi, 1997.

A Hat Full of Sky. Illus. Paul Kidby. London: Doubleday, 2004.

Hogfather. Illus. Josh Kirby. London: Gollancz, 1996.

I Shall Wear Midnight. Illus. Paul Kidby. London: Doubleday, 2010.

The Illustrated Wee Free Men. Illus. Stephen Player. London: Doubleday, 2008.

Interesting Times. Illus. Josh Kirby. London: Gollancz, 1994.

Interesting Times, the Play. Adapt. Stephen Briggs. Illus. Josh Kirby. London: Methuen, 2002.

Jingo. Illus. Josh Kirby. London: Gollancz, 1997.

Jingo, the Play. Adapt. Stephen Briggs. Illus. Josh Kirby. London: Methuen, 2005.

Johnny and the Bomb. London: Doubleday, 1996. ⊗

Johnny and the Dead. London: Doubleday, 1993. ⊗

Johnny and the Dead: Oxford Playscripts. Adapt. Stephen Briggs. Oxford: Oxford University Press, 2003. ⊗

The Josh Kirby Poster Book. Intro. Terry Pratchett. Illus. Josh Kirby. London: Corgi, 1990.

The Last Continent. Illus. Josh Kirby. London: Doubleday, 1998.

The Light Fantastic. Illus. Josh Kirby. London: Colin Smythe, 1986.

Lords and Ladies. Illus. Josh Kirby. London: Gollancz, 1992.

Lords and Ladies, the Play. Adapt. Irana Brown. Illus. Stephen Player. London: Samuel French, 2001.

Making Money. Illus. Paul Kidby. London: Doubleday, 2007.

Making Money. Stage Adaptation. Adapt. Stephen Briggs. London: Samuel French, 2011.

Maskerade. Illus. Josh Kirby. London: Gollancz, 1995.

Maskerade, the Play. 1995. Adapt. Stephen Briggs. Illus. Stephen Player. London: Samuel French, 1998.

Men at Arms. Illus. Josh Kirby. London: Gollancz, 1993.

Men at Arms, the Play. 1994. Adapt. Stephen Briggs. Illus. Stephen Player. London: Corgi, 1997.

Monstrous Regiment. Illus. Paul Kidby. London: Doubleday, 2003.

Monstrous Regiment, the Play. Adapted by Stephen Briggs. London: Methuen, 2003.

Mort. Illus. Josh Kirby. London: Gollancz, 1987.

Mort, a Discworld Big Comic. Illus. Graham Higgins. London: Gollancz, 1994.

Mort, the Play. 1992. Adapt. Stephen Briggs. Illus. Stephen Player. London: Corgi, 1996.

Moving Pictures. Illus. Josh Kirby. London: Gollancz, 1990.

Nation. London: Doubleday, 2008. ⊗

Night Watch. Illus. Paul Kidby. London: Doubleday, 2002.

Night Watch, the Play. 2003. Adapt. Stephen Briggs. Illus. Paul Kidby. London: Methuen, 2004.

Once More, with Footnotes. Ed. Priscilla Olson and Sheila Perry. Illus. Omar Rayyan. Intro. Esther M. Friesner. Framingham, MA: NESFA Press, 2004.

Only You Can Save Mankind. London: Doubleday, 1992. ⊗

Pyramids. Illus. Josh Kirby. London: Gollancz, 1989.

Reaper Man. Illus. Josh Kirby. London: Gollancz, 1991.

Raising Steam. Illus. Paul Kidby. London: Doubleday, 2013.

A Slip of the Keyboard: Collected Non-Fiction. London: Doubleday, forthcoming 2014.

Small Gods. Illus. Josh Kirby. London: Gollancz, 1992.

Snuff. Illus. Paul Kidby. London: Doubleday, 2011.

Soul Music. Illus. Josh Kirby. London: Gollancz, 1994.

Soul Music. The Illustrated Screenplay. London: Corgi, 1997.

Sourcery. Illus. Josh Kirby. London: Gollancz, 1988.

Strata. London: Colin Smythe, 1981. ⊗

Terry Pratchett's The Colour of Magic*: The Graphic Novel.* 1991. Illus. Steven Ross. Adapt. Scott Rockwell. Lettered by Vickie Williams. Ed. David Campiti. London: Corgi, 1992.

Terry Pratchett's The Colour of Magic*: The Illustrated Screenplay.* Adapt. Vadim Jean. Mucked about with by Terry Pratchett. London: Gollancz, 2008.

Terry Pratchett's Hogfather*: The Illustrated Screenplay.* Adapt. Vadim Jean. Mucked about with by Terry Pratchett. London: Gollancz, 2006.

Terry Pratchett's The Light Fantastic*: The Graphic Novel.* Illus. Steven Ross and Joe Bennet. Adapt. Scott Rockwell. Lettered by Michelle Beck and Vickie Williams. Ed. David Campiti. London: Corgi, 1993.

Terry Pratchett's Johnny and the Bomb*: A Time-Tickingly Tremendous Musical.* Adapt. Matthew Holmes. London: A.C. Black, 2012. ⊗

Thief of Time. Illus. Josh Kirby. London: Doubleday, 2001.

Thud! Illus. Paul Kidby. London: Doubleday, 2005.

Truckers. London: Doubleday, 1989. ⊗

The Truth. Illus. Josh Kirby. London: Doubleday, 2000.

The Truth, the Play. 2000. Adapt. Stephen Briggs. Illus. Josh Kirby. London: Methuen, 2002.

The Unadulterated Cat. Illus. Gray Jolliffe. London: Gollancz, 1989. ⊗

Unseen Academicals. Illus. Paul Kidby. London: Doubleday, 2009.

The Wee Free Men. Illus. Paul Kidby. London: Doubleday, 2003.

Where's My Cow? Illus. Melvin Grant. London: Doubleday, 2005.

Wings. London: Doubleday, 1990. ⊗

Wintersmith. Illus. Paul Kidby. London: Doubleday, 2006.

Witches Abroad. Illus. Josh Kirby. London: Gollancz, 1991.

Wyrd Sisters. Illus. Josh Kirby. London: Gollancz, 1988.

Wyrd Sisters. The Illustrated Screenplay. London: Corgi, 1997.

Wyrd Sisters, the Play. 1991. Adapt. Stephen Briggs. Illus. Stephen Player. London: Corgi, 1996.

With Alan Batley and Bernard Pearson

The Unseen University Cut-Out Book. London: Transworld, 2006.

With Bernard Pearson

The Discworld Almanak. Illus. Paul Kidby, Bernard Pearson, and Sheila Watkins. London: Corgi, 2004.

With Ian Stewart and Jack Cohen

The Science of Discworld. London: Ebury, 1999.
The Science of Discworld II: The Globe. London: Ebury, 2002.
The Science of Discworld III: Darwin's Watch. London: Ebury, 2005.
The Science of Discworld IV: Judgement Day. London: Ebury, 2013.

With Jacqueline Simpson

The Folklore of Discworld. London: Doubleday, 2008.

With Neil Gaimon

Good Omens. London: Gollancz, 1990. ⊗

With Paul Kidby

The Art of Discworld. London: Gollancz, 2004.
Death's Domain: *A Discworld Mapp*. London: Corgi, 1999.
The Last Hero. London: Gollancz, 2001.
The Pratchett Portfolio. London: Gollancz, 1996.

With Phil Masters and John M. Ford

GURPS Discworld: Adventures on the Back of the Turtle. Ed. Steve Jackson. Illus. Paul Kidby. Austin: Steve Jackson Games, 1998.

With Stephen Baxter

The Long Earth. London: Doubleday, 2012. ⊗
The Long War. London: Doubleday, 2013. ⊗

With Stephen Briggs

Ankh-Morpork Post Office Handbook and Discworld Diary 2007. Illus. Paul Kidby. London: Gollancz, 2006.
Discworld Assassin's Guild Yearbook and Diary 2000. Illus. Paul Kidby. London: Gollancz, 1999.
The Discworld Companion. London: Gollancz, 1994.
Discworld Fools' Guild Yearbook and Diary 2001. Illus. Paul Kidby. London: Gollancz, 2000.
The Discworld Mapp. Illus. Stephen Player. London: Corgi, 1995.

Discworld (Reformed) Vampyre's Diary 2003. Illus. Paul Kidby. London: Gollancz, 2002.

Discworld Thieves' Guild Yearbook and Diary 2002. London: Gollancz, 2001.

Discworld's Ankh-Morpork City Watch Diary 1999. Illus. Paul Kidby. London: Gollancz, 1998.

Discworld's Unseen University Diary. Illus. Paul Kidby. London: Gollancz, 1997.

Lu-Tze's Yearbook of Enlightenment. Illus. Paul Kidby. London: Gollancz, 2007.

Nanny Ogg's Cookbook. Illus. Paul Kidby. Recipes by Tina Hannan and Stephen Briggs. London: Doubleday, 1999.

The Streets of Ankh-Morpork. Illus. Stephen Player. London: Corgi, 1993.

A Tourist Guide to Lancre: A Discworld Mapp. Illus. Paul Kidby. London: Corgi, 1998.

Turtle Recall: The Discworld Companion ... So Far. London: Gollancz, 2012.

The Wit and Wisdom of Discworld. London: Doubleday, 2007.

With the Discworld Emporium

The Compleat Ankh-Morpork. Additional Illus. Peter Dennis. London: Doubleday, 2012.

Discworld: The Ankh-Morpork Map iPad App. London: Transworld, 2013.

The World of Poo. Illus. Peter Dennis. London: Doubleday, 2012.

Annotated Critical
Bibliography

This Annotated Critical Bibliography comprises three sections: short summaries of Pratchett-related criticism that appears in articles, chapters, and monographs; a list of interviews with both Terry Pratchett and Paul Kidby; and a list of MA theses, dissertations, and equivalents. There is an unavoidable bias towards English-language works, but for the scholarly works we think it is largely representative at the time of writing.

A. Articles, Chapters and Monographs

Baker, Deirdre. "What We Found on Our Journey through Fantasy Land." *Children's Literature in Education* **37:3 (2006): 237–251.**
This article touches on fantasy landscapes of a number of children's authors, including Ursula Le Guin, Philip Pullman, and Diana Wynne Jones, but devotes only two paragraphs to Pratchett. Baker's discussion of *The Wee Free Men* suggests that Tiffany's skepticism about fairy tales allows her to ignore their warnings and think for herself. In this way, Baker claims, Pratchett "re-visions ... both gender and narrative" (249), but the article does not address how he does this beyond stating that Pratchett "provides a different model; he spurs his readers to question" (249).

Bassnett, Susan. "Is There Hope for the Humanities in the 21st Century?" *Arts & Humanities in Higher Education* **1:1 (2002): 101–110.**
This article considers the "current position of research in the Humanities" in light of recent changes in society as well as in verbal and visual literacy (101), and stresses the importance of interdisciplinarity in tertiary education. In addition to commenting on the value of writers such as Pratchett and J. K. Rowling in relation to the larger context of literature, Bassnett notes that Pratchett "maintains that he is now able to write in a much more complex way in terms of narrative" than when he began writing in the 1970s (103).

Briggs, Melody, and Richard S. Briggs. "Stepping into the Gap: Contemporary Children's Fantasy Literature as a Doorway to Spirituality." *Towards or Back to Human Values? Spiritual and Moral Dimensions of Contemporary Fantasy.*

Ed. Justyna Deszcz-Tryhubczak and Marek Oziewicz. Newcastle, UK: Cambridge Scholars, 2006. 30–47.
This article considers the ways in which contemporary children's fantasy fills the spiritual gaps that exist in today's Western culture. The authors discuss *The Wee Free Men* briefly in relation to the Nac Mac Feegles' view of life and death as a cyclical process and their belief that they are already dead when they are in what Tiffany regards as the "real" world. Their belief system "parodies the way in which modern scientific structures claim knowledge about life based on empirical evidence" (35), and Pratchett's text invites readers to assess how they have arrived at their own beliefs about life and death. In this way, the authors claim that Pratchett "foregrounds the constructedness of reality" (35) but, in keeping with postmodern tradition, does not attempt to resolve this issue but merely poses the question. The rest of the article assumes that fantasy authors' fantasy worlds "will inevitably be influenced by their personal beliefs" (36) and then discusses the work of Philip Pullman, Gabriel Nix, and J. K. Rowling, concluding that modern fantasy "fill[s] a gap left by the contemporary marginalization of religion ... [and thus] opens a door to spirituality" (43–44).

Briggs, Stephen. "Introductory Materials." *Turtle Recall: The Discworld Companion ... So Far*. By Terry Pratchett and Stephen Briggs. London: Gollancz, 2012. 1–5.
Briggs provides an overview of the creation of the *Discworld Companion* volumes, noting that this third *Discworld Companion* includes all entries from both the first and the second *Companion*, and has been updated to include entries for books published since then.

_____. "Turtles All the Way Down: Even More Discworld Stuff!" *Turtle Recall: The Discworld Companion ... So Far*. By Terry Pratchett and Stephen Briggs. London: Gollancz, 2012. 325–52.
This section includes a reprint of "Terry Pratchett: The Definitive Interview" that appeared in the original *Discworld Companion*; Briggs notes that this interview is now approximately twenty years old and thus has "taken on the air of an historical document. Almost" (325). A brief piece on "Readers and Fan Mail," also published in the original *Companion*, discusses how things have changed in terms of the kinds of fan mail Pratchett receives since he first began writing and notes the internet's impact on fandom. "The Language Barrier" provides an excellent discussion of translation issues, noting some of the challenges involved in translating the books into Dutch, German, French, and other languages. The section concludes with an extensive overview of the rules for the Discworld card game, Cripple Mr. Onion, which is played with a full pack of seventy-three cards.

Brown, Sarah Anne. "Shaping Fantasies: Responses to Shakespeare's Magic in Popular Culture." *Shakespeare* 5:2 (2009): 162–76.
This article discusses the ways in which Neil Gaiman's *The Sandman*, Pratchett's *Lords and Ladies*, and Gareth Roberts' "The Shakespeare Code" serve as responses to Shakespeare's *A Midsummer Night's Dream*. Utilizing the theoretical frameworks of New Historicism and Poststructuralism, Brown suggests that these works oppose the modern critical trend of participating in a "skeptical demystification" of Shakespeare and instead present responses to his works that demonstrate a more sophisticated awareness

of their complexity. Brown spends the majority of the article discussing Gaiman's work; the sections on Pratchett and Roberts are each quite short, and her comments on Pratchett do little more than point out the correspondence between *Lords and Ladies* and *A Midsummer Night's Dream*, though Brown also briefly mentions a Newtonian reference in relation to Ponder Stibbons.

Buchbinder, David. "The Orangutan in the Library: The Comfort of Strangeness in Terry Pratchett's Discworld Novels." *Youth Cultures: Texts, Images, and Identities.* **Ed. Kerry Malan and Sharing Pearce. Westport, CT: Praeger, 2003. 169–82.**
This article discusses some of the ways in which Pratchett satirizes, ridicules, and deconstructs traditional fantasy's narrative and epic form. Using Tolkien as a touchstone for comparison, Buchbinder observes that Pratchett's world subverts fantasy's traditionally "closed" worlds through their numerous intertextual references and discusses Pratchett's "participation in a British tradition of satiric comedy fiction" (174), targeting greed, fame and celebrity, technology, and managerialism. After a brief discussion of how Pratchett's treatment of such political issues as gender and orientation, power, sex, and age reworks the fantasy genre, the remainder of the article focuses on the ways in which the Discworld series resonates with younger readers. Buchbinder suggests that cultural references including issues of women's rights, racial prejudice, religious fundamentalism, media influence, fantasies of island vacations and Australian travel, and the presence and fear of death are all of interest to younger readers, as are certain threads of Pratchett's stories, including the Cinderella motif and the theme of parental control. The article concludes with a discussion of the Librarian as a representation of the process of male adolescence.

Butler, Andrew. "'A Story About Stories': Terry Pratchett's *The Amazing Maurice and His Educated Rodents.*" *Vector* **227 (Jan./Feb. 2003): 10–11.**
This review article briefly considers Pratchett as an author of children's books, and then discusses the various stories encompassed in *Maurice*. After noting that "stories are double-edged things" (11), Butler concludes that by the end of the novel it becomes imperative for characters to favor dialogue among and between themselves over stories.

_____. *Terry Pratchett.* **The Pocket Essential Series. Harpenden, UK: Pocket Essentials, 2001.**
This relatively short book consists of an introduction and four chapters that consider Pratchett's books from *The Carpet People* to *Thief of Time*. The introduction discusses Pratchett's background and provides a sketch of the history of fantasy before turning to the Discworld novels and their composition; after very briefly mentioning Pratchett's other works, Butler discusses the use of power in Discworld, and concludes with an overview of the book's contents. Two of the book's chapters focus on Pratchett's non–Discworld works: Chapter One on *The Carpet People*, *The Dark Side of the Sun*, and *Strata*, and Chapter Three on *The Bromeliad* and *The Johnny Maxwell Trilogy*. Chapter Two focuses on the Discworld novels, and Chapter Four focuses on collaborations including *The Unadulterated Cat*, *Good Omens*, *The Discworld Companion*, the Maps, *The Science of Discworld*, and *Nanny Ogg's Cookbook*. All of the chapters consist of film-review style entries on individual books and share a similar format: a

sentence noting the book's first British publication, a paragraph on the setting, a plot summary, and a short critical section. This section is divided into "Major Targets," which generally include comments related to the book's theme and its use of comedy, "Cameos," which notes minor characters, and "Subtext," a commentary on the book's meaning which often overlaps or intersects with the "Major Targets" section. Each entry concludes with "The Verdict," Butler's ranking of the book on a 1–5 point scale, the criteria for which is not clearly articulated beyond his comment that "the purpose of this last is clearly to annoy people" (17). The book concludes with a list of Pratchett's books and a very short list of critical materials.

_____. "Terry Pratchett and the Comedic Bildungsroman." *Foundation: The Review of Science Fiction* 67 (Summer 1996): 56–62.
This article applies Bakhtin's notions of the chronotope and the carnivalesque to an analysis of *Mort*. Butler views *Mort* as exemplifying one of the five subtypes of the *Bildungsroman*, one in which both the world and the hero emerge changed from a marked transition point; for *Mort*, Butler locates the transition in the resolution of the paradox the eponymous protagonist creates. Butler also lists several diagnostic features of the carnivalesque—ritual inversion, scatological parody, and insulting friendship—providing examples from the novel to illustrate their presence.

_____. "Theories of Humour." *Terry Pratchett: Guilty of Literature*. Ed. Andrew M. Butler, Edward James, and Farah Mendlesohn. Reading, UK: Science Fiction Foundation, [2004]. 35–50.
This article is constructed so as to provide brief illustrations of five different approaches to explaining humor—Pirandello's, Freud's, Bergson's, Lacan's, and Bakhtin's; each of the five is applied to analysis of *Mort*. In keeping with the "survey" design of the article, each of the theory discussions is quite short, sketching out a few important concepts from each of the five and relating them to several examples from the novel. While Butler notes features common to these five approaches, the presentation does not attempt a synthesis position.

_____, ed. *An Unofficial Companion to the Novels of Terry Pratchett*. Westport, CT: Greenwood, 2007.
This detailed encyclopedia includes entries related to all of Pratchett's writings, not only the Discworld books. Entries focus on a wide range of characters, places, individual novels and book series, genres, authors (including Shakespeare) and significant people, publishers, and topics including fandom, Greek mythology, L-Space, Hollywood films, sexism, and animation, to name only a few. The introduction consists of a short biographical sketch and background on Pratchett's writing, and the book concludes with a Select Bibliography of Primary sources (short works, novels, and other writings by Pratchett) and Secondary sources (anything not written by Pratchett, starting with Douglas Adams' *Hitch-Hiker's Guide to the Galaxy*), finishing with a list of web pages.

Cabell, Craig. *Terry Pratchett: The Spirit of Fantasy*. London: John Blake, 2011.
This full-length biography provides a solid overview of Pratchett's life and work, the latter of which Cabell considers "against the backdrop of [Pratchett's] life, philosophy and career" xvii). After a brief discussion of fantasy, science fiction, and horror genres, the book outlines Pratchett's early history in terms of his schooling and literary influ-

ences, his marriage to Lynn Purves, and his career in journalism. It then traces Pratchett's composition and publication of *The Carpet People, The Dark Side of the Sun, Strata,* and his early Discworld books, including *The Color of Magic, The Light Fantastic, Equal Rites, Mort,* and *Eric*. After a brief "Intermission" that reconsiders *The Carpet People,* Cabell discusses Pratchett's characters and their connection to the history of Discworld, and then moves on to chapters that focus on Pratchett's treatment of cliché, childhood (specifically in relation to *Hogfather*), Pratchett's enjoyment of music and its connections to *Soul Music* and *Maskerade,* and darkness (the Tiffany Aching books). This leads to chapters on Pratchett's writing for children, including *The Bromeliad Trilogy,* the Johnny Maxwell trilogy, and *Nation*. The book's final chapters consider Pratchett's 1995 documentary *Terry Pratchett's Jungle Quest* and his contributions to founding The Orangutan Foundation, his diagnosis with Posterior Cortical Atrophy, a rare form of Alzheimer's Disease, and his activism in the Dignity in Dying organization, as well as chapters on Death and "A Note About Cats," the latter of which discusses *The Unadulterated Cat* and *The Amazing Maurice*. Three appendices provide information about film adaptations, theatrical productions, and book collecting.

Clute, John. "Coming of Age." *Terry Pratchett: Guilty of Literature*. Ed. Andrew M. Butler, Edward James, and Farah Mendlesohn. Reading, UK: Science Fiction Foundation, [2004]. 7–20.
Clute points out the inherent tension between formal Comedy (which returns the world to its original state) and the modern fantasy tradition, which he argues is heavily influenced by Christian authors such as Tolkien and hence does not allow a simple return, instead creating a pseudo-circular linearity by remaking the "return" state a fundamentally transformed version of the initial one; the comic novel is simply transformative. Using the notion of the "incipit"—a term from music denoting a sequence borrowed from another work and used as a kind of seed for further development—he provides a historical discussion of Pratchett's pre–Discworld (*Carpet People, Dark Side of the Sun, Strata*) and Discworld work, connecting particular pieces to authors such as Larry Niven and Gene Wolfe, and arguing that the Discworld has maintained Comedy in the face of modern fantasy, remaining "[f]ree of the dangerous pieties of transformative Healing" (19).

Cockrell, Amanda. "Where the Falling Angel Meets the Rising Ape: Terry Pratchett's Discworld." *Hollins Critic* 43:1 (Feb. 2006): 1–15.
This essay relies heavily on identification rather than analysis. Cockrell notes Pratchett's tendency towards parody, commenting on his treatment of religion and belief in *Small Gods* and *Hogfather,* fantasy in *The Color of Magic,* and war and politics in *Jingo*. In addition to observing Pratchett's ability to create amusing names and perfect phrases, the author comments on his reliance on folklore, popular culture, and the collective unconscious. Cockrell provides a general discussion of Pratchett's characters, including Death and Susan, the Witches, the City Watch, and the Wizards, and briefly comments on his various settings. The essay concludes with a short biographical note on Pratchett and a primary bibliography of his works.

Croft, Janet Brennan. "The Education of a Witch: Tiffany Aching, Hermione Granger, and Gendered Magic in Discworld and Potterworld." *Mythlore: A*

Journal of J. R. R. Tolkien, C. S. Lewis, Charles Williams, and Mythopoeic Literature 27: 3–4 (2009): 129–42.
This essay explores the different sorts of education available to girls who are witches in Pratchett's Tiffany Aching books and J. K. Rowling's *Harry Potter* series. While Tiffany and Hermione both realize that gaining knowledge means gaining power, they achieve their education differently and in fantasy worlds that make different gender assumptions. In the Discworld, males and females study and perform magic differently. Wizards study magic at Unseen University, where their magical education is heavily influenced by book-learning and academic study. In contrast, witches' magical education is considered a more organic type of knowledge, and in the end Tiffany learns that "being a witch is all about doing for those who can't and speaking for those who have no voices" (134). That said, since female characters in Discworld are adopting what have traditionally been considered male Discworld occupations, it is possible that their representation will increase as the series progresses. The gender divisions in the *Harry Potter* series, while less clear, can be seen better through Rowling's presentation of house-elves, who are presented as occupying a space traditionally filled by housewives during the 20th century. Despite their differences, Croft concludes, both series provide role models for readers and suggest that "the truly determined will find a way to thrive under any system" (140).

_____. "The Golempunk Manifesto: Ownership of the Means of Production in Pratchett's Discworld." *Presentations of the 2010 Upstate Steampunk Extravaganza and Meetup*. Ed. Gypsey Elaine Teague. Newcastle-upon-Tyne, UK: Cambridge Scholars, 2011. 3–16.
This article argues that Pratchett's treatment of golems in his "technology" series critiques "the socially transformative power of technological innovation" (3), and that in this way the Discworld series overlaps with both steampunk literature and the Industrial Revolution. Croft suggests Pratchett's primary technological books are *The Truth*, *Going Postal*, and *Making Money*, although she concedes that other books also consider various aspects of technology, including *Monstrous Regiment* (for the effects of the telegraph, the free press, and photography), *Soul Music* (Hex), *Reaper Man* (a combination harvester), *Men at Arms* (firearms in the form of the "gonne"), *Moving Pictures* (motion pictures), and *The Last Hero* (a space-going craft). Croft argues that golems "perfectly represent two essential elements of the Industrial Revolution" in the steam that powered the machines and the lives of the workers (5). After discussing the folkloric origins of golems in medieval Jewish legends and noting their strong connections to community and family, Croft adds that golems often serve as a contemporary metaphor for anxiety about the modern world and the pace of technological change, citing *Frankenstein*, *2001*, and *Blade Runner* as examples. The remainder of the article considers Pratchett's golems in *Feet of Clay*, *Going Postal*, and *Making Money*, relying heavily on close reading to provide their mythological beginnings within Discworld's mythology, their development within Ankh-Morpork's society, and their connections to the economic well-being of the city. Croft concludes by noting the questions that Pratchett's Industrial Revolution series has raised in relation to philosophical and ethical questions about golems, specifically in terms of legal status, identity, and ethics, and modern economic concerns related to unemployment, immigration, and new technology.

_____. "Nice, Good, or Right: Faces of the Wise Woman in Terry Pratchett's "Witches" Novels." *Mythlore* 26:3/4 (Spring/Summer 2008): 151–64.
This article provides an excellent explication of Pratchett's use of the concepts of Nice, Good, and Right to explore the themes of free will, right and wrong, and the ethics of power. The three words act "as shorthand for a complex of ideas about how a witch should or should not deal with this moral imperative: how she should handle her power, treat other people, and face her responsibilities to the world" (155). In the Witches novels, the concept of "Nice" involves the avoidance of making moral choices while not offending people. "Good" means following an externally imposed moral system, while "Right" means seeing past both the concepts of Nice and Good and embracing justice and moral correctness. Croft appears to argue that none of Pratchett's witches are perfectly good or right, and only Magrat is fully Nice (Croft does not discuss her behavior in *Lords and Ladies*), nor are they perfect examples of any single trait. Granny Weatherwax resents having been forced into the role of Good, as she more closely resembles Right, though her "Right is tempered by an understanding of human nature and the willingness to take on the burdens of others" (159). Nanny Ogg also can be considered Right, but "given her more elastic approach to the truth, Nanny has no compunction about hiding her Rightness under a veneer of Niceness when needed" (160). The article concludes that witchcraft's ethics are based on striving for Rightness, which Croft posits as being neutral, at least on the Discworld; this corresponds with the way that magic on the Discworld is also neutral, and is there to be drawn on by anyone who can use it.

Curry, Patrick. *Defending Middle-Earth: Tolkien, Myth and Modernity.* New York: Mariner, 2004. *Google Scholar.* 24 Aug. 2013.
Curry includes a short paragraph distinguishing Pratchett's humanist, comedic, postmodernist fantasy from Tolkien's "mythic fiction."

Dżereń-Głowacka, Sylwia. "Imagery in Terry Pratchett's Discworld." *Imagery in Language.* Ed. Barbara Lewandowska-Tomaszczyk and Alina Kwiatkowska. Frankfurt am Main, Germany: Peter Lang, 2004. 723–32.
This relatively brief article applies concepts taken from Langacker's Cognitive Grammar, and from Gricean linguistic pragmatics, to the analysis of a range of examples taken from Discworld texts, arguing that these frameworks help elucidate elements of Pratchett's humor. Cognitive Grammar accounts for a number of linguistic phenomena by hypothesizing that representations of meaning encoded in language are structured by metaphors ("a city is a person" is one of the examples discussed in the article) and manipulation of figure/ground distinctions; Dżereń-Głowacka is thus able to position the "surprise" underlying examples of Pratchett's humor as being sudden exchanges of metaphor, or figure/ground reversals. The article is designed to provide initial illustrations of the utility of the approach, rather than to argue for a specific interpretation of Pratchett's imagery.

Ekman, Stefan. "Time and Time Again: Pratchett's Djelibeybi." *Here Be Dragons: Exploring Fantasy Maps and Settings.* Middletown, CT: Wesleyan University Press, 2013. 117–124.
This article argues that the quasi–Egyptian kingdom of Djelibeybi in *Pyramids* is a kind of a temporal polder—a domain "whose rules are such that the surrounding world

would destroy them if the boundary were ever breached" (12). Ekman argues that Pratchett's use of the polder differs from typical uses (*cf.* Tolkien's Lothlórien and Holdstock's Ryhope Wood) because of both the way readers become aware of its boundaries and Pratchett's use of "the very nature of time to create the opposition between the polder and the surrounding world" (118). Time in Djelibeybi is converted and stored in the pyramids in much the same way that batteries convert and store energy; both can be turned into light and heat. Time, which is often connected with water metaphors throughout the novel, functions as a duality—dimension versus power—related to quantum mechanics, and uncontrolled buildup eventually causes a shift in the four dimensions of reality. Ekman suggests that Djelibeybi's polder-nature appears in the way it has been sealed away from the rest of the Discworld; his logic here is somewhat inconsistent, but his discussion of Dios is more convincing about the ways that he fails to actively maintain the polder's boundaries, instead focusing on opposing changes in the kingdom in order to protect its reality. The article concludes by noting that the polder is brought to an end not only by Teppic's repeated crossings of its boundaries (during his departures and returns) but also by the foreign education both Teppic and Ptaclusp IIb receive from the outside, which leads to reforms inside the kingdom. However, as Ekman notes, rather than being destroyed, the "anachronistic polder" is re-created as a kind of endless temporal loop of 7,000 years in which Dios "is destined to create Djelibeybi as a changeless polder, maintain it, and finally see it destroyed over and over again" (125); in this way Djelibeybi's polder-boundaries are temporal rather than spatial.

Espinosa Anke, Luis. "Quantifying Irony with Sentiment Analysis Methods: The Case of Terry Pratchett's Discworld." *Current Research in Applied Linguistics: Issues on Language and Cognition,* **Ed. Paula Rodriguez-Puente, Teresa Fanego, Evelyn Gandón-Chapela, Sara Riveiro-Outeiral and María Luisa Roca-Varela. Newcastle-upon-Tyne, UK: Cambridge Scholars, 2013. 220– 239.**
This article discusses disparities between the kind of assignment of ratings of positivity and negativity that are possible with algorithmic approaches such as Sentiment Analysis (a data-mining technique) and those human readers give to Pratchett's novels. Espinosa notes that current implementations of Sentiment Analysis are optimized for short texts, and thus will require alteration to be more useful in the examination of longer literary texts.

Farr, Timothy. "The Subject of Ents, Entwives and Huorns in the Old Forest." *Mythlore* **135 (Sept. 1995): 13–14.**
This short piece points out a variety of Tolkien references that appear in some of the Discworld books, including *Moving Pictures* (the Balgrog, Ridcully the Brown), *Equal Rites* (Granpone the White / Granpone the Grey), *Mort* and *Lords and Ladies* (comments about not meddling in the affairs of wizards), and *Witches Abroad* (dwarves and invisible runes and dwarf bread and a Gollum-like creature).

Fornet-Ponse, Thomas. "'The Gods play games with the fate of men': Zum Verhaltnis von Gottern und Menschen bei Terry Pratchett." *Inklings* **22 (2004): 130–153. [In German]**
Fornet-Ponse analyzes the relationships among gods, humans, and belief in the Disc-

world novels, carefully tracing Pratchett's development of different versions of the quantified "belief/power" dynamic, and the "priest as professional" image across a number of the novels. His primary focus is *The Last Hero*, in which he sees the juxtaposition of Cohen, the Bard, Carrot, Rincewind, and Leonard of Quirm as a device that allows the presentation of five major types of relation to the divine (lacking only the Atheist, who, as he notes Pratchett tells us, tends to have a very brief existence on the Discworld). Fornet-Ponse argues that the "game of the gods," as Pratchett has constructed it, is one that—particularly because of the way belief shapes the gods as they attempt to shape belief—creates a structure in which the gods may restrict humans' ranges of options but not deny free will.

The Greenwood Encyclopedia of Science Fiction and Fantasy: Themes, Works, and Wonders. **Ed. Gary Westfahl. 3 vols. Westport, CT: Greenwood, 2005.**
This encyclopedia includes only a few sporadic mentions of Pratchett's works in the form of book titles or character names.

Gruner, Elisabeth Rose. "Teach the Children: Education and Knowledge in Recent Children's Fantasy." *Children's Literature* **37 (2009): 216–35.**
This article focuses on portrayals of learning in children's fantasy series, and particularly in J. K. Rowling's *Harry Potter* series, Pratchett's Tiffany Aching books, and Philip Pullman's *His Dark Materials*. The three authors depict three different models of education: the traditional boarding school, an apprenticeship, and a "benign neglect of education" (219), respectively. Each of the protagonists finds mentors as well as peers, and each series shows how the making, telling, and reading of stories are central to their educational process. Unlike Harry or Lyra, however, Tiffany must learn to "take control of the stories that form part of the received wisdom of Discworld" (220), since these serve as objects that "require interpretation and revision" (227) rather than merely serving as sources of information. Pratchett's novels demonstrate that acting on stories without thinking carefully first is dangerous, and Tiffany participates in a kind of "unschooling" or "autonomous education" process, as she learns through doing rather than studying. Thus, Tiffany's education as a witch is more of a "socialization into being magical" (229) rather than an education in learning how to perform magic, and in this sense it is akin to an apprenticeship. All three series suggest that the more children direct their own education the more they learn, and thus they seem to "endorse" the concept of autonomous education for not only their protagonists but also for their readers, who become "unschooled" through narrative that teaches children how to read stories while they read them.

_____. **"Wrestling with Religion: Pullman, Pratchett, and the Uses of Story."** *Children's Literature Association Quarterly* **36: 3 (2011): 276–95.**
This article argues that both Philip Pullman's *His Dark Materials* trilogy and Pratchett's Tiffany Aching series link the impulses of narration and religion through narrative causality, and contain protagonists who not only resist narrative causality's extremes but also teach readers to resist its demands. Both heroines "turn story-making into a religious act" and revitalize the traditions or beliefs they appear to be undermining, and in this way become embodiments of "a new theology for a new world" (278). Instead of working from Judeo-Christian traditions, like Pullman, Pratchett works from traditions of English folklore and paganism, and "reanimates what might have

been thought to have devolved into fairy tale, legend, and superstition [by] refresh[ing] and defamiliariz[ing] stories that may form the groundwork of faith" (286). Tiffany's work as a witch "reinfuses her world with a sense of the numinous and a reverence for creation" (290). Both series suggest that the interdependence between the human and the divine results from the storytelling capacity.

Gunelius, Susan. "Terry Pratchett." *Harry Potter: The Story of a Global Business Phenomenon.* **Basingstoke, Hampshire: Palgrave Macmillan, 2008. 134–35.**
This very short piece discusses Pratchett in relation to "branding" and compares the Discworld series with J. K. Rowling's *Harry Potter* series. Gunelius makes some unsupported assumptions about both Pratchett's intentions and readers' responses to the Discworld books, arguing that Pratchett's goal has been "to release two books a year for the past two decades" (135) and that, as a result of the market having been over-saturated with Discworld books, fans were "not able to develop the same level of emotional involvement" with the series and thus do not have the same desire for Discworld books as they had for new books in the *Harry Potter* series. Gunelius also states that the Discworld series "was intentionally written so that readers could pick up any book at any time and enjoy it as a standalone novel" (135), though this assertion is not supported.

Haberkorn, Gideon. "Cultural Palimpsests: Terry Pratchett's New Fantasy Heroes." *Journal of the Fantastic in the Arts* **18:3 (2007): 319–39.**
This article argues that Pratchett's reinvention of heroes from traditions set up by the modern fantasy hero can be regarded as a kind of palimpsest, in the sense that his heroes are superimposed on earlier appearances of cultural heroes. The first half of the article provides background, with a discussion of the theoretical work of Joseph Campbell and J. R. R. Tolkien followed by an overview of the fantasy hero tradition. Haberkorn then turns to an analysis of Pratchett's construction of heroes, and begins with the argument that Pratchett's earlier Discworld novels, especially with the figures of Rincewind and the barbarian heroes Hrun and Cohen, ridicule rather than imitate the typical "uniform, simplified, standardized" (328) fantasy hero mold and portray its inadequacy. With his later protagonists, Pratchett consciously subverts stereotypical traditions and reinvents the heroic figure with Carrot and Vimes, as well as provides alternatives to it with Lord Vetinari. Though the article does not discuss female heroes, Haberkorn notes this is a topic for another paper. The article concludes that Pratchett's changes to the hero stereotype, as part of the cultural discourse on heroism, significantly contribute to shaping the contemporary fantasy hero.

Haberkorn, Gideon, and Verena Reinhardt. "Magic, Adolescence, and Education on Terry Pratchett's Discworld." *Supernatural Youth: The Rise of the Teen Hero in Literature and Popular Culture.* **Ed. Jes Battis. Plymouth, UK: Lexington, 2011. 43–64.** *MyLibrary.* **25 July 2012.**
This chapter considers the ways in which Pratchett's novels use magic and magical education as a metaphor for moving through adolescence and learning to deal with the world. The authors suggest that Pratchett develops a kind of humanistic education that relies on inquiry-based learning and thus stimulates students to think and to explore in order to solve problems (47). After categorizing Pratchett's different systems of education as including apprenticeship, training by a guild, religious education, the

Quirm College for Young Ladies, and Magical education, the rest of the chapter focuses on Tiffany Aching's education as "an argument for a humanistic education in general, and for problem-based learning specifically" (48). The authors note that Tiffany's formal education and vocational training coincide with her personal growth and maturation, and they note that this process stresses the importance of a witch's use of "inquiry and critical thinking, observation and evidence, logic and rational analysis" to understand her world and deal with its problems (50). Tiffany's education as a witch is contrasted with Eskarina Smith's education as a wizard in *Equal Rites*, and the authors note that witch magic and wizard magic are different types: wizardry has a "more sensational effect" that seems to be about show, while witchcraft relies on applied psychology and is about understatement (52). After a brief application of Ginsburg and Jablow's theory of attributes of resilience—competence, confidence, connection, character, contribution, coping, and control—to Tiffany's character, the chapter concludes by noting that, since coming-of-age stories usually are associated with males, Pratchett's four books on the education and adolescence of a girl are thus "very important" (57) because they "provoke" readers to think about magic as well as loss of illusion, humanist values, and virtues essential to adulthood, concluding, "[t]hus, it seems more likely that his books are not so much guides to childhood, but rather guides to adulthood, no matter the age of the reader" (58).

Hanes, Stacie L. "The Nineteenth-Century Foundations of the Discworld, or, More Than You Needed to Know About Granny Weatherwax's Knickers." *New York Review of Science Fiction* 21:11 [251] (July 2009): 11–12.
This essay briefly touches on the connections between aspects of British nineteenth century history and Discworld. Hanes connects Granny Weatherwax's underclothing to Victorian attitudes towards modesty, Nanny Ogg's tin bath and Archchancellor Ridcully's shower to Victorian plumbing and health, and the seamstresses of Ankh-Morpork to the connections between seamstresses and prostitutes in Victorian London. While Hanes' observations are interesting, the article is very general in scope.

Harvey, Graham. "Discworld and Otherworld: The Imaginative Use of Fantasy Literature Among Pagans." *Popular Spiritualities: The Politics of Contemporary Enchantment*. Ed. Lynne Hume and Kathleen McPhillips. Aldershot, UK: Ashgate, 2006. 41–51.
After setting up some terminological distinctions among three different varieties of what he terms "Paganisms" (in rough terms, Wicca/Druidry vs. Germanic Heathenry vs. Animistic Heathenry), Harvey goes on to examine possible reasons for the popularity of Pratchett's Discworld and Holdstock's Mythago Wood among Pagan audiences, and sketches out Pagan readings of particular elements of the texts. In the Pratchett section, Harvey appears to assume as a given that the Discworld is extremely popular among Pagans (perhaps this is common knowledge among scholars who study Paganism, but as Pratchett is extremely popular in general, some evidence that he is *more* popular among Pagans would have been useful). Harvey argues that Pratchett's portrayal of the elves as "bad" is not couched in terms of moral absolutes but rather only in terms of their being bad *for humans* (and bees), a point that raises some interesting questions that the article does not have room to pursue in detail. On a minor point, it refers to Granny, Nanny, and Magrat all as living in Bad Ass; there is a substantive question involved in where each of the characters lives.

Hill, Penelope. "Unseen University." *Terry Pratchett: Guilty of Literature*. Ed.
Andrew M. Butler, Edward James, and Farah Mendelssohn. Reading, UK:
Science Fiction Foundation, [2004]. 51–65.
This essay carefully charts the development of Unseen University and its associated
characters (faculty, staff, students, and in some cases, facilities) across the Discworld
novels up to the time of the essay's publication; along with detailed treatments of the
earlier novels, it includes discussions of *The Last Continent*, and some preliminary
remarks about *The Truth*, but was printed well before *Unseen Academicals*, and because
it was included in a volume with separate discussions of the Librarian, it mentions
him only in passing. Hill details the early inconsistencies in the presentation of the
institution, and discusses its use (and subsequent lack of use) as a backdrop for treatments of sexism, and its role as a stage on which relations of power are played out; she
also relates the novels to their wider literary and cultural contexts in terms of "the academic novel" (anchoring the discussion by reference to authors who are directly mentioned on Pratchett's book jackets or to whose works there are fairly clear allusions in
the Discworld novels themselves) and British academia. Hill does venture a conjecture,
in hindsight mistaken, that Pratchett had perhaps gotten all the use out of UU that
he would likely want, but the texts available at the time supported such a view. The
essay is more concerned with contextualization and with recording UU's development
than with advancing a unitary critical claim, but foregrounds the "uneasy compromise
between the twin images of academia as the refuge of the lazy and as the repository
of intellect and learning" (65).

Hills, Matthew. "Mapping Narrative Spaces." *Terry Pratchett: Guilty of Literature*.
Ed. Andrew M. Butler, Edward James, and Farah Mendlesohn. Reading, UK:
Science Fiction Foundation, [2004]. 129–44.
Hills discusses Pratchett's construction of Discworld in relation to definitions of the
postmodern, noting in particular its emphasis on the vulgar and marginal (e.g. the
sewer system exists for reasons other than narrative), and argues that in this sort of
fantasy, the world will only persist "through the discovery of new lands, or through
the creative and deliberate use of discontinuity" (143). He concludes that "Pratchett
neither radically subverts the conventions of the fantasy map nor merely reproduces
these conventions; his work both observes the co-ordinates of the fantasy genre and
re-places these co-ordinates through a 'postmodern' emphasis on waste and marginality
rather than upon heroic centrality," and comments on fantasy mapping as a moral as
well as spatial project.

Hunt, Peter. "Terry Pratchett." *Alternative Worlds in Fantasy Fiction*. Ed. Peter
Hunt and Millicent Lenz. London: Continuum, 2001. 86–121.
This chapter focuses on Pratchett's first seven non–Discworld children's books—*The
Carpet People*, *The Bromeliad Trilogy* (*Truckers, Diggers, Wings*), and the three Johnny
Maxwell books: *Only You Can Save Mankind*, *Johnny and the Dead*, and *Johnny and
the Bomb*—but also discusses the Discworld series up to 1998's *Carpe Jugulum*. Com-
mending Pratchett as "a satirist every bit as incisive and erudite and wide-ranging"
(87) as Jonathan Swift, Hunt suggests that Pratchett's frequent use of academics as
satiric fodder in their appearance as the Wizards of Unseen University mirrors his dis-
dain for literary research: Pratchett has said that he "'save[s] about twenty drafts....
Once [the final one] has been printed out ... there's a cry of "Tough Shit, literary

researchers of the future, try getting a proper job!" and the rest are wiped'" (87). Hunt briefly discusses Pratchett's fans, observing that they act very like literary scholars in their creation of annotations, discussion boards, and newsletters, but suggests that this behavior is justified since "the Pratchett books belong directly to the fans" (88). Due to their range of allusions as well as their treatment of fantasy, Hunt considers Pratchett's books as "modern fantasy at its most successful" and here mentions the "joke that no British railway train is allowed to depart unless at least one passenger is reading a Pratchett novel" (91). His discussion of Pratchett's children's books notes the way they overturn expectations about Children's literature in their exploration of the differences between literature for children and adults; arguing that what really separates books for children and adults is their point of view, Hunt claims that the Discworld books generally assume an adult point of view, despite their "gnomic pronouncements" as being "for anyone who can understand / for adults of all ages" (114). Ultimately Hunt disagrees with Colin Manlove's contention that Pratchett's books are for entertainment alone, and argues that instead they provide not only a "complete course in narratology" (119) but also astute social and political satire and philosophical insights.

Jakmakejian, Aurélia. "Terry Pratchett, le joker 2003 des 'Utopiales.'" *Rendezvous* **534 (14 Nov. 2003): 60–64. 15 June 2012. [In French].**
This brief article in French, whose title translates as "Terry Pratchett, the 'Utopiales' 2003 Joker," discusses Pratchett's appearance at the Utopiales Festival in Nantes, France in November 2003. It provides a brief introduction to Pratchett, and corrects French misperceptions that he isn't "nice" and that he doesn't like the French, noting that both were proven untrue during his visit. It also discusses the fame of the Discworld series, commenting on the 32 million copies of his books sold in countries ranging from Estonia, Germany, the United States, Australia, New Zealand, and Czechoslovakia to the Netherlands, Italy, Spain, and France; Pratchett comments that the only holdout is China, perhaps due to the Western flavor of his novels. Jakmakejian also mentions Pratchett's perennial presence on the bestseller lists in Britain and his wide and varied readership. The article then segues into a discussion of the Festival and the topic of science and parascience before concluding with a discussion about fantasy author James Morrow, who is agitating in favor of the translation of more European fantasy novels for American markets.

James, Edward. "The City Watch." *Terry Pratchett: Guilty of Literature.* **Ed. Andrew M. Butler, Edward James, and Farah Mendlesohn. Reading, UK: Science Fiction Foundation, [2004]. 112–28.**
James juxtaposes Vimes as hero with Carrot as Hero, framing both as parodic extensions of media tropes: the American detective or cop for Vimes, the British bobby for Carrot (with the "Destined King" trope, of course, added in for good measure). James views the City Watch novels as "the most political of Pratchett's works" (119), and provides numerous examples of ways in which the novels address issues of political power, community, and prejudice.

James, Edward, and Farah Mendlesohn, eds. *The Cambridge Companion to Fantasy Literature.* **Cambridge: Cambridge University Press, 2012.**
Several among this collection of essays make passing mention of Pratchett, although none focus on him in any detail.

Langford, David. *Josh Kirby: A Cosmic Cornucopia*. Illus. Josh Kirby. Foreword
   by Tom Holt. London: Paper Tiger, 1999.
This lavishly illustrated book provides a detailed history for and critical commentary
on the work of fantasy artist Josh Kirby, a prolific fantasy and horror artist best known
for his *Discworld* covers. After a brief biographical sketch, six chapters—organized
loosely by genre—discuss Kirby's art, and two of these focus on Discworld illustrations.
Although Langford notes that his discussion starts with *Reaper Man*, since the earlier
Discworld covers are discussed in Nigel Suckling's *In the Garden of Unearthly Delights*,
he nevertheless includes occasional comments about Kirby's earlier Discworld art and
general observations about Kirby's style, such as information about Kirby's artistic
influences, which include Titian and Rubens for form, Hogarth for characterization,
Hieronymus Bosch and Pieter Bruegel the Elder for a sense of an overflowing "abundance of bustling, imperfect humanity" (6), and muralist Frank Brangwyn for the use
of bold color. Langford discusses Kirby's composition process, his choice of media,
his preferred size of paintings for covers, and his policy "'not to do a Discworld cover
that does not have a frameable painting at the end of it'" (99). He also provides a
detailed analysis of Kirby's paintings from *Reaper Man* through *The Fifth Elephant*,
along with his illustrations for other Discworld stories, including four computer games,
short stories, the musical CD *From the Discworld*, and Kirby's illustrations for Pratchett's illustrated novella, *Eric*.

_____. "Pratchett, Terry." *The Encyclopedia of Fantasy*. 1997. Ed. John Clute and
   John Grant. New York: St. Martin's Griffin, 1999. 783–85.
This encyclopedia entry lists Pratchett's publications to 1996, mentions Pratchett's
concepts of "narrative causality" and "morphic resonance," and then provides an
overview of the novels according to their groupings and themes. In addition to the
Rincewind sequence, the Witch sequence, the Death stories, and the City Guard or
Night Watch sequence, Langford discusses Discworld books that do not fit tidily into
one of the main story arcs, including *Moving Pictures, Pyramids,* and *Small Gods.* In
addition to pointing out various authors parodied in the Discworld series, such as H.
P. Lovecraft, Fritz Leiber, and Anne McCaffrey, along with topics including astrology,
druids, dwarfs, heroic fantasy, magic shops and spells, and trolls, Langford also notes
that "a steadfast seriousness in matters of life and death underpins the humour of the
finer novels" (784), and that the Discworld series is becoming increasingly shaped by
Pratchett's "interplay of belief and Story" (784).

_____. "Pratchett, Terry (David John)." *St. James Guide to Fantasy Writers*. Ed.
   David Pringle. New York: St. James, 1996. 486–88.
This encyclopedia entry provides a brief summary of Pratchett's life and work to 1996,
and comments that the Discworld novels "offer the most recognizable brand image
of funny fantasy in Britain today" (486).

Lewis, Helen. "The Politics of Pratchett." *New Statesman* 21 Nov. 2012. Web. 15
   July 2013.
This very short piece notes that the Discworld books, despite being fantasy, are not
irrelevant to real world concerns but instead have become increasingly political. Lewis
then cites several Discworld novels' treatment of political issues, including power (*Feet
of Clay*), capitalism (*Going Postal*), religion and the strength of belief (*Small Gods*),

and war (*Jingo*), and then briefly summarizes their content before noting Vimes and Granny Weatherwax as the series' "moral cores."

Mackey, Margaret. "The Survival of Engaged Reading in the Internet Age: New Media, Old Media, and the Book." *Children's Literature in Education* **32:3 (Sept. 2001): 167–189.**
This article considers the spin-off texts engendered by J. K. Rowling's, Philip Pullman's, and Pratchett's series, and argues that "extended reading is supported rather than undermined by many of these associated texts" (167). Mackey's discussion of Pratchett is far less extensive than the discussions of Rowling and Pullman, and does little other than providing an incomplete list of some of the offshoots of the Discworld books, including one of the maps, one *Companion*, a graphic novel, an illustrated compendium, and two computer games. Mackey does note two interesting statistics about Pratchett: his books "account for an astonishing 1 percent of all fiction sold in the Dillons chain [and] he rises to the status of legend by being regularly nominated as the most shoplifted author in Britain" (168).

Manlove, Colin. *The Fantasy Literature of England.* **New York: St. Martin's, 1999. 135–37.**
Despite introducing him as "a parodist of 'genre' fantasy," Manlove acknowledges Pratchett to be "a highly inventive fantasist in his own right" (135) and credits him with popularizing the genre of comic fantasy. Manlove briefly summarizes *The Color of Magic*, noting Pratchett's use of Tolkien, Robert E. Howard, and Anne McCaffrey as his sources of parody, calling Pratchett a "creative comic genius" (136). After a lengthy quotation describing the Rimfall, Manlove concludes that Pratchett's fantasy, despite being "a display of inventive pyrotechnics: it asks only that we enjoy, it does not seek to change us" (137), mixes textual realities in postmodern ways similar to Salman Rushdie and Robert Irwin.

Mendlesohn, Farah. "Faith and Ethics." *Terry Pratchett: Guilty of Literature.* **Ed. Andrew M. Butler, Edward James, and Farah Mendlesohn. Reading, UK: Science Fiction Foundation, [2004]. 145–61.**
Mendlesohn argues in this essay that Pratchett's work can be read as constructing a consistent theory of morality, one that positions an identity-derived (rather than image-defined) valuation of life, and the acceptance of the potentialities and responsibilities of choice, as the locus of the Good (or the Better than Otherwise, at least). The article develops this reading by an examination of *Jingo*, *Small Gods*, and the first and third *Johnny and the Bomb* novels in particular (although the Agataeans of *Interesting Times* enter the discussion as well), focusing on Pratchett's treatment of evil as objectification of human life and how this treatment interacts with the complex of motifs with which Pratchett surrounds notions of warfare and honor.

_____. *Rhetorics of Fantasy.* **Middletown, CT: Wesleyan University Press, 2008.**
Mendlesohn refers to Pratchett several times in this work, but he is positioned primarily as one among many sources of examples to illustrate categories in the typology of fantasy that she develops in the volume. For example, she connects Ankh-Morpork citizens' "city mindset" (in the Watch sequence and later novels) to the notion of a pocket universe (91–2) and the parodically unsubtle clue-dropping in *Carpe Jugulum* to the more earnest preceding versions in what she terms intrusion fantasies (126).

She and Edward James consider Pratchett in more detail in *A Short History of Fantasy*.

Mendlesohn, Farah, and Edward James. *A Short History of Fantasy.* **London: Middlesex University Press, 2009. 167–84.**
Most of the discussion of Pratchett in this highly readable volume is in the tenth chapter, titled simply "Pullman, Rowling, Pratchett." In keeping with its title, the book is designed to provide historical contextualization rather than to argue for a particular theoretic framework for a specialist audience. It provides a particularly useful, brief, but non-reductionist discussion of the relation between these authors' "blockbuster" status and shifts in the economics of the fantasy book market—for example, the advent of Amazon, and changes in British law controlling book-pricing—and discusses some of Pratchett's impact on the genre itself, noting that "while sword-and-sorcery makes an impressive reappearance in the twenty-first century ... it looks very different, at least in part because Pratchett mocked some of the older clichés to death" (183). Its other mentions of Pratchett are primarily as illustrative examples.

Moody, Nikianne. "Death." *Terry Pratchett: Guilty of Literature.* **Ed. Andrew M. Butler, Edward James, and Farah Mendlesohn. Reading, UK: Science Fiction Foundation, [2004]. 99–111.**
Focusing primarily on the novels in which Death is a central character, such as *Mort, Reaper Man,* and *Hogfather,* this article considers Pratchett's construction of Death, and of the contexts Death becomes a participant in, as critiques of Thatcherian political/enterprise discourse and as statements about the relationship between work and identity. Moody contextualizes the books' popularity with discussions of changes in the science fiction book market (which became the "fantasy and science fiction market") and in wider British culture, concluding that "by insisting on and achieving an integrity for the character of Death, Pratchett disrupts the terrain proposed by political rhetoric of the 1980s and 1990s, which had established itself as the only agenda for debating everyday life, social change, and consensus" (111).

Moorcock, Michael. *Wizardry and Wild Romance: A Study of Epic Fantasy.* **London: Gollancz, 1987. 63–4; 117–19.**
Moorcock makes two short mentions in passing of Pratchett, the first of which notes Pratchett's emphasis on landscape as being like that of other sorts of sword and sorcery tales, the second of which positions Pratchett relative to authors such as Pratt, de Camp, and Leiber.

Noone, Kristin. "Shakespeare in Discworld: Witches, Fantasy, and Desire." *Journal of the Fantastic in the Arts* **21:1 (77) (2010): 28–40.** *OmniFile Full Text Select.*
This article discusses the correspondences between Shakespeare's *Macbeth* and *A Midsummer Night's Dream* and Pratchett's *Wyrd Sisters* and *Lords and Ladies,* and argues that "while desire is an unavoidable, powerful, and ambivalent part of life, with all attendant dangers and strengths, the heart of successful magical thinking lies in human response and choice" (10 of 12). Noone defines desire in *Wyrd Sisters* and *Macbeth* as a craving for power, and in *Lords and Ladies* and *A Midsummer Night's Dream* as a love of beauty and glamour. Noone notes that magic is paradoxical since it is invoked only when desire cannot be realized in reality, and suggests that Pratchett's witches

provide a resolution to this problem in the shape of human response. The article concludes that Pratchett uses Shakespeare like Shakespeare used fantasy: to provide "a space for the exploration of human desires and choices" (10 of 12).

"Out of This World: The Art of Josh Kirby. 15 June–30 September 2007." *Walker Art Gallery Exhibition*. 2007. Liverpool, UK. 10 Oct. 2012.
This art exhibition overview discusses Kirby in light of his reputation for having created cover art for "some of the most iconic science fiction and fantasy novels" as well as film posters for *Star Wars: Return of the Jedi* and *Monty Python's Life of Brian*. The catalogue provides biographical material, a discussion of his fantasy artwork, and a lengthy discussion of his Discworld paintings, suggesting that Pratchett's novels in translation were "re-branded when books that had originally been launched with artwork by other artists were given new Josh Kirby covers, guaranteeing their saleability on the foreign market." It claims that Kirby's covers are "synonymous with [Pratchett's] work, capturing the frenetic pace of life in the Discworld," and notes that some of his Discworld illustrations became "iconic within Kirby's output," including "Rincewind Running" as well as the universe's creation in "The Big Bang," both from *Eric*.

Oziewicz, Marek. "'Into Our Hands They Are Absolutely Delivered?' Animal Fantasy as a Form of Affirmative Action." *Relevant Across Cultures; Visions of Connectedness in Modern Fantasy Literature for Young Readers*. Ed. Justyna Deszcz-Tryhubczak, Marek Oziewicz and Agata Zarzycka. Wroclaw: Oficyna Wydawnicza, 2009. 119–32.
This article focuses on four works of rat fantasy—Robert C. O'Brien's *Mrs. Frisby and the Rats of NIMH*, Ursula Le Guin's "Mazes," Philip Pullman's *I Was a Rat*, and Pratchett's *The Amazing Maurice*—and argues that anthropomorphism is the alternative to animal degradation, since it encourages empathy and helps promote a sense of interconnectedness between animal life and reader. After tracing historical attitudes towards degradation of animals, Oziewicz discusses each of the stories in turn, providing a brief plot summary for each. He suggests that Pratchett's view of inter-species relationships and evolution of the animal consciousness theme "offers a look at the human world through non-human eyes" (129) and that this perspective creates anthropomorphism for both the rats and Maurice.

_____. "'We Cooperate, or We Die': Sustainable Coexistence in Terry Pratchett's *The Amazing Maurice and His Educated Rodents*." *Children's Literature in Education* 40 (2009): 85–94.
This article invokes Fritjof Capra's concept of ecological sustainability and his usage of the terms "ecoliteracy" and "ecodesign" as scaffolding for Oziewicz's argument that *The Amazing Maurice* presents "a modern example of environmentally informed social dreaming about sustainable coexistence" (85). Moreover, it considers the problem of connecting economic, social, and political discourses to things that are non-human, and thus functions as "a work with a transformative purpose. It suggests that cooperation and coexistence are workable beyond what we assume to be their limits" (85). Oziewicz concludes by suggesting that Pratchett's novel illustrates his conviction that "we can learn how to recondition ourselves to accept attitudes and priorities compatible with ecological sustainability."

Parker, Vic. *Terry Pratchett (Writers Uncovered)*. London: Heinemann, 2007.
The Writers Uncovered series is aimed at schoolchildren and provides background on
Pratchett, an introduction to his works for children, and "tips" to inspire younger
readers' own writing. Printed in color and including numerous photographs and text-
boxes, it opens with a biographical sketch that traces Pratchett's schooling, his earliest
publications, and his jobs as a journalist and as Publicity Officer for the Central Elec-
tricity Generating Board. After noting his creation of Discworld, it shifts to short sections devoted to the children's books; each section provides plot summary and a short
paragraph of "Inside Information" with related interesting facts. These are followed
with pages on Pratchett's honors and awards, the adaptations of *Truckers* as an animated film and *Johnny and the Dead* and *The Amazing Maurice* into plays, and an
example of a book review of *The Amazing Maurice*, coupled with a suggestion that
readers try to write their own book review. After briefly discussing future projects, the
book concludes with a timeline, further resources, a glossary (keyed to words that
have appeared in bold throughout the text, such as "conventions," "extra-terrestrial,"
"draft," "parody," and "touch-typing"), and an index.

Petty, Anne C. "Terry Pratchett: Funny Side Up." *Dragons of Fantasy*. Cold Spring
Harbor, NY: Cold Spring, 2004. 96–121.
This chapter discusses Pratchett's dragons in *The Color of Magic, Guards! Guards!*,
and *The Last Hero* and notes their parodic correspondences with dragons in Anne
McCaffrey's *Pern* tales, Ursula Le Guin's *Earthsea* tales, and J. R. R. Tolkien's *The
Hobbit*. Petty notes several examples of Pratchett's humor, his ironic reversals, and his
comic technique of shifting focus before moving to a detailed discussion of *The Color
of Magic* and the correspondences between its dragons and McCaffrey's. After noting
similarities between Pratchett's dragons in *Guards! Guards!* and those in Tolkien and
McCaffrey, the chapter discusses their correspondences with western dragon mythology. Several paragraphs are devoted to the Dragon of Ankh-Morpork's characterization, physical description, and sound imagery before the chapter segues into a
discussion of swamp dragons and the ways in which they parody British dog and horse
breeders, as well as briefly mentioning the moon dragons in *The Last Hero*. Petty concludes with praising Pratchett's parody.

Petzold, Dieter. "'A Christian Atheist': Religion in Terry Pratchetts Post-Mod-
erner Fantasy Fiction." *Spiritualität und Transzendenz in der modernen
englisch-sprachigen Literatur*. Ed. Susanne Bach. Paderborn: Schöningh,
2001. 49–69. [In German]
This chapter is cited in Fornet-Ponse's "'The Gods play games with the fate of men'"
but was unobtainable at date of writing.

Pratchett, Terry, and Jacqueline Simpson. *The Folklore of Discworld*. Illus. Paul
Kidby. London, UK: Transworld, 2008.
The entries in this work are written from a "faux-real" stance (with the Discworld and
Earth as two environments within a multiverse) and position selected Discworld topics
in relation to general information from folklore studies. In keeping with its stance, it
is intended for a popular audience, not researchers—it does refer to several specific
studies, and often includes excerpts from collected folktales, but uses these as illustration instead of focusing on argumentation or documentation issues (of course, one
could argue that actual folklore rarely focuses on argumentation or documentation

issues either). Its relatively brief bibliography is designed to be a list of suggested further reading for those with no specialized knowledge of folklore or mythology.

Pringle, David, ed. *Ultimate Encyclopedia of Fantasy: The Definitive Illustrated Guide.* **1998. Foreword by Terry Pratchett. London: Carlton, 2006.**
This colorful illustrated encyclopedia is divided into eight main sections, of which the two largest contain alphabetically arranged entries on major authors and fantasy characters and entities. The other six sections, which are not arranged in a discernible order, comprise entries on fantasy types, cinema and television fantasies, games, settings, and fantasy magazines. The book concludes with a short glossary of terms. The entry on Pratchett is quite short, providing a brief overview of the various clusters of the Discworld books—Rincewind, the Witches, Death, and the Watch—as well as the books that do not clearly fit into these clusters. In the Fantasy Characters section, the only entry relating to Discworld is the entry on Death, which lists the books he appears in, while the entry on Discworld in the Settings section is somewhat longer but essentially descriptive.

"Rhianna Pratchett on Reclaiming Lara Croft and Having Discworld Creator Terry as a Dad." *Metro.* **4 Mar. 2013. Web. 6 Mar. 2013.**
In this interview with Pratchett's daughter, a videogame scriptwriter, she comments on her father's love for "electronics, robotics and computers" and comments that, despite having been diagnosed with Alzheimer's in 2007, Pratchett is doing well and now writes using "TalkingPoint speech software because he can't type any more." She regards herself as "the protector of Discworld and that means protecting it from myself as well," and also notes that she and her father are working with BBC Worldwide on a television series of The Watch books.

Rusnak, Marcin. "Playing with Death: Humorous Treatment of Death-Related Issues in Terry Pratchett's and Neil Gaiman's Young Adult Fiction." *Fastitocalon: Studies in Fantasticism Ancient to Modern* **2:1–2 (2011): 81–95.**
Rusnak examines the intersection of humor and depictions of death in Gaiman's *The Graveyard Book* and Pratchett's *The Amazing Maurice and His Educated Rodents*, using Freudian interpretations of humor as a basis. Drawing on work by Philippe Ariés, Douglas Davies, and Benjamin Noys, he notes that Western attitudes toward death have changed dramatically in the past fifty years, and argues that the increase in death/dying motifs and "black humor" in YA fiction represent attempts to develop new means of dealing with an increasingly taboo topic, since "humour in its numerous forms may alleviate fear and other negative emotions usually associated with death and death-related issues" (84). Rusnak particularly notes as stylistic devices the casual attitude Pratchett's characters frequently adopt about death, the ways in which discussion shifts from the abstract to the corporeal, and, of course, Pratchett's memorable personalization of Death himself. The article does not address criticisms of Freud's theory of humor, or of additional/competing explanations for the increase in death themes in YA literature, but such would have been beyond its practical scope, and Rusnak does an excellent job of stating his grounds.

Rüster, Johannes. *All-Macht und Raum-Zeit: Gottesbilder in der englischsprachigen Fantasy und Science Fiction.* **Berlin, DE: Lit Verlag, 2007.** *Google Books.* **18 Aug. 2013 [In German]**

This detailed analysis of the ways in which science-fiction and fantasy authors have constructed theories about the nature of divinities and the divine incorporates examinations of a number of Discworld novels (including *Eric, The Color of Magic, Small Gods, The Last Hero,* and *Pyramids,* as well as the non–Discworld novel *Good Omens*), in addition to analyses of a number of texts by other authors (e.g., Gaiman, Bradbury, Lem, Vonnegut). It should therefore be of particular interest to scholars contextualizing Pratchett within the wider field of science-fiction/fantasy studies.

_____. "'It's Alive!': Der Mad Scientist als Amoralapostel." *Inklings: Jahrbuch für Literatur und Ästhetik.* 26 (2008): 119–137. [In German]
Rüster examines the figure of the "mad scientist," contextualizing the discussion by placing mad scientists into relation with both the "wizard" and "evil genius" images. By Rüster's definitions, the distinguishing feature of mad scientists is their amorality—unlike evil geniuses, they are not primarily concerned with the pursuit of power, but rather of knowledge; the danger they pose is constituted by their disinterest in the wider consequences of that pursuit. Pratchett is brought into the exposition as an example of postmodern conceptions of the mad scientist (following discussions of *Frankenstein* as a pre-modern case and *Dr. Strangelove* as a modern exemplar). After tracing the origin of "the Igor" in film, Rüster argues that while Pratchett's Igor trope is obviously connected to the mad scientist motif, it acts as a "magic mirror" to it, by virtue of Igors' application of their knowledge to addressing community needs and by their humanity in contrast to that of their masters. Teatime, on the other hand, evinces a number of mad-scientist traits without so obviously fitting the image.

Sawyer, Andy. "The Librarian and His Domain." *Terry Pratchett: Guilty of Literature.* Ed. Andrew M. Butler, Edward James, and Farah Mendlesohn. Reading, UK: Science Fiction Foundation, [2004]. 66–82.
Sawyer discusses Pratchett's Librarian as an affectionate and celebratory parody, pointing out the Librarian's (and librarians') crucial role as facilitator and guardian. The article includes a brief but nuanced overview of the history of library science and some of its major figures (Edwards, Dewey, Ranganathan), noting the rapid reconfigurations made possible by the internet's potential to decouple content from physical artifact and by database technologies' emancipation of organization from a single sort order. Sawyer sets up a three-way distinction of Clever vs. Skilful vs. Knowledgeable as a parallel to Martin's Right, Good, and Nice, and then goes on to argue that the appeal to librarians of the Knowledgeable Librarian—whose overwhelmingly positive reaction to a parody might seem odd—is tied to Pratchett's obvious understanding of their mission. Pratchett has, for example, an unusually clear grasp of the relative social value of librarians and academics, for whom Sawyer argues the Librarian is a foil. Thus, Pratchett's parodic figure is one that reclaims it, that loudly but silently wrests it from the distinctly unpassionate grasp of the standard cultural stereotype. As the article can be read as rather slyly performing a number of the points it makes about librarians while describing them, it is interesting from a general rhetorical standpoint as well.

_____. "Narrativium and Lies-to-Children: 'Palatable Instruction' in *The Science of Discworld." Journal of the Fantastic in the Arts* 13:1 [49] (2002): 62–81.
In this examination of the first volume of *The Science of Discworld* sequence, Sawyer places Pratchett, Stewart, and Cohen's treatment of the science/fiction relationship

into opposition with a unidirectional, didactic one he characterizes as Gernsbeckian, arguing that in Science, "the threads of the 'fiction' and 'science' aspects are there to illuminate and interrogate each other rather than merely to be 'entertaining' or 'instructive'" (63). His argument has bearing both on typologies of science fiction and on discussions of science as explanatory narrative.

Sayer, Karen. "The Witches." *Terry Pratchett: Guilty of Literature*. Ed. Andrew M. Butler, Edward James, and Farah Mendlesohn. Reading, UK: Science Fiction Foundation, [2004]. 83–98.

Sayer examines the status of Pratchett's witches in relation to the tripartite maiden/mother/crone figure as presented in popular syntheses such as Dexter's *Whence the Goddesses*, which Sayer uses extensively, noting that in Pratchett's novels, "[t]here is an adherence to the (reproductive) pagan model of maiden, mother, crone, yet women's sexuality is not constructed simply—there are various models of motherhood (Magrat and Gytha), maidenhood (Granny, Agnes, and Magrat), and of being a crone (Gytha and Esme)" (97). Using concepts from Lacan and Kristeva, the article also examines ways in which Pratchett's witches lend themselves to being read as feminist (their independence, their power, their physicality) or resist such a reading (their connection to domestic sites such as their huts).

Schanoes, Veronica L. "Book as Mirror, Mirror as Book: The Significance of the Looking-Glass in Contemporary Revisions of Fairy Tales." *Journal of the Fantastic in the Arts* 20:1 (2009): 5–23. *ProQuest*. 3 June 2012.

After reviewing feminist analyses of the mirror as a symbol of patriarchal objectification, making specific reference to Gilbert and Gubar's as well as Irigaray's theories, Schanoes examines Angela Carter's presentation of mirrors in detail. She argues that Carter has transformed the mirror as a symbol for later fantasy writers such as Tanith Lee and Terry Pratchett, supporting the argument with critical analyses of *Wyrd Sisters* and Lee's *White as Snow*. Schanoes argues that the mirrors in these feminist revisions of fairy tales function as symbols that represent reflections—comprising stories, which are in turn composed of memories of the past and fantasies for the future—and that, despite their ephemeral nature (because they are constructed by and contained in the mind), these reflections are necessary to how one constructs and relates to the world; similarly, "fantasy is utterly necessary to our understanding of reality."

Scholz, Thomas. "The Making of a Hilarious Undead: Bisociation in the Novels of Terry Pratchett." *Fastitocalon: Studies in Fantasticism Ancient to Modern* 1:2 (2010): 141–52.

Scholz applies Arthur Koestler's notion of creativity as "bisociation"—the juxtaposition of two frames of reference that conflict, with the dissolution of the conflict resulting from application of a consistent but novel logic—to an analysis of Discworld's undead characters, such as zombies (Reg Shoe and Windle Poons), the vampires, and the ghost of Verence I. After pointing out the devices by which bisociation is accomplished in a number of examples and discussing the frames being juxtaposed, he refers to increasing frequency of humorous undead, citing J. K. Rowling's *Harry Potter* series particularly. The article does not attempt to trace the history of humorous undead, and it is unclear whether he considers them as essentially a recent phenomenon.

Simpson, Jacqueline. "On the Ambiguity of Elves." *Folklore* 122:1 (Apr. 2011): 76–83.
Simpson discusses Pratchett's, Tolkien's, and Rowling's construction of "elf" figures in relation to folkloric depictions from northern Germanic texts, specifically Norse, including Sturluson's *Edda*, and Old English, including *Beowulf* and several of the metrical charms. She confines the discussion to direct cognates of "elf" (*ælf, álfar*), thus excluding in a principled way a discussion of similar figures from neighboring cultures / linguistic groups, and highlights the extent to which folkloric elf-figures have persistently retained both benevolent and malefic traits. Her discussion of Pratchett's elves occupies a comparatively small portion of the argument, using them primarily as an example of a modern author's employment of their negative characteristics. The article is likely to be particularly useful to those unfamiliar with northern European folklore, as it provides a highly accessible overview of material treated in greater detail in scholarly monographs.

Smith, Eve. "Selling Terry Pratchett's Discworld: Merchandising and the Cultural Economy of Fandom." *Participations: Journal of Audience and Reception Studies* 8.2 (Nov. 2011): 239–256.
Smith applies Bourdieu's notions of economic and cultural capital to the analysis of the results of a 2007 online survey of fan ownership of merchandise and collectibles. The discussion of the survey itself is focused on integrating a few of the major findings with a summary of Bourdieu's theory and details about the fan base; it does not focus on survey construction or statistical analysis, and appears designed to clearly introduce the areas of discussion and connect them, rather than to address a specialist audience of social scientists. One of Smith's major points is that Pratchett's fan base values openness, so this non-specialization may be a statement as well. The survey results indicate that level of education (a proxy for cultural capital) does not predict ownership patterns except in the case of very hard-to-obtain items, with "items" here including abstract ones, e.g., "having a Discworld character named after you" (254).

Smith, Kevin Paul. "Battling the Nightmare of Myth, Terry Pratchett's Fairytale Inversions." *The Postmodern Fairytale: Folkloric Intertexts in Contemporary Fiction*. New York: Palgrave, 2007. 133–163.
This extended essay on Pratchett applies Baudrillardian concepts to a detailed examination of *Witches Abroad*, arguing that the novel effectively addresses social concerns with "the reign of the hyper-real and the way that fairytales can become repressive myths that, like the panopticon, are part of a society's power structures" (160). He notes that Pratchett's undermining of fairy tales' efficacy as vectors of ideology works in some ways like feminist revisions of fairy tales do: by making figures that were previously simply narrative objects central and dynamic, and by (simultaneously) drawing readers' attention to narrative conventions through this shift. After examining each of the prototypical fairy tale scenarios that the witches cheerfully demolish on their way to Genua (and how Pratchett accomplishes the destruction), Smith draws detailed parallels between Genua and Disney Land in a discussion of the hyper-real and dystopia.

Smythe, Colin. "A Short Biography." *L-Space Web*. 1996–2011. 3 July 2012.
This short biographical essay provides an overview of Pratchett's education, his job

history prior to becoming a full-time writer, his honorary degrees, his marriage and the birth of his daughter, his diagnosis with early-onset Alzheimer's disease in 2007, and the ever-increasing rise of Discworld fandom. Progressing chronologically, Smythe focuses on Pratchett's publications and their history, beginning with his first publication at the age of thirteen—a short story entitled "The Hades Business" appearing first in his school magazine *Technical Cygnet* and then commercially two years later in *Science Fantasy* magazine—and concluding with *Snuff.* Smythe notes Corgi's publication of *The Colour of Magic* in 1985 as "the turning point in Terry's writing career," and adds that Pratchett began writing full-time in 1987 after finishing *Mort.* The essay also notes Pratchett's work for the Orang-Utan Foundation. It concludes with a discussion of the recent live-action films of *Hogfather, The Colour of Magic, Going Postal,* and the upcoming production of *Unseen Academicals.*

Suckling, Nigel. *In the Garden of Unearthly Delights: The Paintings of Josh Kirby.* **Foreword by Brian Aldiss. 1991. London: Paper Tiger, 1995.**
This book traces artist Josh Kirby's career from its beginning until 1991. Essentially a collection of color reproductions of Kirby's artwork, each chapter begins with a short essay discussing the different themes that appear in his work, ranging from "Vapours of Forgotten Worlds" through "Maidens and Monsters" and "Sword and Sorcery" to "Hitchcock, Poe and Horror." Of the eight chapters, only the sixth focuses on the illustrations for Pratchett's Discworld, though Kirby's illustrations for the covers of Pratchett's *Bromeliad* trilogy as well as *The Dark Side of the Sun* and *Strata* are also included. Kirby's understanding of the Discworld books appears nicely in his comment that "humour and shrewd social comment and airy philosophy and droll science thread their way through the frantic, even manic, efforts of the inhabitants of the Discworld to survive.... Here perhaps we have Bruegel in literary form" (92). One chapter of the book highlights Kirby's "Voyage of the Ayeguy," his *magnum opus,* and the book concludes with a selection of his science fiction illustrations.

Thomas, Melissa. "Teaching Fantasy: Overcoming the Stigma of Fluff." *English Journal* **92:5 (May 2003): 60–64.**
This short piece provides a surface-level overview of the history of fantasy and its topics, mentioning wizards, gender roles, and heroism. Its paragraph on Pratchett notes his popularity, his humor, and his social commentary, concluding that his fantasy "has come a long way from theological speculation to a sort of human spiritual spanking" (63).

Tiffin, Jessica. "Structured Sword and Sorcery: The Popular Fairy Tales of Lee, Pratchett, and Tepper." *Marvellous Geometry: Narrative and Metafiction in Modern Fairy Tale.* **Detroit: Wayne State University Press, 2009. 131–178.**
In this well-contextualized essay drawing on a number of theorists of fairy tales (Bettelheim, Tatar, Zipes), popular fiction (Cavetti), and orality (Ong, Harres), Tiffin points out similarities between the fairy tale and popular narrative (both, for example, rely on minor surface variations on very fixed generic structures) and notes that within the "SF Ghetto," literary fairy tales and innovative popular fantasy novels exist in a state of tension: the audience expects a level of predictability that the works seek to undermine. She goes on to examine how the three authors listed in her title may be read as negotiating this tension; for Pratchett, she argues that "the Discworld's nar-

rative structures ... provide the necessary element of familiarity which enables the popular audience comfortably to consume the disrupted view of modern culture the novels provide" (161). The subsection on Pratchett focuses on *Witches Abroad*, with its deflation of the Disneyesque by the witches' ironic realism, stating that "the use of fairy tale in [Pratchett's] novels is inevitable; like Byatt, he appears to be drawn to structural narrative which counteracts the fragmentary nature of the modern culture he parodies" (161).

Washington, Linda, and Carrie Pyykkonen. *Secrets of The Wee Free Men and Discworld: The Myths and Legends of Terry Pratchett's Multiverse.* **New York: St. Martin's Griffin, 2008.**
This fan-created appreciation piece relies heavily on Wikipedia as a major source for its information, and adopts a conversational style throughout. The authors provide their rationale for writing with "Call us crazy, but we really like Pratchett's books and are dying to tell you why—hence this book" (2). Its three loosely-organized sections address the literary roots of Discworld, Pratchett's characters, and other aspects of the Discworld including magic, power, time, the City Watch, and Pratchett's use of technology.

Watt-Evans, Lawrence. *The Turtle Moves! Discworld's Story Unauthorized.* **Dallas: BenBella, 2008.**
Watt-Evans is a well-established fantasy author, and the volume is constructed rather like an informal travel guide: the reader is presented with the author's comments about the text couched *as* the author's comments about the text. It does not attempt to construct a scholarly critique (in the traditional sense) or connect observations to formal critical theory, although Watt-Evans does provide stylistically-aware commentary grounded in intimate practical and historical knowledge of the field. One major section presents individual plot descriptions and comments on each of the novels to the time of publication, and another examines development across "sequences" (e.g., the Watch books); Watt-Evans accompanies these with shorter sections, some focused on particular elements occurring in multiple texts (e.g., the Luggage) and others involving Discworld's status as a whole. The edition includes links to online resources.

Webb, Caroline. "'Change the Story, Change the World': Witches/Crones as Heroes in Novels by Terry Pratchett and Diana Wynne Jones." *Papers* **16:2 (2006): 156–61.**
This article discusses the positive portrayals of the witch/crone figures in *The Wee Free Men* and Diana Wynne Jones' *Howl's Moving Castle* and suggests that, by showing how their protagonists gain power by identifying with the role of the witch, young readers realize "that stories, and the social conventions they represent, may themselves be resisted in the course of establishing individual identity" (156). In Pratchett's novel, Tiffany realizes that a witch is someone who has responsibility for the community's well-being and indeed its life; her understanding that the power of story changes one's vision of the real world allows her to resist this power of story and claim her identity as her community's witch. In Jones' novel, Sophie is liberated by her new identity as crone, and her acceptance of this new identity eventually leads to her power and her liberation. Webb briefly contrasts both novels with treatments of the witches in E. L. Konigsburg's *Jennifer, Hecate, Macbeth, William McKinley, and Me, Elizabeth* (1967)

and Elizabeth George Speare's *The Witch of Blackbird Pond* (1958). She then argues that both Pratchett's and Jones' novels invite re-valuation of our conceptions of the witch/crone figures and critique fairy tale conventions as well as the power of story to shape and reflect "potentially destructive social conventions" (160).

B. *Interviews*

1. Interviews with Terry Pratchett

"'Discworld' Author Terry Pratchett." Book World Live. *Washington Post*, 1 Oct. 2008. Web. 21 Feb. 2009.

"Fantastic Voyager." By John Gilbey. *Times Higher Education Supplement,* 16 Sept. 2010. Web. 23 Oct. 2010.

"'Fantasy is the whole cake': An Interview with Terry Pratchett." By Aleandra Rehfeld, Jan Schnitker, Matthias Schröder. *"Do you consider yourself a postmodern author?" Interviews with Contemporary English Writers.* Ed. Rudolf Freiburg and Jan Schnitker. Münster: Transaction, 1999. 173–200.

"Humour Can Exist in the Most Dreadful Trials." By Alison Flood. *The Bookseller* 5328 (18 Apr. 2008): 26. *Academic OneFile.* 4 June 2012.

"I know the books have their heart in the right place." *Bookwitch*. 24 Apr. 2012. Web. 15 July 2013.

"I will always be the fellow who writes funny books." *Bookwitch*. 10 Sept. 2010. Web. 15 July 2013.

Interview. National Book Festival. 29 Sept. 2007. Library of Congress. 15 July 2013.

Interview. *SFX*. 14 Sept. 2010. Web. 16 Sept. 2010.

"An Interview with Sir Terry Pratchett." By Neil Gaiman. *boing boing*. 10 Oct. 2011. Web. 15 July 2013.

"A Life in Writing: Terry Pratchett." By Alison Flood. *Guardian,* 15 Oct. 2011. Web. 3 Nov. 2011.

"My Hols." By Cally Law. *The Times*. 29 July 2001. Web. 2 Jan. 2002.

"Profile: Terry Pratchett." *BBC News*. 31 Dec. 2008. Web. 2 Nov. 2011.

"Promotional Interview for *The Amazing Maurice and His Educated Rodents*." Harper-Collins. N.d. Web. 19 Oct. 2004.

"The SF Kick: Terry Pratchett Talks to Stella Hargreaves About SF, Fantasy and Why He Won't Be Taking the Devil's Bargain Just Yet." *Interzone* 81 (1994): 25–28.

"Sweet Fantasy: 25 Years of Terry Pratchett's Discworld." By Neil Gaiman. Waterstones. N.d. Web. 4 Mar. 2013.

"Terry Pratchett." By Linda L. Richards. *January Magazine*. Aug. 2002. Web. 10 Mar. 2011.

"Terry Pratchett." By Liz Holliday. *Science Fiction Chronicle* 13:7 (Apr. 1992): 5, 26–27.

"Terry Pratchett." *The Wand in the Word: Conversations with Writers of Fantasy*. By Leonard S. Marcus. Cambridge, MA: Candlewick, 2006. 153–166.

"Terry Pratchett: Discworld and Beyond." *LOCUS* 43:6 (Dec. 1999): 4, 73–76.

"Terry Pratchett: 'Fantasy Is Uni-Age.'" By Stephen Moss. *Guardian* 21 Apr. 2013. Web. 21 Apr. 2013.

"Terry Pratchett: 'I had a stroke—and I didn't even notice.'" By Moira Petty. *Daily Mail*, 29 Oct. 2007. Web. 9 Jan. 2011.

"Terry Pratchett: 'If I'd known what a progressive brain disease could do for your PR profile I may have had one earlier.'" By Deborah Orr. *Independent,* 29 Nov. 2008. Web. 9 Jan. 2011.

"Terry Pratchett on His Latest Visit to Discworld, Alzheimer's, and Where He Got That Hat." By Sanjida O'Connell. *New Scientist* 2732 (31 Oct. 2009): 30–31. Web. 28 Feb. 2013.

"Terry Pratchett: Sex, Death and Nature." By Laurie Penny. *New Statesman,* 21 Nov. 2012. Web. 12 May 2013.

"Terry Pratchett: Truth Is Stranger Than Fiction." By Sanjida O'Connell. *New Scientist,* 31 Oct. 2009: 30–31. Web. 28 Feb. 2013.

"Words from the Master." *L-Space Web.* 2 Feb. 2008. Web. 26 Jan. 2011.

2. Interviews with Paul Kidby

"Design Q&A with Paul Kidby." By Rachel. *Talk About Random.* 20 June 2013. Web. 21 June 2013.

"Entrevista a Paul Kidby, magia con las manos y mucho cuteness." *Beliterature.* Np. 4 Mar. 2013. Web. 14 May 2013. [In Spanish].

"Fantastic Fantasy Artwork #2: *Night Watch* (Discworld: Book 29) by Paul Kidby." By Lee. *Fantasy Book Review.* 11 Oct. 2011. Web. 27 Oct. 2011.

"Как се рисува светът на Тери Пратчет 'How to Paint the World of Terry Pratchett.'" By Asia Vladimirova. *Culture* [Култура]. 2 Feb. 2013. Web. 15 May 2013. [In Bulgarian].

"The Illustrator Who Makes Terry Pratchett's Characters Come Alive!" By Ms. Z. *The Genius Salon.* 27 Nov. 2012. Web. 30 Nov. 2012.

"Paul Kidby." By Lloyd Harvey. *Inside the Artist's Studio.* 4 Mar. 2010. Web. 30 May 2012.

C. MA Theses and Dissertations

Abbott, William T. "White Knowledge and the Cauldron of Story: The Use of Allusion in Terry Pratchett's Discworld." MA thesis. East Tennessee State University, 2002. *ProQuest.* 20 Jan. 2011.

Andersen, Dorthe. "Bewitching Writing: An Analysis of Intertextual Resonance in the Witch-Sequence of Terry Pratchett's Discworld." MA Thesis. Aalborg University, 2006.

Andersson, Lorraine. "Which Witch Is Which? A Feminist Analysis of Terry Pratchett's Discworld Witches." MA thesis. University of Halmstad, 2006.

Crowe, Jen. "A War of Words: Humour in the Novels of Terry Pratchett." MA thesis. University of Birmingham, 2003. Cited in Kristiansen's "Subverting the Genre" but unobtainable at date of writing.

Hall, Carey Olive. "The Consumer/Contributor Role of Discworld Fans: The Uses and Gratifications of Online Community Membership." MA thesis. Royal Roads University, 2006. *ProQuest.* 12 Aug. 2013.

Hudson, Walter C., IV. "When Can I Read That? Changing Literacy Goals in Children's Literature." MA thesis. University of Arkansas, 2007. *ProQuest.* 12 Aug. 2013.

Ipfelkofer, Alexander. "Formen und Funktionen von Zitaten und Anspielungen in ausgewählten Romanen Terry Pratchetts." Magisterarbeit. Friedrich-Alexander-Universität Erlangen-Nürnberg, 2000. *Google Books.* 18 Aug. 2013. [in German]

Kristiansen, Andreas. "Subverting the Genre: Terry Pratchett's Discworld as a Critique of Heroic Fantasy." MA thesis. Department of Modern Languages, NTNU, 2003. *L-Space Web.* 1 Feb. 2011.

LaHaie, Jeanne Hoeker. "Girls, Mothers and Others: Female Representation in the Adolescent Fantasy of J. K. Rowling, Philip Pullman, and Terry Pratchett." Diss. Western Michigan University, 2012. *ProQuest.* 12 Aug. 2013.

Lawless, Daphne Antonia. "Weird Sisters and Wild Women: The Changing Depiction of Witches in Literature, from Shakespeare to Science Fiction." MA Thesis. Victoria University of Wellington, 1999. 7 Aug. 2013.

Rüster, Johannes. "The Turtle Moves! Kosmologie und Theologie in den Scheibenweltromanen Terry Pratchetts." Thesis. Wetzlar: Förderkreis Phantastik, 2003. Cited in Fornet-Ponse's "'The Gods play games with the fate of men'" but unobtainable at date of writing. [In German].

Stypczynski, Brent A. "Evolution of the Werewolf Archetype from Ovid to J. K. Rowling." Diss. Kent State University, 2008. *ProQuest.* 12 Aug. 2013.

Walther, Nichole. "Fantasie als Parodie: Humorvolle Verfremdung in diversen Themenbereichen und Figurenkonstellationen der Discworld-Romane." Diplomarbeit. Fachhochschule Köln [Cologne], 2007. *Google Books,* 2010. 15 Aug. 2013. [In German].

Additional Resources

The Colin Smythe Ltd. Terry Pratchett page. http://www.colinsmythe.co.uk/terry pages/tpindex.htm.

The Colin Smythe Terry Pratchett Archive, University of London, Senate House Library. http://www.senatehouselibrary.ac.uk/our-collections/historic-collec tions/printed-special-collections/pratchett/.

Discworld Monthly Newsletter. http://www.discworldmonthly.co.uk/.

L-Space Web, including The Annotated Pratchett File v.9.0. http://www.lspace.org/.

Wossname: Newsletter of the Klatchian Foreign Legion. http://groups.yahoo.com/group/WOSSNAME/.

About the Contributors

Anne Hiebert **Alton** is a professor of English at Central Michigan University, where she teaches literature of all sorts. Her research interests include British and children's literature, illustration, and interdisciplinarity. In addition to essays on the *Harry Potter* series and on Arthur Rackham, recent publications include edited scholarly editions of *Peter Pan* and *Little Women*.

Gideon **Haberkorn** teaches English, ethics and philosophy in Germany's secondary education system and has written articles about popular culture, fantasy fiction, realism, rhetoric and humor. He is co-editor of *Comics as a Nexus of Cultures* (McFarland, 2010). He is a member of the International Association for the Fantastic in the Arts.

Gray **Kochhar-Lindgren** is a professor of interdisciplinary arts and sciences and associate vice chancellor for undergraduate learning at the University of Washington, Bothell. He is the author of *Narcissus Transformed*, *Starting Time*, *TechnoLogics*, *Night Café*, and *Philosophy, Art, and the Specters of Jacques Derrida* and is working on projects on philosophy in the streets, global noir, and the emerging global university.

Roderick **McGillis** is an emeritus professor of English at the University of Calgary. Along with Yan Wu and Kerry Mallan, he has edited the collection of essays *(Re)imagining the World: Children's Literature's Response to Changing Times*.

William C. **Spruiell** is an associate professor of English at Central Michigan University, where he teaches English linguistics, Old English, and science fiction and fantasy literature. His research interests include functional theories of grammar and theories of creative language use. He has co-edited *Relations and Functions Within and Around Language* and *The Speculative Grammarian Essential Guide to Linguistics*.

Caroline **Webb** is a senior lecturer in English at the University of Newcastle, Australia. She specializes in study of British modernism and contemporary fiction, and is interested in fantastic fiction, including fantasy for children. Her articles include discussions of works by Virginia Woolf, James Joyce, Angela Carter, Terry Pratchett, Diana Wynne Jones, and J. K. Rowling.

Index

Page numbers in **bold italics** indicate pages with illustrations. A dagger
symbol (†) after a name indicates a Discworld character